LUTHER:
THEOLOGIAN FOR
CATHOLICS AND
PROTESTANTS

LUTHER: THEOLOGIAN FOR CATHOLICS AND PROTESTANTS

Edited by

GEORGE YULE

T. & T. CLARK

59 GEORGE STREET, EDINBURGH

Copyright © T. & T. Clark Ltd., 1985

Typeset by C. R. Barber & Partners, Fort William, Scotland,
printed and bound by Billings, Worcestershire, England.

for
T. & T. CLARK LTD., EDINBURGH,
SCOTLAND

ISBN 0 567 29119 7

FIRST PRINTED 1985
REPRINTED 1986
REPRINTED 1988

PREFACE

To mark the occasion of the 500th anniversary of Luther's birth we have written these essays which together reflect something of the remarkable contribution he made to the understanding of the Christian faith. None of the contributors is a member of the Lutheran church but are Anglican, Roman Catholic, Methodist or Presbyterian, yet all see in him one who, by concentrating on the uniqueness of the grace of God in Jesus Christ, deepens the perception of the Catholic faith of the whole Church.

My thanks are due to my fellow contributors who have gone to such pains to make this a worthy contribution for the occasion and to Professor T. F. Torrance for permission to reprint his essay on Luther's Eschatology, now long out of print. Especially I should like to thank Mr John Todd for his unfailing kindness and helpfulness and also Mrs Jean Henderson for her care in typing and retyping sections of the manuscript.

George Yule,
All Saints' Day
Reformation Sunday 1982

CONTRIBUTORS

Basil Hall, formerly Professor of Church History at the University of Manchester, Dean of St John's College, Cambridge, and author of many articles on the Reformation.

Harry McSorley, Professor of Religious Studies, University of Toronto, author of *Luther: Right or Wrong.*

Gordon Rupp, formerly Dixie Professor of Ecclesiastical History, University of Cambridge, author of *The Righteousness of God: Luther Studies.*

Ian Siggins, Visiting Professor, Harvard University, Divinity School, author of *Martin Luther's Doctrine of Christ.*

John Todd, publisher and writer, author of *Luther – A Life.*

Thomas Torrance, formerly Professor of Christian Dogmatics, New College, Edinburgh, author of *Kingdom and Church: A Study in the Theology of the Reformation.*

George Yule, Professor of Church History, University of Aberdeen, formerly of Ormond College, University of Melbourne.

CONTENTS

INTRODUCTION

'Luther – theologian for Catholics and Protestants' is a title that would have perplexed if not angered many, both Catholics and Protestants, of former ages. Even in our age of ecumenical dialogue the emphasis on the term 'theologian' would seem to many to be irrelevant. Is not theology the cause of our unhappy divisions? But it is the thrust of this book to show that Luther, whose theology ostensibly caused the disruption of Christendom, has probed the central area of Christian theology which alone can unite us.

It is a great temptation of Protestant historians to fail to take account of how Luther was moulded by the Mediaeval Church. But he insisted that the Mediaeval Church 'is our mother', who has nourished us with word and sacraments and taught us the faith handed down by generations of faithful men. Luther was a product of Mediaeval piety, an emphasis developed in three of these essays. If aspects of this piety posed theological problems as the first and fourth essay show, John Todd, in the third essay, reveals very clearly how this piety provided a vast treasury of spirituality which helped resolve these same problems, while the first essay shows how much Luther built upon the great theologians of the past. This is one aspect of the truth of the title.

Joseph Lortz in his great work in 1939 *The Reformation in Germany* was one who began to change the direction of the Catholic theological assessment of Luther. Luther, he insisted, rightly rebelled against a decadent Catholicism that was no true Catholicism. Since Vatican II this insight has been developed and greatly extended and one can gauge the significance of this in Harry McSorley's essay which points out where both Catholics and Protestants, by re-examining what Luther himself had to say rather than taking it from the interpretations of scholastic, pietist or liberal Protestant interpreters on the one hand or Catholic polemicists on the other, will find much more common ground than they supposed. This essay stresses the central significance of

the sacraments for Catholics and for Luther and it is this theme
which is taken up by Basil Hall who shows how fundamental the
sacraments were for Luther as promises of God undergirding the
gift of salvation and an essential aspect of the life of the Church.

From the Reformed side a new approach to Luther became
possible with Karl Barth's recalling the Church to the centrality of
the incarnation. This is what undergirds all other Christian
doctrines. This too was Luther's approach. 'We preach much and
write much', said Luther's colleague, Bugenhagen, 'but we say but
one thing "Christ our righteousness".'[1] That justification was by
grace alone and that this grace of God was itself Christ our
righteousness, was the great insight of Luther on which all other
doctrines depend. 'For if the doctrine of justification is lost', he
wrote, 'all doctrine is lost'.[2] This reconciling work of God is
summed up, said Luther, in the Nicene creed where it points to
Jesus Christ as 'Very God of Very God . . . who for us men and for
our salvation came down from heaven and was made man'. This
emphasis of Luther is explored in detail in the sixth essay. This is
not just a protestant perception. Father Daniel Olivier, Professor
of Lutheran studies at the Institut Superior d'Etudes
Oecumeniques at Paris, who, except for the exigencies of time
would have contributed to these essays, has also shown how
Luther's understanding of justification was bound up with
Christ's incarnation where on the cross he stands in the place of
sinful man.[3]

The centrality of justification by grace was the issue from which
Luther never varied. In his vast range of writings and the many
crises which beset him, this remained constant, and this is the
theme of Gordon Rupp's essay.

Luther himself pointed out that he was only to be heeded when
he spoke in accordance with the Word of God and we should
therefore not be true to Luther himself if we were uncritical of his
shortcomings, a point emphasised in a number of these essays. But
it is our judgement that Luther's remarkable insights into the
nature of God's grace revealed in the coming of Christ is the basis
for the unity and renewal of the Church and it is to this we point.

The final piece is Professor T. F. Torrance's distinguished
article 'The eschatology of faith: Martin Luther', written in 1955
in *Kingdom and Church* and long out of print, and it seemed

important once again to make it available. It was not written with
the title of this book in view, but it deals with many issues which
Catholics and Protestants will have to face if they wish together to
seek the fulness of the faith and it does so by exploring the ways in
which Luther approached them. It should therefore be seen both
as an important article in its own right and as an addendum to
these essays, deepening them in various ways and pointing to
issues with which they have not dealt. There is little writing on
Luther's thought on eschatology, so in this Luther year we trust
we have made a genuine contribution from British theology by
republishing it.

NOTES

1. Pomeranus Bugenhagen, *A Compendious Letter which John Pomeranus, curate of
   the Congregation at Wittenburg sent to the faithful Christian congregations in
   England*, London, 1536.
2. *Luther's Works*, (American Edition), hereafter *LW*, 26:9.
3. Daniel Olivier, *Luther's Faith*, translated by John Tonkin, Concordia, 1982.

For Father Noel Ryan S.J. and Professor Harry Wardlaw, United
Faculty of Theology, Melbourne

This essay formed the basis of the Archbishop of Canterbury's
Luther Commemoration lecture, Lambeth Palace, November
1983.

LUTHER: THEOLOGIAN FOR CATHOLICS AND PROTESTANTS

George Yule

'When the artist Grünewald died he left among his belongings various works of Luther and a rosary. And if that other great religious artist Dürer had been asked if he were a Catholic or a Protestant, he would have been perplexed by the question. Even at the Council of Trent there was a sizeable group of able theologians who wanted to state the path of salvation in ways much more akin to Luther than to his opponents. Subsequently, however, positions hardened. Secondary considerations became primary ones and it became unthinkable that a Catholic should favour Luther's theology. Even since Vatican II, with the increasing amount of goodwill, the real reason for such polarised positions is still rarely perceived.

We need not be surprised, for this lack of perception came almost immediately after the posting up by Luther of the Ninety Five theses. In his reply to Erasmus in 1525 Luther said 'moreover, I praise you highly for this also, that unlike all the rest, you alone have attacked the real issues and have not wearied me with irrelevancies about the papacy, purgatory, indulgences and such trifles, for trifles they are rather than the main issue ... If those who had attacked me hitherto had done the same, and if those who boast now of new spirits and new revelations would still do it, we should have less of sedition and sects.'

Reformation in the commonly accepted sense of the word was not Luther's concern. His interest was concentrated on the piety of the Church, not its impiety. This gives the clue to the significance of Luther as a theologian both for Catholics and Protestants, for in effect he offered solutions to a number of mediaeval religious concerns which were of basic importance but very difficult of solution.

The commonly held view that the Reformation occurred

1

because of the corruptions of the Church and that Luther was merely following the path of a number of forerunners is demonstrably inadequate. The age, in the words of Lucien Fébvre, had *un appetit pour le divin*.[2] This is particularly true of the Rhineland and the cities of northern Germany and the Low Countries. This religious intensity had come out of the whole ecclesiastical life of mediaeval Christendom, heightened particularly by the great age of mystical religion, with its emphasis upon the personal awareness of God that had so dominated the spiritual life of the fourteenth century on the one hand with the influence of Tauler, Suso, Master Eckhart, Hildergard of Bingen, and on the other by the emphasis on the return to apostolic simplicity of the Fransiscans.

The great age of the mystics and the stir caused by St Francis had passed but with the advent of printing and the increasing literacy of the urban population their influence, though less direct, was more pervasive.[3] Particularly is this true of the Rhineland and Northern Germany, where there are many signs of a deep spirituality, especially among the laity.[4] It was all within the orbit of the Church, with little trace of heresy of any kind. 'Our cause', said the German Hussite, Reiser in 1456, 'is like a fire going out',[5] while the last trials for heresy in Germany prior to the Reformation were before 1470.[6]

One can see the direction of this spirituality portrayed vividly in the paintings, especially those depicting the sufferings of Christ, of Grünewald, Roger van der Weyden, Tilman, David and many others – a Christian art form that has no parallel for its devotional intensity, particularly in depicting the passion of Christ.[7] There was a great increase in devotional literature – works of piety, portions of the Psalter and Gospels and sermons.[8] Indeed there were twenty-two editions of the Bible in German prior to Luther's great translation.[9] The most popular work of edification was Thomas à Kempis' *The Imitation of Christ*, which together with the paintings on the sufferings of Christ show the direction this piety was taking – meditating on Christ and imitating his life and suffering. Along with this deeply felt internal piety went many external expressions of religious devotion – pilgrimages, the collecting of religious relics, the building of churches,[10] new endowment of masses, the founding of brotherhoods, and the sale of endulgences all on an unprecedented scale as Bernd Moeller has shown in his important essay.[11] The rise of the *Brethren of the Common Life*, a type of lay order seeking to practice a monastic style of piety within the life of their daily occupations illustrates the commitment of the laity to the devotional life at this time.[12] Its founder, Gerard Groote, was steeped in the works of the mystics, but left the monastery where he had been for three years to devote his life to preaching.[13]

There was a constant cry by preacher, mystic and humanist for deeper and deeper devotion. The attack on scholastic theology by many humanists and mystics was not that it was untrue but that it did not make people pious. 'I see the simple multitude', wrote Erasmus, 'longing after food for their souls, desiring how they can return to their homes better people, and then the lecturer (theologaster) ... ventilates some frigid or perplexing question from Occam or Scotus', [14] while the slogan of the mystical writer Nicholas of Clemanges would be 'deeds before doctrine'.[15]

This highlights a serious break between theology and the devotional life. Whereas the Greek Fathers with their concentration on the incarnation wove piety and theology together, as in the earlier middle ages, did St Anselm whose theology blends into prayer, there was a tendency to aridity in later mediaeval scholasticism which strikingly divorced the two so that worship became the preserve of the mystics and lacked the proper undergirding and controls which incarnational theology should have given it. In the well-known words of Thomas à Kempis 'Of what use is it to discourse loftily on the Trinity if you lack humility and thus displease the Trinity. Truly lofty words do not make one holy and righteous but a virtuous life makes one dear to God.'[16] We have moved a long way from Anselm's 'fides quaerens intellectum', in order that it may lead to deeper faith. The rise of the Devotio Moderna was a reaction to the devotional aridity of later scholasticism.[17] There were of course notable exceptions, like Gerson whose great examplars were Bernard and Bonaventura, who 'inflame the affections while at the same time instructing the mind'.[18] But this attitude was not common and piety and theology had become separated to a serious extent, so there was little theological guidance given to this increasing emphasis on piety in the Christian life, and indeed what guidance was given was, as we shall see, baneful, for it ploughed a strongly Pelagian element into an area that was already susceptible to such an attitude.

It was however not the theologians and not even the humanists who mainly stimulated this piety, but the preachers. Dr Siggins in his essay has drawn attention to this much neglected aspect of the religious life of the late mediaeval church, to the vast numbers of sermons that were printed, an indicator of their popularity, and also to the large numbers of books on homiletics and model sermons that left the presses between 1470 and 1520. This would be the chief and continuing source of inspiration for most people. Few would be unaffected by it, and they would hear, as Siggins shows, a broad range of topics throughout the Christian year calling for uprightness of life and the application of the church's teaching to their lives. But two emphases stand out; the inevitability of death and to prepare for this by being truly contrite for their sins.[19]

The theme of death dominated many sermons and much contemporary writing and even popular songs, and was vividly expressed in series of woodcuts on the 'Dance of Death'.[20] The effects on popular religion were obvious. Count Werner of Simmer in 1483 left a legacy for one thousand masses to be said for him. The sale of indulgences went up steeply throughout the century despite the qualms of some theologians.[21] It was an age of spiritual anxiety, and Huizinga has remarked on the melancholic expression of the portraits painted in Northern Europe at this time.[22]

How does one prepare for death and the judgement? This, urges Siggins, was the main concern of the preacher. One must be truly contrite and then God will forgive. It was virtually salvation, *sola contritione*, by contrition alone. Sincere contrition brings God's forgiveness before and apart from sacramental penance, provided that the penitent was resolved to confess and to perform his allotted penance. To be truly contrite called for the deepest and humblest self-examination. This was the atmosphere in which Luther's spiritual life was moulded. How does one prepare to face death and judgement with assurance? This was Luther's and the Western Churches' basic problem, and it was virtually impossible to resolve in the terms it was posed in Western theology.

For the whole Western Church had inherited from Tertullian and Jerome a legalistic framework for its theology. Tertullian, a remarkable and creative man, had almost single handed worked out Latin equivalents for the Greek theological vocabulary of the Early Church. He is now credited with having coined over nine hundred words.[23] Latin is the most precise language in Europe and one of its richest areas is its judicial vocabulary. To this Tertullian frequently resorted but this gave the theological vocabulary in its new Latin form a legalistic twist which it did not have in its original Greek form. For example, the Greek *metanoein*, repent, turn around, was rendered in Latin as *poenitentiam agitur*, a duty required of the guilty party in the Roman law courts—'to do a penance'. Luther specifically mentioned the difficulty that this false translation caused him.[24] Sin of the New Testament, an attitude of hostility to the love of God, tended to become sins, a list of particular transgressions of the law of God. When Jerome translated the New Testament into Latin about the year 400 he used basically Tertullian's vocabulary and this, until Erasmus' editing of the Greek text of the New Testament in 1516, was the Bible of the whole Western Church from which its prayer books, its devotional literature and its church law was derived.[25] This has given the devotional life of the Western Church and its theology a legalistic and moralistic twist and has led to a higher emphasis being placed on the juridicial metaphors of the Bible than on the more appropriate personal ones in its understanding of the way of salvation. This tendency was heightened further by the most unfortunate view of Latin Christianity, bolstered up by St Augustine's own usage, to think of the grace of God as a non-personal religious essence instead of as God's giving of his gracious presence in Jesus Christ. Several serious results followed. Under the rigorous and exact process of mediaeval scholasticism, theology took on a strangely impersonal ring which tended to obscure the love of God behind impersonal logical categories and so tended to drive a wedge between theology and piety which was the last thing the great scholastics like Anselm or Bonaventura wanted to do. One of the merits of mystical theology was that it partly overcame this defect and this was why Luther, for example, praised Tauler, not because of the actual mysticism, which he distrusted, but because it led to a personal knowledge of God.

5

Where, for example, Tauler had written 'the spark of the soul or man's highest part,' Luther put 'faith' in a marginal note.[26]

An even more serious result was that the way of salvation was presented in an extremely legalistic and Pelagian way. All realised man sinned; all realised that grace was necessary to rememdy this. But in this legalistic, impersonal and forensic *schema* the view became dominant that God's forgiveness is conditional on our true repentance of which our contrition is an essential ingredient. It was fully realised that grace was necessary and the relationship of grace to man's repentance was expressed in a variety of ways but almost always there was left a residue of human effort so that contrition itself became 'our work' and the nagging doubt remained—and this as we shall see was Luther's problem—'was I contrite enough'. This was an attitude characterised later by Calvin was 'legal repentance'.[27] The descriptive 'ifs' of the New Testament had become legal prescriptive 'ifs' so that it was thought that God's forgiveness was dependent upon our repentance.[28] But the grace of God is unconditional, and because of this it calls forth unconditional obligations of gratitude. These, however, are never conditions for the grace of God. God's forgiveness is always prior to man's repentance and indeed makes it possible, as Augustine so well knew. Making conditions for repentance, especially when coupled with a legalistic view of sin and an impersonal view of grace, make Pelagianism almost inevitable. As Dr Siggins has shown so clearly in his essay, even contrition for Luther had been cast into a Pelagian mould. The concentration of mediaeval, and indeed of most Western, theology is on the 'means of salvation'—that is on the 'how' question, rather than with the Greek Fathers, on the 'who' question which spells out the fact of the incarnation, seen especially in Irenaeus, Athanasius and Cyril, of Christ taking on Himself fallen humanity and redeeming it.[29] That approach is essentially personal so that the very statement of the theology is doxological in character, which means that a divorce between theology and piety is less likely to occur. But in the Western Church, with its legalistic cast, and with grace itself being talked about as if it were one of the categories of this legalistic equation of the way of salvation, almost inevitably Pelagianism came in, and the mediaeval dogmatic statement was that grace given through the sacraments enabled one to do works that were worthy of salvation. This led to very detailed discussions about how grace was received. It could be expressed, as with Gregory of Rimini, in an entirely anti-Pelagian way, but it ended up under the Occamist, being suggested that an initial act of love on man's part, (that is doing the best one can on the basis of natural ability), was rewarded by God with an infusion of grace which then enabled man, co-operating with grace, to do works worthy of salvation.[31] Some recent Catholic scholarship has suggested that Luther knew only this Occamist tradition and it was this which he was attacking, but Luther is quite explicit on the point. 'In the name of the Church and of Christ the mediaeval theologians themselves became Pelagians, not to mention Occam and his school who shortly afterwards became worse' (Pelagians).[31]

Under these self defeating constraints much of the greatness of mediaeval theology was obscured, and it needed a new theological orientation to bring forth the fuller significance of Anselm, of Bernard, of Bonaventura and indeed particularly, of Augustine himself.

This was the situation in which Luther lived and these were the theological problems which confronted him. Why was he not content with this intense but theologically incoherent piety? Until the importance of this issue is recognised no true assessment of Luther's achievement is possible, either by Catholic or Protestant historians on the one hand, or by secular historians on the other, whose frequent attempts to rationalise his motives at the critical points of his life seem singularly misguided. He has been described as the mouthpiece of the *petite bourgeoisie* or the product of a harsh upbringing by his father.[33] Many people, no doubt, had harsh fathers; many were members of the burgher classes of the towns, but they did not resolve the problem that was so pressing to a vast variety of people. Luther gave a genuine answer to a genuine theological dilemma, and it would be just as silly to rationalise this answer as, for example, to say that Einstein made his discoveries because of a harsh parental upbringing or because of his social situation.[34] It was not for nothing that Dürer wanted to paint that man who saved him from so great fear.[35]

Luther saw the problem in clearer focus than his contemporaries because he saw with greater clarity the

7

implications of the simple Gospel demand to love God with heart and soul and mind and strength and to love one's neighbour as oneself. This insight made things not easier, but infinitely harder for him. 'I was always thinking', he wrote, 'when will you do enough that God will be gracious with you. Such thoughts drove me to the monastery.'[36] He realised the depth of the command and began to experience the impossibility of keeping it. The monastic life had been urged by St Bernard as the only way in which it could be kept, so he entered a monastery.

'I myself was a monk', he wrote, 'for twenty years I tortured myself with prayers, fasting, vigils, and freezing; the frost alone might have killed me. It caused me pain such as I will never inflict on myself again, even if I could. What else did I seek by doing this but God, who was supposed to note my strict observance of the monastic order and my austere life? I constantly walked in a dream and lived in real idolatry. For I did not believe in Christ; I regarded Him only as a severe and terrible Judge, portrayed as seated on a rainbow. Therefore I cast about for other intercessors, Mary and various other saints, also my own works and the merits of my order. And I did all this for the sake of God, not for money or goods.'[37] His problem at this stage was how could he be truly contrite and so be forgiven.

At first things in the monastery went well. 'I know from my experience, and that of many others, how peaceful and quiet Satan is accustomed to be in one's first year as a priest or monk.' Then his troubles began again – not the temptations of the flesh that tormented many other monks. Indeed he marvelled that St Jerome should have been thus harassed while he himself was vexed 'not with women but with the really knotty problems'.[38]

What was this knotty problem? 'Although I readily listened to the flattering appreciation of my own works on the part of the prior and the brethren, and allowed myself to be esteemed a marvellous fellow ... I never-the-less failed to stand the test of even a small attack of death and sin. When such trials came I straightway fell and found no help either in my baptism or in my monkery'.[39]

This knotty problem was how to overcome an attack of sin and death. Baptism by which he had been marked with the forgiveness of sin and his union with Christ, and monasticism in which he had given himself into the care and service of God should have been sufficient. A little later in his life baptism became sufficient to overcome these attacks, for whenever he came under their spell he would say 'I have been baptised'.[40] But at this stage it proved of no avail, because he still was enthralled by the notion of legal repentance and the conditionality of God's forgiveness.

He knew better than most of his contemporaries the desperate nature of the human condition because he realised, like St Augustine that the sins which people worried about were merely a manifestation of something much more intractable. It was the orientation of one's whole personality towards oneself. Augustine had described how this meant that with this orientation one converted even the good things of life into idols. Luther went deeper at this point and saw how one converted even one's religious strivings also into an idol. 'For Scripture describes man', he wrote, 'as bowed down to himself (*incurvatum in se*) so that not only bodily goods, but spiritual goods also he turns to himself and seeks himself in all things.'[41] 'For man makes himself', he wrote, 'a final and ultimate object, an idol ... This crookedness and depravity and iniquity is described many times in Scripture under the name of fornication or idolatry . . . and is in the hidden depths of our nature, nay rather is nature itself wounded and in ferment, throughout the whole, so that it is not only impossible to remedy without grace, but it is impossible fully to recognise it.'[42]

Like Augustine he realised that to love God with his heart and soul and mind and strength meant that he had to desire to do God's will, and all that did not have this motivation was sin. 'It is said that human nature has a general notion of knowing and willing good, but that it goes wrong in particulars. It would be better to say that it knows and wills the good in particular things, but in general neither knows nor wills the good. This is so because it knows only its own good or what is good, honourable, and useful for itself, but not what is good for God and for others.'[43] Luther's biblical understanding had advanced so far that by the time of the Romans Commentary (1515–16) he saw that when the Bible spoke of flesh it was basically speaking of self-idolatory of which sensuality was just one manifestation. 'The flesh', he wrote, 'is the whole man, with body and soul, reason and will. And every man has fleshly senses, moods, affections and will who is not born of the Spirit. For the soul is so embedded in the flesh which seeks to guard and protect it that it is indeed more flesh than the flesh itself.'[44]

In this dilemma, knowing he was called to love God with heart and soul and mind and strength, the means of absolution prescribed by the Church were, and could be, of no final avail. Like St Anselm, Luther realised that there could be no limit to the First Commandment to love God,[45] and therefore the suggestion that one could be sufficiently contrite for not so doing was impossible. Luther's early years in the monastery had been spent in a vain endeavour to fulfil the impossible. God's forgiveness as we have said was thought to be conditional upon confessing all one's sins, being truly contrite for them, and then performing a *satisfactio* to show that one indeed was truly contrite. Looking back in 1535 upon his life as a monk, Luther saw this attitude akin to that in which St Paul placed the Judaizing Christians in Galatia. Commenting on Galations 5:3, 'every man who receives circumcision is bound to keep the whole law.' Luther wrote, 'What I am saying here on the basis of the words of Paul I learned from my own experience in the monastery about myself and others . . . The more someone tries to bring peace to his conscience through his own righteousness, the more disquieted he makes it. When I was a monk, I made a great effort to live according to the requirements of the monastic rule. I made a practice of confessing and reciting all my sins, but always with prior contrition; I went to confessions frequently, and I performed the assigned penances faithfully. Nevertheless, my conscience could never achieve certainty but was always in doubt and said: "You have not done this correctly. You were not contrite enough. You omitted this in your confession".'[46] Posed in the framework of the legalism and moralism of the time these questions were unanswerable. Confronted with the absolute demand of the love of God, within his framework, these practices could yield no certainty. For Luther had passed into a different realm and was devoting himself to trying to love God. He realised that this love, as St Bernard had shown, had to be for God's sake, and not for the sake of winning heaven or escaping hell, because that would be self love.[47] Consequently, 'however irreproachably I lived as a monk, I felt myself in the presence of God to be a sinner'. He was caught in a vicious circle. In order to be absolved he had to love God, but in order to love God he had to be absolved.

Then over the period of a number of years Luther came to realise that the grace of God shown in Jesus Christ was both the beginning and the end of the Christian life, so that salvation could only be described as *sola gratia* from beginning to end. A chain is as strong as its weakest link, but in this chain every link was the grace of God as revealed in Jesus Christ, and he came to realise that this was the essential teaching of the Catholic faith. Flashes of illumination came to him in this long search as he wrestled with the Bible and the Fathers and listened to the comfortable words of Staupitz and the mystical theologians.

This insight came to Luther by degrees. He was like a man trying to complete an intricate jigsaw with only a hazy notion of what the final picture should be, for his contemporary religious scene was so jumbled. The language of the grace of God was so confused with ideas and practices of moralism and legal repentance that the very intensity of religious life led inevitably to a Pelagianism which undercut grace, and to the assumption that religious works were the way to salvation. As Dr Siggins points out in his essay, Luther's first great step forward 'was a protest against the present state of penitential practice' so that any idea of putting pressure on God to forgive one by means of prayers, penances, pilgrimages or other religious practices he now saw as totally misguided and lacking in faith.[48] He took up the emphasis of the late mediaeval preaching on contrition and expressed it in terms of humility not in this case so much as humble obedience but of accusing oneself in the presence of God in line with the thought of Gerson and Biel.[49] In his comment on Psalm 51 in 1513–14, he worked this out in a *schema* that judgement of self is in substance the justification of God while justification of oneself is in opposition to the judgement of God.[50] This paved the way for his fine expositions of humility in his Romans commentary. On Romans 2:11 he wrote 'Thus the Jews always incline to make God a respecter of persons. It is this foolishness of theirs which the heretics and all the spiritually proud imitate . . . They do not know that, on the contrary God elects and favours only a soul that despises itself and considers itself worthy only to be rejected . . .'[51] And later 'For this is the whole business of the Apostle and his

Lord, that he should humble the proud and bring them to a knowledge of this thing and teach them to need grace, that he may break down their own righteousness, so that when they are made humble they may seek Christ and confess themselves to be sinners and thus perceive grace and be saved'.[52]

This is certainly an essential part of Luther's understanding of salvation and this is why in the *Ninety Five Theses* he insisted that the whole of life of the believers be one of penance.[53] But this emphasis could still become another way of self justification. One saved oneself by being truly humble.

The final solution came to him when he realised that the whole of our salvation was the gift of God, given to us in Jesus Christ, *sola gratia*. Indeed that Jesus Christ himself was this grace of God, Christ our righteousness, who being truly God showed completely 'the mind and heart' of the Father and being truly man was completely united with sinful man, so that nothing more could be added.

This solution came to him when he resolved the problem posed by the conjunction of ideas in Romans 1:16, 17.[55] 'The righteousness (*iustitia*) of God is revealed in the Gospel' and 'the just shall live by faith'. He had hitherto, along with the mediaeval exegetes, assumed that *iustitia*, the justice of God, was the demand of God the judge – His law. And how could that conceivably be the Gospel, good news? And what then could one make of the next phrase 'The just shall live by faith'? In mediaeval theology the righteousness (*iustitia*) earned by Christ was seen as being granted to the sinner as a gift, but this was separated from the justice (*iustitia*) of God, which was His law, demanded by God at the last judgement against which man had to measure up with the appropriation of help from the righteousness (*iustitia*) of Christ given through sacramental grace. It suddenly dawned on Luther that the *iustitia* of Christ and the *iustitia* of God coincide and are granted simultaneously.[56] That is Christ Himself was the righteousness of God. It was all of grace – *sola gratia* – and therefore the only appropriate human response was gratitude, *sola fide*, faith only. Anything else would be Pelagianism. 'There I began to understand' he wrote many years later, 'the *iustitia* of God as that by which the just live by the gift of God, namely by faith; and this sentence "the justice of God is revealed in the

Gospel" to be that passive justice with which the merciful God justifies us by faith as it is written "the just shall live by faith . . ." From then on the whole face of scripture appeared different. I ran through the scripture then as memory served me and found the same analogy then in other words, as the work of God, that which God works in us; the power of God, with which He makes us strong, wisdom of God with which He makes us wise, fortitude of God, Salvation of God, glory of God'.[57]

Many of Luther's insights into the nature of God's forgiveness pre-date this illumination, but this now made everything cohere and in so doing resolved many of the problems that had bedevilled the Western Church.

He now saw that he was 'accepted though unacceptable', to use Paul Tillich's perceptive phrase, (though Luther would have emphatically added to it 'in Jesus Christ'). This acceptance in Christ applied to the whole of a Christian's life so that he summed it up as 'simul iustus et peccator' or better 'semper peccator, semper penitens semper iustus'.[58]

This insight that the righteousness of God and the righteousness of Christ are identical is nothing other than seeing the implication of what Athanasius had insisted upon during the formulation of the Nicene Creed where he had, in contradiction to Arius stressed that the being of God cannot be separated from His action in Christ.[59] Hence, if the acts of Christ are sheer love then the being of God is sheer love. One cannot set God's justice over against Christ's love. That is a form of Arianism, proclaimed inadvertently by many Catholics and Protestants alike.

From all these strivings with the knotty problem of loving God without an ulterior motive Luther came to see that *sola gratia* is an essential aspect of the Catholic faith. If man is sinful in the way Augustine has shown, and if God, the Holy Trinity, sought the welfare of mankind to such an extent that God the Son stood beside the enemy and the helpless, then the only way to state this was *sola gratia*.[60] Any form of Pelagianism or legalism cuts across this. An inadequate legalistic view of sin involves an inadequate view of grace. 'But he who teaches and understands aright what it means that Christ is both true God and true man, on the basis of the verses already heard and those we shall hear later, such as "He who has seen Me has seen the Father" and "Believe Me that I am in My Father and the Father in Me" – such a person can surely conclude and say: "I will hear and know of no other God, but I will look and listen solely to this Christ. And if I hear Him, I already know on what terms I am with God; and I need no longer torment myself, as I did before, with my anxiety about atonement and reconciliation with God." For in this picture all wrath and terror vanish, and only grace and comfort shine forth. Now I can gain a real and genuine trust in God, console my conscience in all trials and adversity, judge all life and conduct properly, and teach and instruct everybody.'[61]

It is clear from the latter part of his 'Tower experience' which we have formerly quoted that the whole emphasis is on the sheer grace of God – God *pro nobis*, on our behalf for Christ Himself is the *iustitia Dei*. That faith is the only appropriate and truly possible response to this. When he speaks therefore of justification by faith he is using a shorthand expression for the whole Gospel. So in his *Commentary on Galations* he writes 'Paul wants to establish the doctrine of faith, grace, the forgiveness of sins or Christian righteousness'.[62] At various times Luther used each phrase in this shorthand fashion to comprehend the whole work of salvation and did so, after 1518, almost invariably in Christological terms a topic on which I enlarge in a later essay. In this Luther differs both from many mediaeval Catholics and from many Protestants. The commonest word used to translate 'faith' in mediaeval theology was *assensus*, assenting to the truths of the Bible or the Creed. But Luther instead used *fiducia* – trust or reliance upon God's faithfulness in Christ. The consequences of this were very far-reaching and show the profundity of Luther's thought in this area.[63] All mediaeval theology, mystic or scholastic, Thomist or Occamist, believed that becoming like God was the indispensible condition of salvation. Only like could truly know like.[64] 'Our becoming like God', wrote Gerson, 'is the cause of our union with Him'. So the way of salvation was *fides caritate formata*, faith formed by love. So when many heard Luther speak simply of *sola fide* they assumed that he was speaking about *fides informis*, a dead faith like that which 'the demons have but tremble',[65] as described by Jacob Hochstraten in his *Disputation* with Luther in 1526 when he wrote that 'Luther lists no preconditions for the spiritual marriage of the soul with

Christ except only that we believe in Christ . . . Not a single word is said about the mutual love by which the soul love Christ'.[66] But this fails to take account of the significance of Luther's change from using *assensus* to *fiducia*. He discusses this issue at some length in his 1535 *Commentary on Galations*. 'But where they' [the Scholastics] 'speak of love we speak of faith. And while they say that faith is the mere outline but love is its living colours and completion, we say in distinction that faith takes hold of Christ and that he is the form that adorns and informs faith as colour does the wall. Therefore Christian faith is not an idle quality or an empty husk in the heart, which may exist in a state of mortal sin until love comes along to make it alive. But if it is true faith, it is a sure trust and firm acceptance in the heart. It takes hold of Christ in such a way that Christ is the object of faith, or rather not the object but, so to speak, the One who is present in faith itself'.[67] Faith and love coalesce in its object, Jesus Christ.

Many Protestants assume that when Luther said justification by faith alone he meant that we are saved not be our works but by our existential decision of faith. But this, as Cranmer remarked, makes faith into a work, and it would have been for Luther just another type of Pelagianism.[68] 'Faith', he wrote, 'is something done to us rather than by us (magis . . . passio quam actio) for it changes our hearts and minds.'[69] The essential point of Christian faith is its object Jesus Chirst. Without its object all that remains of faith is 'merely froth and uncertain opinion or dreams'. Faith is merely the husk but Christ is the kernel.[70] 'Even if I am feeble in faith, I still have the same treasure and the same Christ as others have. There is no difference . . . It is the self-same Christ we possess whether you or I believe in Him with a strong faith or a weak faith'.[71] The function of faith was to point away from one's self and one's works to Christ only, and hence Luther's preference for *fiducia* rather than *assensus*, for it was a word implying personal allegiance.

Consequently in any detailed discussion of faith Luther never speaks about it without its object, Jesus Christ. 'Faith unites the soul with Christ', he wrote, 'as a bride is united to her bridegroom'.[72] 'Observe' he wrote to Latomus, that 'faith is not enough, but only faith which hides under the wings of Christ and glories in his righteousness'.[73] This was a constant perception and

15

it comes out just as strongly in his early Romans commentary as it did in his later sermons on John. The Apostle speaks, he wrote on Romans 5:2, 'against those presumptuous persons who think they can come to God apart from faith, as though it was sufficient for them to have believed and thus *sola fide*, but not through Christ ... But it is necessary to have Christ always hitherto and to eternity as the mediator of such faith'.[74]

At point after point, because he was wrestling with the text of the Bible with its strongly personal and historical orientation, Luther at first, probably unwittingly, personalised the whole theological approach which under scholasticism had become so abstract. Faith, as we have shown, was now seen not the assenting to propositions, but as trust in the promises of God. Grace now became the saving activity of God in the person of Christ rather than an abstract spiritual essence. It was a hard lesson to learn and the next generation saw the rise of a Protestant scholasticism, almost as abstract as the later mediaeval variety (and with the similar virtue of precision) which fastened on Protestantism many of the mediaeval problems from which the insights of Luther and Calvin had begun to free it, and from which it was eventually freed by an odd mixture – the warmth of evangelicalism, the blood letting of liberalism which sometimes proved fatal, and the incarnational emphasis of Karl Barth. With Catholics, Vatican II has begun a similar process also with a variety of ingredients.

One other major problem of the Mediaeval Church on which Luther's discovery gave light was his transforming of Christian ethics into the ethics of gratitude. We have seen how he had come to realise with St Bernard that to love God meant loving Him for His own sake and not for the ulterior motive of being saved, and with St Augustine that we do not do His will until we delight to do it. The legalistic framework, the Pelagianism that had infiltrated so much of scholastic theology, coupled with the fact that the grace of God was thought of as an abstract quality, made the call to love God with heart and soul and mind and strength an impossible demand in the sense that the more one strove the more self-absorbed one tended to become. But putting the emphasis on the iniative of God, *sola gratia*, and coupling this with the cost of redemption in the cross of Christ transformed the situation. One was now freed to do good without the ulterior motive of earning salvation.[75] As he put it in *The Freedom of a Christian* 'Although I am an unworthy and condemned man, my God has given me in Christ all the riches of righteousness and salvation without any merit on my part out of pure free mercy ... Why should I not therefore freely, joyfully with all my heart, and with an eager will do all things which I know are pleasing and acceptable to such a Father'.[76] This spills over into works of compassion 'Just as our neighbour is in need and lacks that in which we abound, so we were in need before God and lacked his mercy. Hence as our heavenly Father has in Christ freely come to our aid, we also ought freely to help our neighbour'.[77] This gives the Christian life a spontaneity that is lacking in one caught up in doing meritorious works. In his *Treatise on Good Works*, he gave the fine illustration that when two people love each other the size of the gift to each other is of no consequence. Where there is doubt in love however then 'he searches within himself for the best thing to do; then a distinction of works arises by which he imagines he may win favour'. Likewise a Christian man living in confidence towards God 'does everything gladly and willingly not to gather merits and good works but because it is a pleasure for him to please God'.[78] He almost echoed one of Augustine's riskiest and profoundest sayings 'Love God and do what you like'. For now one was free 'to delight to do His will'. One is indeed free to do those things which when regarded as meritorious were highly dangerous. Now one was free to live a monastic life, to collect relics, to go on pilgrimages if they were a joyful response to the grace of God.[79]

So Luther's great contribution in recalling the Church to make central the cost of our redemption in Christ and to realise that it was by grace only, broke through the suffocating legalism of the Western Church. In this attack all legalists suffer – both Catholics and Protestants. In many places he lumps them together with gusto. 'For if the doctrine of justification is lost, the whole of Christian doctrine is lost. And those in the world who do not teach it are either Jews or Turks or papists or (Protestant) sectarians'.[80] He was scathing about those Protestants who made the Bible into a book of precedents and tried to reform the Church by this method. When a Puritan style of reformation was being brought into the Wittenburg church by Carlstadt, Luther came out of hiding in the Wartburg and preached eight telling sermons against its legalism. The Pope had ordered the laity not to touch the sacramental vessels, he said, 'but now you go ahead and become as foolish as the pope in that you think a person must touch the sacrament with his hand'. 'It is right that the sacrament be in both kinds, but this must never be made compulsory . . . Where this is done the sacrament becomes an outward work'.[81]

Luther summed this attitude up in his comment on Romans 7:7–6. They therefore who interpret the Gospel as something else than good news do not understand the Gospel. Precisely this must be said of those who have turned the Gospel into a law rather than interpret it as grace and set Christ before us as a Moses'.[82] It was radical stuff and not even Luther worked out fully what happens when one takes the Nicene creed out of a museum and begins to spell out the implications of the God standing beside and in the place of 'the enemy'. That man is a sinner is important and has to be taken seriously, but what is more important and what has to be taken more seriously is that in Jesus Christ God 'became like us that we might become like him' – by grace alone. This is the basis and indeed the only basis for the unity of all Christians as a pledge for the unity of mankind. This, too, Luther at times glimpsed. The ministers of Nuremberg were having a quarrel over the not unimportant issue of ordination and he wrote to them as follows:

> Suppose you saw Jesus Christ standing bodily in the midst of you and by his very eyes speaking thus unto your hearts. What do you O my dear children, whom I have redeemed by my blood, renewed by my Word that you might mutually love one another? . . . There is no danger in your difference but there is much in your dissension . . . Do not thus sadden my spirit. Do not thus spoil the Holy Angels of their joy in heaven. Am I not more to you than all your matters of difference than all your affections, than all your offences? Can any unjust trouble pierce your heart so much as my wounds, as my blood, as I the whole Saviour Jesus Christ?[83]

That indeed is the question the divided churches must put to each other.

NOTES

1. Luther's Works, American Edition, (*LW*) 33:294.
2. Lucien Fébvre 'The Origins of the French Reformation' in *A New Kind of History*, ed. Peter Burke, (Harper Torchback, 1973), 55.
3. The fifteenth century has been called the inflation period of German mystic literature. G. Pickering, *Bulletin of the John Rylands Library*, XXII, (1938), 458.
4. It is obviously very difficult to measure evidences of true piety, but it is undeniable that there were many signs of it in many places in Europe in the fifteenth century, particularly in the towns of the Netherlands, the Rhineland and in Northern Germany. Other parts of Europe showed signs of spiritual laxity, like the low figures for church attendances in Scotland. This complex scene has been well surveyed by S. Ozment, *The Reformation in the Cities*, (Yale, 1975) Ch. 2. Many stress that this religious life was formal and mechanical but as E. Delarnelle observes, beneath these numerous external observances lay a spiritual cry for religious security, *L'Eglise au temps du Grand Schisme et la crise conciliaire*, (Paris, 1964), 656.
5. Quoted by B. Moeller, 'Religious Life in Germany on the Eve of the Reformation', in *Pre-Reformation Germany*, ed. G. Strauss, (Harper, New York, 1972), 15.
6. ibid.
7. This deeply moving late mediaeval art of Northern Europe shows the same lack of theological control as in the other forms of piety. In the various paintings of the Crucifixion by Van der Weyden, for example, Mary, St John and even the mourning donor take up positions of almost as central importance as Christ.
8. Moeller, op. cit., 21.
9. ibid.
10. The fifteenth century saw the building of many of the largest and finest churches of Europe. In England, it was the greatest era of church building since the Normans. In East Anglia and Lincolnshire alone some hundreds of major churches were built. In the Low Countries many of the finest urban churches were rebuilt.
11. Moeller, op. cit., 16, 33, note 16.
12. For the Brethren of the Common Life and their style of piety see *History of the Church* vol. IV 'From the High Middle Ages to the eve of the Reformation', eds. H. Jedin and J. Dolan, 429–32.
13. Gerard Groote, *The Following of Christ*, ed. J. Malaise, (New York, 1937), Introduction xiii.
14. Quoted J. W. Aldridge, *The Hermeneutic of Erasmus*, (Richmond, Virginia, 1966), 27.
15. Quoted S. Ozment, *The Age of Reform*, 78.
16. *Imitation of Christ*, 1.i.7.
17. In one sense there is nothing original in the *Devotio Moderna*. It merely stresses the pious practices of the Church but it emphasised that there must not be either just intellectual apprehensions of the truth of Christianity, or external observances. It was practical experience of God that was to lead to godly living. The humble following of Christ was the basis of their piety. *History of the Church*, ed. H. Jedin, vol. IV, Ch. 47.
18. S. Ozment, *Age of Reform*, 74–7.
19. I. D. K. Siggins in the following essay.
20. See Huizinga, *The Waning of the Middle Ages*, Ch. XI; and paintings on death and judgement by Holbein, Nicholas Manuel, Dürer, Bosch and Brueghel et. al.
21. Moeller, op. cit., 18 and H. Boehmer, *Road to Reformation*, (Philadelphia, 1946), 172–3.

22. Huizinga, op. cit., Ch. 2.
23. Ian Balfour, *The Relationship of Man and God in the writing of Tertullian*, Edinburgh, Ph.D. Thesis.
24. Luther, Letter to Staupitz, May 30, 1518, *LW*, 48:65–8.
25. W. Ullmann, *A History of Political Thought: The Middle Ages*, (Pelican, 1965), 22 ff. for an illuminating discussion of this Latinising effect on the Church by the Vulgate.
26. S. Ozment, *The Age of Reform*, 241.
27. John Calvin, *The Institutes*, III-iii-1 to 4. Luther, as so often, had anticipated Calvin in this attack. In *The Babylonish Captivity of the Church*, he attacked St Jerome for describing penitence as a second plank of safety after shipwreck instead of relying on the promises of God in Baptism. 'God . . . cannot deny himself if you confess him and faithfully cling to him in his promise. But as for contrition, confession of sins and satisfaction, along with all those carefully devised exercises devised of men: if you rely on them and neglect this truth of God, they will suddenly fail you and leave you more wretched than before', *LW*, 36:58 and 60–1.
28. For this point and also the impersonal view of grace in the Latin West, and the priority of law over grace that recurred in Protestant scholasticism in the seventeenth century see J. B. Torrance 'Strengths and Weaknesses of the Westminster Theology' in *The Westminster Confession in the Church Today*, ed. Alasdair I. Heron, (Edinburgh, 1982), 52, 53.
29. It is most significant that Luther in his wrestling with the problem of the 'how' question saw its solution when he related it much more closely to the 'who' question. After 1518 he more and more discussed justification in terms of the incarnation.
30. S. Ozment, *Age of Reform*, 233–8 and H. Oberman, *Forerunners of the Reformation*, (1967), Ch. 3.
31. Luther, W. 39/1, 419:17–19 quoted H. Oberman, 'Iustitia Christi and Iustitia Dei', in *Harvard Theological Review*, LIX (1966), 6.
32. R. Pascal, *The Social Basis of the German Reformation*, (1933).
33. Erik Erikson, *Young Man Luther* (1958), made popular in John Osborn's play.
34. For a detailed critique of Erikson, see S. Ozment, *Age of Reform*, 223–37, and for Osborn E. G. Rupp, *Luther and Mr. Osborn*. One seeks a rationalisation for irrational behaviour, not rational, and the assumption behind most of these endeavours is that religion is irrational and therefore one seeks a rationalisation. But this shows a complete failure to see that Luther was giving a rational theological answer to a theological problem.
35. Dürer in a letter to Spalatin 1520, quoted G. Strauss, *Nuremberg in the 16th century*, (New York, 1966), 168.
36. *W* 37, 661:22.
37. *LW*, 24:23–4.
38. *TR* 1, 240:12, quoted E. G. Rupp, *Luther's Progress to the Diet of Worms*, 27.
39. *W* 38:148, quoted J. Mackinnon, *Luther and the Reformation*, 1:102–3.
40. *The Babylonish Captivity of the Church*, *LW*, 36:60.
41. *LW*, 25:345; see also E. G. Rupp, *The Righteousness of God*, 165. I am deeply indebted to this splendid chapter on Luther's *Commentary on Romans*. Luther had previously used this expression *incurvatum in se* in his *Commentary on Psalms*, 1513–14.
42. *LW*, 25:350–1.
43. *LW*, 25:345.
44. *W* 10.1-ii.301.27. Sermon on John 20:19 quoted E. G. Rupp, *The Righteousness of God*, 167.

45. Anselm, *Cur Deus Homo*, Bk. 1:20–1. Luther had read Anselm but not, I think, deeply; *LW*, 13:90.
46. *LW*, 27:13.
47. Bernard, 'On the Love of God', in *Late Mediaeval Mysticism*, (*LCC*, XIII), 62, 63.
48. I. D. K. Siggins, next essay, p.70 .
49. E. G. Rupp, *The Righteousness of God*, 148.
50. *LW*, 10:238.
51. *LW*, 25:182; *LCC*, translation, 48.
52. *LW*, 25:191; Rupp's translation, *The Righteousness of God*, 168.
53. *LW*, 31:25 and 83–5.
54. *LW*, 27:13. From his *Commentary on Galatians* of 1535, where he sets out his understanding of *sola gratia* and *sola fide* in its most considered form.
55. The date at which Luther came to this discovery is at present the subject of a substantial controversy. Some insist that he must have resolved this issue prior to his lectures on *Romans* 1515–16. Others, notably U. Saarnivaara, *Luther discovers the Gospel*, (Concordia, 1951), point out that the comment on this verse in 1515 is singularly slight for something so crucial to him and advance other reasons for the specific illumination of this part of his problem which came at the end of 1518. This issue does not affect my particular argument here, but I discuss it in my later essay p. 98–9.
56. See S. Ozment, *The Reformation in Mediaeval Perspective*, (Chicago, 1971), 144 ff.
57. This section is in a long autobiographical fragment of 1545, *LW*, 34:327–38.
58. Luther, 'Commentary on Romans' 7.8, *LW*, 25:336, 434; see also *LCC*, edition, Introduction by W. Pauck, xlv.
59. T. F. Torrance, *Theology in Reconciliation*, (1975), 224 ff.
60. J. Pelikan, *Obedient Rebels*, (1964) 47–8, begins a discussion of this issue.
61. *LW*, 24:98.
62. *LW*, 26:4.
63. See G. Ebeling, *Luther*, Ch.10, and *LW*, 24:146, where Luther shows the integral relation of faith and love.
64. S. Ozment, *The Age of Reform*, 242, 43.
65. Quoted ibid., 242.
66. Quoted S. Ozment, *The Reformation in Mediaeval Perspective*, 150.
67. 'Commentary on Galatians', 2:16, *LW*, 26:129.
68. Cranmer, 'Homily on Salvation' in *Cranmer, Miscellaneous Writings*, (Parker Society), 131.
69. 'Commentary on Genesis', *LW*, 2:267. There is a long discussion on the active nature of faith and of the relationship of faith to the promises of God in this section.
70. *W* 8, 519:19. Quoted I. D. K. Siggins, *Luther's doctrine of Christ*, 147. I am indebted to this work with its rich range of quotations.
71. 'Commentary on John', 6:29, *LW*, 23:8.
72. 'The Freedom of a Christian', *LW*, 31:351.
73. 'Against Latomus', *LW*, 32:235–6.
74. 'Commentary on Romans', *LW*, 25:287, (Rupp's translation).
75. G. Wingren, *The Christian's Calling: Luther on vocation*, (ET 1957), 37 ff.
76. *LW*, 31:367.
77. ibid.
78. *LW*, 44:27.
79. See his 'Sermons at Wittenberg 1522', *LW*, 51:79–81.
80. 'Commentary on Galatians', preface, *LW*, 26:9. See also p. 150.
81. Sermons of 1522, *LW*, 51:88–90.

82. *LW*, 25:327 on.
83. Luther, *Brief Wechsel*, ix, 322–7, July 1533. Translated by M. Schild, *Lutheran Theological Journal* (Adelaide), vol. VII, No. 1, 38–41. So great was the strife within the Lutheran church soon after Luther's death between the 'orthodox' Lutherans and the followers of Melanchthon, and between them and the Reformed, that those who understood Luther on this issue published pamphlets containing extracts from his letters such as this one to help reconcile the differences. Some of these were translated into English and used for a similar purpose during the controversies between Presbyterians and Independents during the English Civil War. I came across several extracts from these letters, including the one just quoted, in Samuel Bolton's irenic work, *The Arraignment of Error*, January 1646. It is instructive that when I showed this letter to some 'orthodox' Lutherans before I had found it in Luther's works, they decided that it could not possibly be by Luther despite his obvious phraseology at certain points.

LUTHER: MODEL OR TEACHER FOR CHURCH REFORM?

Harry McSorley

To speak of Luther as a theologian for Catholics and Protestants requires qualifications in order to safeguard historical and theological truth and, consequently, to provide a firm – that is, a historically and theologically sound – basis for restoration of full communion among Christians. Such a qualified reception of Luther may help offset any unjustified euphoria accompanying the perfectly justifiable spirit of positive appreciation that will be voiced in virtually every room of the Christian household on the occasion of the fifth centenary of Luther's birth. Moreover, it is only through an assessment of Luther that is both critical and fair that one will dispel the notion that ecumenical theology itself is some kind of 'romantic' enterprise.[1]

I shall introduce this assessment of Luther by pointing out in part I in a rather general way some of the senses in which he is *not* a theologian for all Christians, not even for all Lutherans. This will lead to a more specific examination, in section II, of a sense in which Luther does not seem ecumenically 'receivable' – namely, as a model or exemplar of church reform. The path will then be clear for us to look in part III at the positive way in which Luther can serve both Protestants and Catholics today as a 'common doctor' who can help them bring about that which he was unable to do – the restoration of unity between the Roman Catholic Church and the churches resulting from the Protestant reformation.

I

Luther was clearly not a theologian for such Catholics as Pope Leo X, who first censured, then excommunicated Luther. Nor was

23

he a theologian for such Catholic adversaries as Prierias, Eck, Cochlaeus and their twentieth century heirs, Denifle, Grisar and Maritain.[2] There were also critical Catholic humanists who wanted reform, but not in Luther's manner.

Neither was Luther a theologian for those fellow reformers whom he called 'Anabaptists' and worse, to the extent that he and they refused to accept the position of the other on such matters as infant baptism, the permissibility of images and traditional liturgical forms. Nor was he a theologian for Zwingli and his followers, and the Calvinists, to the extent that each side found the eucharistic theology of the other unsatisfactory. A considerable portion of English Protestantism also balked at Luther's sacramental theology.[3]

Luther is not even a theologian for all Lutherans in the important sense that only three of his hundreds of works, the *Catechisms* and the *Smalcald Articles*, have been received into the normative Lutheran collection known as the *Book of Concord*.[4] When Luther's other writings are drawn upon in the *Formula of Concord*, the final part of the *Book of Concord*, the qualification is made that the Holy Scripture is the sole rule and norm of all doctrine and that even Luther's writings are subject to it.[5] Here we have embedded in the official Lutheran confessions and important qualification concerning the manner in which Luther's theology is to be regarded by Lutherans. To accept all of Luther's theology without subjecting it to a scriptural critique is un-Lutheran![6] When the *Formula of Concord* was taking shape in the late 1570s, strong Lutheran pressure was exerted to limit the number of Luther's works that were to be received officially because of the problems that arise when 'human writings' are set alongside 'the Word of God'.[7]

The official or formal reception of Luther's works by Lutherans is even more restricted when one considers that many Lutheran churches – those of Denmark, Norway and France as well as some of the smaller non-European Lutheran churches – do not include in their constitutions the *Formula of Concord* with its limited reception of Luther's writings.[8] Among these churches Luther's 'Catechism', sometimes more specifically his 'Small Catechism', is often but not always singled out as a secondary interpretative norm along with the *Augsburg Confession*.[9] There are, then, some

Lutherans who do not put *any* of Luther's works on the same level as the *Augustana*.

The rather formal facts mentioned in the two previous paragraphs disclose a deliberate attitude of critical reserve and sobriety toward Luther even among those who link their form of Christian life with his name. With this attitude Lutherans have thus heeded well Luther's own critical view of his work.[10]

II

> 'I have said more than once: Let anyone attack
> my person however he will. I don't claim to be an
> angel . . .' *WA* 7, 275:1–2 (Against Emser, 1521).

I am not going to accept Luther's invitation to 'attack his person'. I intend, rather, to raise some questions about Luther's justification of an aspect of his personal behaviour that many Christians, not just Roman Catholics, still regard as an obstacle which prevents them from recognizing the father of the reformation as the exemplar of church reform 'for all seasons'. The barrier of which I speak is Luther's polemical manner of reviling and disparaging his 'opponents', be they Roman Catholics 'papists' (to use the most mild epithet he hurled at them), Protestant 'enthusiasts', 'fanatics', 'sacramentarians' or 'false brethren', or Jews and 'Turks'.[11] I shall take it for granted that the average reader knows what I'm talking about and that I need not rehearse examples of Luther's invective. For those who wish a quick review, Luther's 1543 treatise against the Jews and his 1545 tract against the papacy are generally regarded as the low points of his verbal abuse of those deemed by him to be in the power of Satan. It also goes without saying that Luther was not the only master of the art of verbal assault in the sixteenth century, nor was his anti-semitism any greater than John Eck's. But no one is proposing Eck or Cochlaeus as theologians for Catholics and Protestants. Nor do they have the kind of place in Roman Catholicism that Luther has in Lutheranism and in Protestantism.

Before his excommunication Luther could confess with

apparent sincerity, though not without some persuasion by the Roman emissary, Charles von Miltitz, that he had spoken the truth too heatedly and too sharply and had gone too far in his criticism of the Roman Church.[12] Despite the hard-hitting tracts of 1520, Luther followed the advice of his friends and of his prince-protector and assumed a reserved posture at the Diet of Worms in 1521.[13] He soon regretted having been mild there when he should have spoken out like a prophet.[14] The 'civil' criticism of the church made by Erasmus, Capito and others, which abstains from 'chiding, biting and giving offense', accomplishes nothing, argues Luther, for the pontiffs thus think they can continue in their ways uncorrected.[15] His 'reprehending' of papal and ecclesiastical abuse and false teaching will thus become increasingly sharp and vituperative, culminating in the tracts of the 1540s mentioned in the preceding paragraph.

The acerbity of Luther's polemic, especially that directed against the papacy, has alienated Roman Catholics from the sixteenth century to the present, including such irenic interpreters as Joseph Lortz, Albert Brandenburg and Cardinal Jan Willebrands.[16] In a recent study of Luther's critique of the papacy which, in my judgment, fails to bring out that Luther's critique was conditional, not absolute,[17] Scott Hendrix points out, as did Holl,[18] that Luther was able to find some precedent for his offensive speech in the language of the prophets and even in that of Jesus and Paul.[19] Moreover, contends Hendrix, it was Luther's conscientious conviction that the papacy was doing serious harm to the church – and not some 'abysmal hatred' – that led him to his passionate critique of the papacy.[20]

I find this, at least to some extent, a plausible line of explaining, if not excusing, Luther's polemical behaviour. It also seems to me that the view articulated by Melanchthon in his oration at Luther's funeral, and embraced most recently by both Edwards[21] and Hendrix,[22] is also a just and ecumenically appropriable way of interpreting and relativizing Luther's hard-line polemics. While refusing to dispute the observation made in his day even by people who were 'not evil' that Luther was harsher (asperior) than he ought to have been, Melanchthon responded with a sentiment he said Erasmus had spoken often: that, in view of the magnitude of its ills, God has given this age a severe physician (acrem medicum).[23] Not just Erasmus, but other Catholics such as Eck, Pope Adrian VI and speakers at the Council of Trent, even if they did not offer positive assessments of Luther's teaching, could also see God chastizing the church through Luther.

Melanchthon himself seems to be granting that Luther's harsh style of reform is not the remedy for the less glaring reforms of which the church constantly stands in need.[24] For one reason, as Luther himself foresaw and then acknowledged after the fact: his reformation had about it a tragic dimension,[25] a division of the western church that has proliferated and persisted.[26] But there is another reason. Precisely because the ecumenical movement of our age is showing signs of becoming God's instrument in overcoming Christian discord, Christians are going to have to think together about the way a future 'church uniting and reforming' is continually to be open to reform and renewal. This justifies us in looking a bit more deeply at some of the rationale Luther used to justify his polemic mode of reform so that we can distance ourselves from it while remaining open to what he has to say to us as a common teacher.

Were God so to have intervened at Luther's death as he did at Lazarus's, I think Luther would have leaped from his coffin to denounce Melanchthon for suggesting that he had spoken too harshly against his opponents. By what standard did Melanchthon and other good people then and later regard Luther's polemic as offensive? By the standard of Christian love, of course, especially as the radical implications of that standard were disclosed by Jesus in the Sermon on the Mount. This critique of Luther's harshness ignores the hard fact, however, that Luther did not think he or any Christian preacher was bound by those standards when confronted with enemies of the Gospel.

As Luther proceeded on his course of sharp opposition to the Roman Church, he consistently exempted parents, preachers and public officials from the command of Matthew 5:22 – not to be angry with our brother or call people names – when they are exercising their 'office' or acting as 'public persons'.[27] By 1545 the exception extends to *all* Christians as Luther asks: 'Should not I as a Christian, and should not all lovers of our Lord Christ rightly be impatient, angry and intolerant, and moreover curse the accursed papacy and call it the most shocking names, a papacy which is not ashamed to blaspheme our Lord most disgracefully and turn his promises into lies?'[28]

Nor, for Luther, does the command to love our enemies, to bless those who curse us, to do good to those who hate us and pray for those who persecute us in Matthew 5:44 apply to those in the preaching ministry or to other public persons when they are acting as such.[29] In this sermon Luther first states without qualification that the Christian person 'shows no hatred nor enmity whatever toward anyone and has no anger in his heart – only sheer love, gentleness and kindness, just as our Lord and His heavenly Father do, whom he here even offers as an example.'[30] But why is it, asks Luther, that so many holy people in the Scriptures curse their enemies, even Christ and his apostles?[31] 'Or how can I love the pope, whom I daily rebuke and curse, and rightly so?' The answer, says Luther, is that 'the office of preaching is not ours, but God's. But what is God's is not our doing, but his, through the Word and ministry as his own gift and activity. But since it is written in John 16 that it is the office of the Holy Spirit to reprove the world . . . He can't just tell the world what it wants to hear but must rebuke it and speak sharply against evil.'[32] Luther sums up his interpretation of Matthew 5:44 by saying: If someone interferes with our love and service of God, 'neither love nor service applies to him, since the text says: 'You shall love and do good to *your* enemy.' But I must be an enemy to *God's* enemy so that I do not rise up with him against God.'[33]

The great Luther scholar, Paul Althaus, takes note of the distinctions and the exceptions Luther makes when dealing with the love requirement of the Sermon on the Mount, yet makes the astonishing claim that 'Luther does not weaken the Sermon on the Mount in the slightest. He accepts it in its full rigor.'[34] It would seem truer, I think, if Luther's name were to be added to the long list of those who, as Gunther Bornkamm puts it after reviewing the history of exegesis of the text, have sought to interpret the Sermon on the Mount by trying 'to limit its validity'.[35]

Gordon Rupp, the renowned Methodist Luther scholar, is confident that he is expressing the attitude of virtually all his fellow British Free Churchmen when he rejects Milton's view that Luther's animosity on behalf of his great cause should be ranked among the Christian virtues.[36] Many of Luther's own followers then[37] and now[38] have found his polemical manner offensive. In 1970 the Lutheran World Federation in fact seized the opportunity presented by Cardinal Willebrand's historic positive statement concerning Luther[39] to make history itself by formally repudiating the sub-Christian aspects of the reformation polemics. Since that statement does not seem to have received the publicity it deserves, I take the liberty of citing it here:

> It is . . . in accordance with [the] commandment of truth and love that we as Lutheran Christians and congregations be prepared to acknowledge that the judgment of the Reformers upon the Roman Catholic Church and its theology was not entirely free of polemical distortions, which in part have been perpetuated to the present day.
>
> We are truly sorry for the offense and misunderstanding which these polemic elements have caused our Roman Catholic brethren. We remember with gratitude the statement of Pope Paul VI to the Second Vatican Council in which he communicates his plea for forgiveness for any offense caused by the Roman Catholic Church. As we together with all Christians pray for forgiveness in the prayer our Lord has taught us, let us strive for clear, honest, and charitable language in all our conversations.[40]

In closing this critique of Luther's polemical manner, justice requires that attention be drawn to at least one great moment in his career when Luther demonstrated that he could identify with a style of reformation writing that was markedly different from his own. I refer to his attitude toward the *Augsburg Confession*, the great unifying document of virtually all Lutheranism. In the doctrinal section of the *Augustana*, even though several 'Anabaptist' doctrines are condemned, no dogma of the Roman Church is attacked. More important for the point of this section is the fact that the *Augustana* is free of Luther's characteristic polemic. We thus have a reception of Luther's key reformation insights along with a non-reception of Luther's polemical style by the most authoritative utterance of the Lutheran reformation. This analysis by no means advocates an ecumenism at the expense of Luther,[41] but rather, a reformation theology which overcomes that which most Catholics and many Protestants think is the most objectionable aspect of Luther's reformation – its polemical style. That Luther, too, was capable of disengaging his reformation teaching from the polemical armour and assault weapons with which he surrounded it is evident from the fact that, despite some early grumblings, Luther was able not only to embrace enthusiastically the content of the *Augustana*,[42] but also to point with pride at its irenic character![43] The latter point provides further evidence that Luther's comments about Melanchthon's 'soft-pedalling' (Leisetreteri) during the Diet of Augsburg was meant not as a rebuke but as a genuine compliment.[44]

III

'. . . but I will let no one attack my doctrine without responding, because I know that it is not mine, but God's.' *WA* 7, 275:3–5 (Against Emser, 1521).

Having criticized the less than angelic manner in which Luther carried out his reform, we are now in a position to see him as a teacher for Protestants and Catholics. One more caveat is needed, however. When Luther says his teaching is not his, but God's, it should be clear from what has been said in the first section that this refers to that teaching of Luther which is in conformity with the Scriptures. Luther certainly did not exempt himself from his own canon: 'The saints have often sinned in their own lives and erred in their writings, but the Scriptures cannot err. . . . [Therefore] nothing is more dangerous than the works and the lives of the saints which are not grounded in the Scriptures.'[45]

With that guideline in place, I can proceed to mention some basic ways in which Luther can serve as a teacher for all Christians. Then I shall single out certain of Luther's teachings which I think are particularly appropriate today, first for Protestants, then for Roman Catholics, from the point of view of Christian reconciliation.

In his funeral oration for Luther, Melanchthon listed several teachings of Luther that, in his mind, represented a blessing for the whole church. I think it fitting to mention them and in the order Melanchthon chose: In the first place, Luther was one who overcame the 'very obscure' teaching in the church of his day about 'penitence' by unfolding a doctrine of 'true penitence' which pointed to the One who is the source of our firm spiritual consolation in the face of anxiety about God's judgment. Luther also illumined Paul's 'doctrine which says we are justified by faith.' Luther showed the distinction between law and gospel and between the 'justice of the Spirit' and civil justice. He taught the true invocation of God based on faith and a good conscience, an invocation directed to the one mediator, the Son of God, sitting at the right hand of the Father interceding for us. He enobled civil life by showing that it, too, is pleasing to God. He separated necessary works from ceremonies, rites and laws that impeded the true invocation of God. His German translation of the bible was of such clarity that its readers derive more light from it than from a number of commentaries. His own commentaries, as even Erasmus admitted, excelled by far those of previous authors.[46] Can any Christian, Catholic or Protestant, who is to any extent conversant with Luther's teaching on the above matters, as well as with Luther's German Bible, fail to agree with Melanchthon that 'the light of the Gospel has been made to shine more brightly by the voice of Luther?'[47]

The list of those aspects of Luther's theology that have gained, or deserve to gain ecumenical acceptance can be considerably lengthened I wish to use the remaining space, however, to suggest some ways in which Luther's theology has been heard and still might be heard by Protestants and by Catholics so as to facilitate reform and reconciliation among the still separated churches of the West.

A.   *Luther: A Theologian for Protestants*
The ecumenical movement of our time has given rise to a new appreciation of the sacraments by Protestants, at least, but by no means exclusively, on the level of theology and church leadership. This does not represent some kind of latter-day catholicizing of Protestantism, but rather the recovery of evangelical and catholic substance that is integral to the New Testament and to the reformation theology of Luther, Calvin and other reformers. It does represent the overcoming of one of the most baleful effects of

what might be crudely called 'enlightenment' theology, which introduced into Protestant thought a disastrous disjunction between 'Word' and 'Sacrament', to the detriment of the latter. No one can study the theology of the Father of the Reformation, or Calvin for that matter, and conclude that Protestantism is a church of the 'Word' and Catholicism a church of the 'Sacrament'.

Accompanying this new awareness that sacraments are integral to Christian life are strong signs that Christians are on the way to concord in the matter of baptism, the Lord's Supper and the ministry to a degree that is without precedent since 1520. This rapprochement includes the prospect of surmounting the historically ugly division between at least some of the heirs of those who, in the sixteenth century, were uncharitably and unjustly called 'Anabaptists' and virtually all other Christian churches. Historic divisions between Lutherans, Catholics, Calvinists and Baptists concerning the sacrament of unity, the Eucharist, also appear to be in the process of being overcome as a result of prayerful, sustained dialogue and study between previously estranged members of the Christian household.[48] Luther's voice has been appropriately heard in all these discussions, along with other Christian voices, and the central thrust of his teaching has had a significant impact on the emerging consensus on the sacraments.

I draw attention here to Luther's teaching on both Baptism and the Eucharist only to point to something else to which it is intimately related that is just beginning to find a place on the ecumenical agenda: the importance of 'right teaching' and the doctrine of infallibility. Just as one cannot read Luther and fail to see that the sacraments were integral to the original form of Protestantism, neither can one read him carefully and overlook the centrality of right – and inerrant – teaching for his theology. The development of Protestantism into so-called 'Orthodoxy' followed by 'Pietist' and 'Enlightenment' and 'Liberal' reactions to it, turned much of Protestantism away from something that was at the very heart of Luther's teaching, a concern for true doctrine. Some of those who admired him for diverse reasons from the eighteenth century to the present have even seen in Luther's critical stance toward the canonicity of biblical books as well as his critique of such biblical authors as James grounds for first criticizing and then rejecting the Christian articles of faith concerning the divinity of Jesus, the Trinity and other articles of the creed – in the name of Luther![49] The popular consequence of this radical 'Protestant' critique of the Christian faith is that the ordinary protestant in the nineteenth and much of the twentieth century assumed a stance of doctrinal tolerance if not indifference, while seeing Catholics as 'dogmatic'. This was an exact reversal of the roles which Luther saw being played by himself, on the one hand, and the Catholic, Erasmus, on the other during their historic exchange. The 'new' Protestants, who wanted to be extremely reticent in making doctrinal assertions were thus on the side of Erasmus, while the Catholics were found offensive because they were (unwittingly) following Luther's injunction: 'Not to delight in assertions is to cease to be a Christian.'[50]

Just as Luther's realistic sense of the sacraments has been a stimulus, certainly not the only one, to helping contemporary Protestants regain their Reformation sacramental roots, so also Luther's appreciation of doctrine and of ecclesial infallibility may help overcome post-Reformation Protestant attitudes that render difficult dialogue with Roman Catholics on the question of ecclesial and papal infallibility. Protestant-Catholic discussion about papal infallibility is often in difficulty at the outset because those on the Protestant side do not share with their Catholic partners the belief that the whole visible church, that is, the church that baptizes infants and celebrates the Lord's Supper, is in any meaningful sense infallible. Here is where Luther might be of help. For the founder of Protestant Christianity firmly believed in the infallibility of the church and its 'articles of faith'. Included in these 'articles' is the Christian legitimacy of the practice of infant baptism and the true, sacramental presence of the body and blood of Jesus Christ in the Lord's Supper.

When his various biblical arguments on behalf of infant baptism failed to have effect, Luther could say quite confidently: 'All of Christianity from East to West has baptized infants for more than a thousand years ... Because the church is holy, if it had erred it would not be holy.'[51] This kind of argument throws light on what Luther understands by a scriptural proof. Obviously clear biblical warrant is desirable. But even if such evidence is not available, if there is a universal Christian practice that is not opposed to Scripture, this is a strong indication that it is right.[52]

In the debates over the true presence of Christ in the Eucharist, Luther was convinced he had 'clear' biblical proof for the traditional doctrine. Nonetheless he did not hesitate to appeal to the fact that this doctrine was an article of faith held by the whole church, as is attested by the writings of the Greek and Latin Fathers and by daily 'use' right up to his time:

> [Such] testimony of the entire holy Christian Church (if we had nothing else) ought of itself [allein] be sufficient for us to abide by this article ... For it is dangerous and dreadful for us to hear or to believe contrary to the united testimony, faith and doctrine of the entire holy Christian Church as it has unanimously taught from the beginning for over fifteen hundred years ... Whoever doubts [this article] in effect does not believe the Christian Church. Such a person not only condemns the entire holy Christian Church as a damned heretic but also Christ himself with all the apostles and prophets who have given the basis and the powerful testimony for this article that we confess: 'I believe one holy Christian Church,' ... One may trifle with papal or imperial laws or other human tradition of the Fathers or councils, but not with articles of faith which have been with us from the beginning and which have been unanimously upheld throughout Christendom.[53]

This scratching of a relatively untapped mine of Luther's theology already enables us to conclude: (1) the concept of the inerrancy of the whole church, often called ecclesial infallibility, is integral to Luther's evangelical-catholic reformation theology;[54] (2) that the 'holy Christian Church' of which Luther speaks in *this* connection is not some invisible reality (except in the sense that, as an object of faith we believe it and don't 'see' it) but the very concrete church that baptizes babies, celebrates the eucharist and studies the Bible; (3) It is erroneous to say that Luther's critical scriptural principle brought to a close the history of dogma, for this overlooks the crucial truth that Luther felt bound not only by God's Word, but also by the divinely grounded and sustained articles of faith which mediated that Word to him and which led him to interpret Scripture in the light of those articles. Just as Luther invoked the innerancy of the 'entire holy Christian Church' against opponents of his day, so too, *per impossibile*, would he have invoked the same principle against 'neo-Protestants' from the enlightenment through Harnack and beyond who thought that in the name of Luther's critical scriptural principle they could discard this or that article of the faith of the whole Christian Church. This overlooks a core aspect of Luther's theology: ecclesial innerancy.[55] (4) Recovery of this basis reformation doctrine of the innerancy of the entire church will surely facilitate dialogue on the question of conciliar[56] and papal infallibility which can only be understood as instruments and signs of the basic inerrancy of the whole church.

B. *Luther: A Theologian for Catholics*

Luther has long been a theologian for Roman Catholics, though this has seldom been acknowledged. For example, although some of the disciplinary reforms at the Council of Trent may have been thinkable apart from Luther – for example the dissociation of almsgiving from indulgences, provision for proper education and discipline of the clergy, the crucial requirement that bishops be pastors of but one diocese and that they reside in it – it is quite unlikely they would have been enacted without Luther's prophetic exposure of the harm done the church by the lack of such reforms. Luther's central doctrinal concern, the doctrine of justification by faith through grace, and its corollary, the unfreedom of the sinner to do anything for justification apart from the liberating grace of Christ was unquestionably heard and appropriated by Trent, to be sure, in its own idiom.[57]

The influence of Luther's theology on the Second Vatican Council is also discernible, even if Luther's name is not found in the footnotes to the council documents. One thinks here of the council's teaching on the primacy of the Word of God over all of church life; the attendant recognition that the teaching ministry in the church is not above God's Word, but ministers to it; the fostering of a biblical piety in the church, the use of the vernacular in the liturgy as one aspect of an overall reform of the eucharistic liturgy; emphasis on the preaching of the Gospel as integral to the duties of the ordained ministry; restoration, albeit only on a limited basis, of the chalice to the laity; elaboration of a fuller doctrine of the priesthood of all believers than one can find in even the *Book of Concord*; situation of papal primacy and infallibility within the context of the whole church and of episcopal collegiality, thereby overcoming a serious deficiency caused by the unanticipated adjournment of Vatican I;[58] recognition that reform of both church doctrine and discipline are necessary; and, finally, the very crucial acknowledgment that the one Church of Christ extends beyond the boundaries of the Roman Catholic Church.

The last point is one that accords fully with Luther's view of the church and its inerrancy. A doctrine or a practice that has been held by the entire holy church, if it is in harmony with Scripture, is, for Luther, inerrant. But if such a doctrine or practice has only been received by part of the church, can it be required of the whole church if it does not seem to be clearly in conformity with Scripture? The implications of this particular point of Vatican II's – and Luther's – teaching seem to me to be far-reaching, though as yet little-appreciated by Catholic theologians. Does not such a doctrine require Roman Catholics to do some retroactive thinking? Are the western councils of the second millennium truly ecumenical if they did not involve or have not yet been received by the rest of the church?[59] If they are not, this does not automatically mean everything they said was false. But it would give Roman Catholics some leeway in deciding upon the authoritativeness of the various doctrines taught by all those councils, something which could bode well for Christian reunion.

There are many other aspects of Luther's theology which might still be heard with profit by Catholics. On the occasion of the anniversary of the Diet of Worms, for example, a representative group of Catholics from that city requested Pope Paul VI to issue a clarifying word about Luther that would take into account the findings of recent Catholic Luther scholarship, in a fuller manner than Cardinal Willebrands had done the year before at the assembly of the Lutheran World Federation. This would not only serve the cause of justice, they said, but would also make it easier for Catholics to follow those parts of Luther's theology that are cherished by many Christians of all confessions. They cited Luther's theology of faith, his insights into biblical interpretation, his doctrine of sin and of the paradoxes of the Christian life, his doctrine of the hiddenness of God and 'what is perhaps most important, his theology of the cross.'[60]

Each of these themes could become the object of reflection, but I shall resist that urge and draw attention to still another point, or complex of points, where Luther's theology still needs to be heard by Catholics as they undergo internal renewal in preparation for reconciliation with other Christian churches. I refer to Luther as the doctor par excellence of Christian liberty.

If Protestants can derive from Luther a renewed sense of reverence for the church's 'articles of faith', Catholics have much to learn from him about 'unity in necessary things, liberty in doubtful things', a principle to which Vatican II subscribed. The Roman Catholic Church has just promulgated a new code of canon law at a time when Lutheran and Anglican theologians are beginning to see the desirability of a universal Petrine ministry exercised by the Bishop of Rome, provided Christian liberty be safeguarded.

How central the question of canon law is for Christian reunion can be gathered by simply recalling: (1) it was the canon law procedures in force in Luther's day that provided the machinery for his excommunication; among other things, the law required retraction from Luther rather than fraternal dialogue and it allowed such avowed, literally prejudiced opponents of Luther as Eck and Prierias to be involved in forming the judgment against him; (2) it was the canon law text of his day that Luther sent to the flames in 1520 along with the papal bull threatening his excommunication.

Christian liberty, as Luther expounded it, does not mean there is to be no canon law or discipline in the church. Indeed, as early as the great treatise *On Christian Liberty* of 1520, Luther warned against those who, as soon as they hear of the liberty of faith, turn it into a fleshly liberty, thinking that if they believe, they are now permitted to do anything they like. 'They want to show they are free Christians only by despising and rejecting ceremonies, traditions and human laws.'[61]

We cannot find in Luther nor derive from his works a new canon law. In fact, Luther confessed that the question of church ordinances was 'the most difficult question of all, variously addressed by many, but actually settled by no one.'[62] In many quarters of the Roman Catholic Chruch, particularly among canon lawyers, I am happy to say, there is an appreciation of the fact that all church discipline and law must reflect the Gospel of Christ if it is to be worthy of the Christian people. To the extent that the new code does not measure up to the norm, one can hope confidently that the Catholic people and their bishops will not receive it. One can also be confident that when the *next* revision of the code is undertaken, the evangelical insights of Luther will play a significant role.

Closely related to Christian liberty, if not one of its components, is loving, loyal, yet courageous criticism of church leasers, pronouncements, preaching, worship and structures whenever these obscure the gospel, impede the mission or infringe Christian liberty. Whether he was speaking sarcastically or whether it was through uncharacteristic lack of imagination, the only way Luther could see a Christian minister responding to ecclesiastical abuse *if* he were bound by the Sermon on the Mount is as follows:

> Am I to say to our enemies, the pope, the bishops, princes and whomever, who persecute the gospel and trample on the people who hold on to it: Dear lords, may the dear God reward you. You are pious people and holy fathers, etc., or should I keep silence, show them reverence, or kiss their feet, etc.? No, dear brothers – here is what we should say: I am a preacher who ought to have teeth in his mouth, to bite them and irritate them and to tell them the truth, and if they don't want to hear it, to excommunicate them, to bar them from heaven, to send them to hell's fire and give them to Satan for God's sake, etc.'[63]

Surely the way of Jesus lies between these extremes of dishonest, fawning flattery on the one hand and verbal assault on the other. Is it not the Christian standard to be watchful, to stand firm in the faith, to be courageous and strong, while at the same time letting all that we do, including reproving, rebuking and other occasionally painful acts of church discipline, be done in love?[64]

One of the key factors contributing to the rise of an uncritical attitude toward the papacy on the part of many Catholics was precisely the unbridled criticism hurled at it during the reformation. This Catholic over-reaction on behalf of the papacy, as distinct from the theological case for the Petrine ministry that is gaining ecumenical acceptance in our day, has probably contributed as much to the continuance of Christian division as has the excessively critical reformation rejection of the papacy.

Luther was not uncatholic in criticizing the one who held the place of Peter. There have been Catholic precedents since the rebukes to Peter administered by Jesus and Paul. Thomas Aquinas, for example, to the objection that it isn't proper for a subject to admonish a prelate, says: 'To argue with and to scold *irreverently* is prohibited, but he can admonish *charitably* as Paul did to Peter in Galatians 2:11.'[65]

One may justly ask: where were these 'charitable admonishers' during the scandalous period of the church in which Luther found himself? Luther soon learned that his 'reverent' attempts at reform were getting nowhere. In fact, they only seemed to incite vituperative responses, which unfortunately drove him to reply in kind, thus giving rise to the tragic and sinful dimensions of what had originally been a Catholic reform of the church. Five hundred years after his birth Catholics are increasingly coming to see Luther as a 'beloved praeceptor' not just for Protestants, but also for themselves. And they will even increasingly be able to appropriate the image of Luther as the courageous and conscientious reformer when it is purified and itself reformed by the principle: 'in all things, charity.'

NOTES

1. Steven Ozment, *The Reformation in the Cities* (New Haven and London, Yale University Press, 1975), pp. 5 and 169, note 18 applies this term to the impressive ecumenical studies of Hans Küng and Otto Pesch. If Küng's book on Karl Barth's doctrine of justification is 'romantic', so is Barth's acknowledgment that Küng has understood his thought *exactly*. To call Pesch's rigorously argued thousand-page study of Luther and Aquinas on justification 'romantic' is surely to redefine that term. It is, moreover, not true that the conclusion of Pesch's work is that Luther and Aquinas are 'saying the same thing in different ways'. For Pesch they are often saying *really different* things as a result of a basic opposition in their very understanding of the nature of theology. Even where there are unbridgeable

differences between the two – this is Pesch's main point – these differences ought not to be seen as church-dividing: *Die Theologie der Rechtfertigung bei Martin Luther und Thomas von Aquin* (Mainz, Mathias-Grünewald Verlag, 1967), pp. 941–8, 950, conclusion 4; cf. pp. 529 and 537–52, 885–90. Three things might be said about Ozment's verdict, pp. 3–4, that the very title of my own book, *Luther: Right or Wrong?* (New York-Minneapolis, Paulist and Augsburg, 1969) expresses 'the strong apologetic undercurrent' of the 'Lortz school': (1) I do not belong to that school; (2) the title for the American edition was chosen by the *Lutheran* co-publisher; (3) those who read the sub-title, which *is* mine, will see that it is not an exercise in apologetics, but in ecumenical theology, the unromantic nature of which is explained at length by Heinrich Fries in the foreword to the American version. Heiko Oberman, *Luther: Mensch zwischen Gott und Teufel* (Berlin, Severin und Siedler, 1982), p. 325 shows little awareness of what actually goes on in ecumenical dialogues when he insinuates that they 'pass over in silence those questions which separate Christians'.

2. One cannot say with equal ease that Luther was not a theologian for the Council of Trent. See my essays 'Luther, Trent, Vatican I and Vatican II', *McCormick Quarterly*, XXI (1967), pp. 95–104 and 'Luther and Trent on the Faith Needed for the Sacrament of Penance', *Concilium*, 61 (1971), pp. 89–98. At Trent no less a person than the future Pope Urban VII had to point out that Luther and Calvin taught many things that were true, including their agreement with St Jerome's teaching that the distinction between bishops and priests is the result of church decision, not divine precept, *Concilium Tridentinum*, ed. S. Ehses, IX, 2nd ed. (Herder, Freiburg, 1965), p. 54, lines 25–39.

3. See B. A. Gerrish, 'John Calvin on Luther', and William A. Clebsch, 'The Elizabethans on Luther', in: *Interpreters of Luther*, ed. Jaroslav Pelikan (Philadelphia, Fortress, 1968), pp. 67–96 and 97–120.

4. *Formula Concordiae*, Solida Declaratio, Von dem summarischen Begriff, VI, 9 in: *Die Bekenntnisschriften der evangelisch-lutherischen Kirche*, 4th ed. (Göttingen, Vandenhoeck and Ruprecht, 1959), pp 836–7. Henceforth cited as BSLK. Cf. T. G. Tappert, tr. and ed., *The Book of Concord*: The Confessions of the Evangelical Lutheran Church (Philadelphia, Fortress, 1959), p. 505, § 9. Henceforth cited as Tappert.

5. BSLK, p. 837, lines 3–16 (Latin). The text states that this critical view of Luther's works comes from Luther himself! Tappert, p. 505, § 9.

6. Hubert Jedin's admonition, 'Whoever wants to make all of Luther Catholic becomes a Lutheran himself', implies a standard for 'being Lutheran' that is foreign not only to the *Book of Concord* but also to Luther. 'Zum Wandel des katholischen Lutherbildes', in: H. Gehrig, ed., *Martin Luther: Gestalt und Werk* (Karlsruhe, Badenia, 1957), p. 46. In prefaces to collections of his works in 1533 (*WA*, 38:133 f.) and 1539 (*WA*, 50:657–8; *LW*, 34:283–4), Luther sincerely laments that his works are being collected because precious time will be spent studying them instead of Scripture.

7. BSLK, p. 837, note 1.

8. Hans Weissgerber, 'The Valid Confessional Symbols', in: V. Vajta and H. Weissgerber, eds., *The Church and the Confessions* (Philadelphia, Fortress, 1963), pp. 1–22.

9. For example, the Lutheran churches of Denmark, Norway, Brazil, Bolivia, Ethiopia, the Sudan, Hong Kong and Taiwan; Weissgerber, pp. 9–11, 15–21.

10. In addition to the texts mentioned in note 6 above, *WA*, 58/1:79–84 provides dozens of citations attesting Luther's genuine humility in criticizing his own writings. See also Karl Holl, 'Luthers Urteil über sich selbst', in his *Gesammelte*

Aufsätze zur Kirchengeschichte, Bd. I, 2nd and 3rd ed. (Tübingen, Mohr, 1923), pp. 398–401, English tr. by Erik Midelfort in: Jaroslav Pelikan, ed., *Interpreters of Luther*, pp. 20–22.

11. For a survey of Luther's polemical style see Bernard Lohse, *Martin Luther: Einführung in sein Leben und sein Werk* (München, Beck, 1981), pp. 91–6. Miriam Usher Chrisman, 'From Polemic to Propaganda: The Development of Mass Persuasion in the Late Sixteenth Century', *Archive for Reformation History* 73 (1982), pp. 175–96 offers evidence which helps us to see how second-generation 'propagandists' tore asunder the seamless garment of Christ that had only been ripped by earlier 'polemicists'. However, by restricting the term 'polemic' to 'a controversial argument' which 'connotes a two-way ... dialogue, although it may be a dialogue between the deaf' and excluding from it any 'systematic attempt to propagate a particular opinion or doctrine [whose] purpose is to influence men's opinions and thus their actions and behaviour' which, following L. Doob, she calls 'propaganda', p. 175, she thereby disjoins things that were, at least in Luther, intimately related, if not indistinguishable. Mark U. Edwards, Jr., *Luther and the False Brethren* (Stanford, Calif., Stanford Univ. Press, 1975) carefully analyses the polemical exchanges between Luther and the Protestants who disagreed with him. His introduction and conclusion, however, contain insufficiently grounded assertions about the allegedly different nature of the polemic between Luther and the Catholics of his day. For example, as will be shown in the next section, Luther, too, could argue 'from Scripture and tradition as interpreted by the church'; cf. Edwards, pp. 1–2. Furthermore, in view of the collection of texts assembled in *WA*, 58/1:136–7 about Luther's reference to himself as a prophet, it is incorrect to say 'he made no special claim about himself' to Catholics, but only to Protestants; p. 2.

12. *WA* Br 1, 290:20–2, 29; 293:42–4; *LW*, 48:98 and 102 (letter to Elector Frederick and draft of letter to Leo X, January 5 or 6, 1519).

13. Richard Friedenthal, 'Hier stehe ich ... Luther und das Lutherverständnis', in: *Luther in Worms: 1521–1971*, ed. Fritz Reuter (Worms, Norberg, 1973), pp. 60–72. Though he speaks of 'Roman tyranny' in his famous speech at Worms, Luther still acknowledges that he was more acerbic than was fitting in his replies to its defenders: *WA*, 7:834, 5–6.

14. *WA* Br 2, 387:5–388, 25. *LW*, 48:306–7 (Letter to Spalatin, September 9, 1521). For similar texts see Holl, pp. 409–17; Midlefort, pp. 25–30.

15. *WA* Br 2, 387:16–388, 1; *LW*, 48:306–7. According to Luther it was the pope, not he, who first resorted to unpeaceful tactics: *WA* Br 2, 245:15–16; *LW*, 48:192 (letter to Spalatin, January 14, 1521).

16. For references to Lortz and Brandenburg see Remigius Bäumer, *Martin Luther und der Papst*, 2nd ed. (Münster, Aschendorff, 1970), p. 99. In his historic address to the Lutheran World Federation, after giving what amounts to the first official, positive Roman Catholic pronouncement on Luther's person and teaching, Willebrands used rhetorical silence to express the depth of Catholic feeling on this point: 'It is a consolation for me to think that we also share the same sentiments if in these joint reflections I prefer to say nothing about certain particularly sharp attacks that Martin Luther made against the Roman Pontiff; they sadden my heart and I feel sure that you, too, regard them as a burden.' In: *Sent into the World*: The Proceedings of the Fifth Assembly of the Lutheran World Federation, Evian, France, July 14–34, 1970, ed. LaVern Grosc (Minneapolis, Augsburg, 1971), p. 64. I can only agree with Otto Pesch in his magnificent book, *Hinführung zu Luther* (Mainz, Grünewald, 1982), when he applauds the way in which Willebrands is able to speak of Luther as 'our common teacher' (cf. German text in *Evian 1970*, ed. H.-

W. Heßler [Witten-Frankfurt-Berlin, Eckart, 1970], p. 99) and when he calls for a more extended application of this term to Luther's teaching; pp. 272–9. But in view of the words of Willebrands cited above and in terms of the critique that I offer in this section, I cannot agree with his recommendation: 'Don't worry about [Luther's] sharp polemic! One may read this as a reflection of the conditions in the church of his day and as the angry expression of a deep suffering in respect to the church!', p. 279. As we shall see, Luther's polemic involves more than this.

17. See my essay, 'Luther's Ecclesiological Significance for the Twentieth Century Ecumenical Movement', *The Springfielder* 35 (1970), pp. 131–9 and Harding Meyer, 'Das Problem des Petrusamt in evangelischer Sicht', in: Karl Lehmann, ed., *Das Petrusamt* (München-Zurich, Schnell and Steiner, 1982), pp. 110–25, esp. pp. 119–21.
18. Holl, p. 414; Midlefort, p. 28.
19. S. Hendrix, *Luther and the Papacy* (Philadelphia, Fortress, 1981), pp. 152–6. Luther's invocation of St Paul in his 1531 *Lectures on Galatians* as a model for his own polemics is presented at length, but without critical comment, by Edwards, pp. 112–26. Theological critique is necessary, however, when we are looking at Luther from an ecumenical perspective. For the moment I simply put the question, with respect to the *Lectures on Galatians*, whether Luther truly reflects the standard of Jesus when he teaches that 'charity can sometimes be neglected without danger' or that, in defense of the Gospel, 'charity is certainly not to be exercised toward those who teach lies and errors': *WA* 40/2, 48:12–13, 18–21; *LW*, 27:38–9. On the different behaviour that is allowed 'according to faith' and 'according to charity' see *WA* 40/1, 188:12–15; *LW*, 26:103. Cf. *WA* 40/1, 193:20–194, 12; *LW*, 26:107. Highly important, by way of contrast with the kind of behaviour Luther elsewhere defends for himself and urges on others, is Luther's acknowledgment here that Paul 'does not inveigh against Peter sharply, but treats him with sufficient reverence': *WA* 40/1, 193:14–15; *LW*, 26:106.
20. Hendrix, pp. 152–6. Lohse, *Martin Luther*, p. 194 speaks of Luther's 'unimaginably deep hatred of the papacy'.
21. p. 205.
22. p. 152.
23. *Corpus Reformatorum*, ed. C. G. Bretschneider (Halle, Schwetschke, 1843), vol. XI, col. 729.
24. Second Vatican Council, *Decree on Ecumenism*, note 6.
25. *WA Br* 2, 388:35–9: Satan is trying to cause a dreadful tragedy in Germany (letter to Spalatin, September 9, 1521); *LW*, 48:307–8. Tetzel was 'the primary author of this tragedy': *WA* 54, 184:31–2; *LW*, 48:355 (preface to his Latin works, 1545).
26. Müntzer formed the first 'sect', Carlstadt, the second, the Baptists, the third. Luther predicts many more sects will arise after his death, 'God help us': *WA TR* 5, 49:15–50, 3 (October, 1540). Cf. *WA* 40/1, 681:3–9 (*Galatians*, 1531), *LW*, 26:455.
27. *WA*, 45:112, 8, 12, 13 (Sermon on Mount 5, July 8, 1537): 'Ibi semper excipiendus magistratus die mussen zurnen . . . Ideo [being angry] est virtus apud magistratum et etiam Christianos in officio, in parentibus'. Cf. *WA* 20, 455:37–456, 15; 34/2, 6:19–8, 27. Luther's concern in making these exceptions is that evil not go unpunished. The exception is also allowed for the same reason in his otherwise restrained treatment of the 5th and 8th commandments in the *Large Catechism*: *WA* 30/1, 157:34–6; 172:3–5; cf. BSLK 606:21–7; 629:25–30; Tappert, 289:182; 401–402, 274.
28. *WA* 54, 262:12–16; *LW*, 41:331 (*Against the Roman Papacy*). Hendrix, p. 155, cites this passage without referring to the exegetical principle by which Luther justified such polemics.

29. *WA* 32, 397:26–407, 4 (Sermon on Mount 5, 43–8 of 1532).
30. *WA* 32, 398:17–20.
31. He cites Matthew 23:13; Acts 7, 51; 13, 10 and the 'anathema' of Galatians 1:8: *WA* 32, 398:31–7. Whether Jesus occasionally 'neglected' to practise charity (see note 19 above) or saw himself exempt in his preaching ministry from the demands of his own Sermon on the Mount is a question on which New Testament scholars may be able to enlighten us.
32. *WA* 32, 398:25–31.
33. *WA* 32, 400:19–23; my emphasis.
34. *Die Ethik Martin Luthers* (Gütersloh, Mohn, 1965), pp. 68–84; my translation from his pp. 69–70; E.T. p. 64.
35. *Jesus von Nazareth* (Stuttgart, Kohlhammer, 1956), p. 204. More recent studies of the Sermon on the Mount by Lutherans either don't mention Luther's interpretation—John H. Elliott, 'Law and Eschatology: The Antitheses of the "Sermon on the Mount",' *Lutheran World* 15 (1968), pp. 16–24—or mention it briefly and only in connection with the opening it has provided for later Lutherans to be too passive(!) in the face of abuse by the 'worldly regiment': Leonhard Goppelt, 'Das Problem der Bergpredigt', in: Goppelt, *Christologie und Ethik* (Göttingen, Vandenhoeck & Ruprecht, 1968), pp. 28–43, esp. 34–5. Pesch, *Hinführung*, pp. 237–40 and 322–3 likewise raises questions about Luther's exemption of public life from the requirements of the Sermon on the Mount, but doesn't touch the problem caused by exempting 'preachers' from it when they are defending the Gospel. See above note 16.
36. Rupp, 'Luther außerhalb des Luthertums: Freikirchliche Sicht', *Concilium* 12 (1976), p. 509. This is coupled with the hope that the polemic of Luther and Milton may be relegated to the distant past, along with other old, unhappy battles.
37. Ernst Bizer, *Luther und der Papst* (München, Kaiser, 1958), p. 47; Edwards, p. 205.
38. R. Bäumer, p. 99 lists Peter Meinhold and K. G. Steck among the Lutherans who have distanced themselves from Luther's polemic.
39. See note 16 above.
40. 'Statement on the Visit of Cardinal Willebrands' adopted by the Fifth Assembly of the Lutheran World Federation, 1970, in: L. K. Grosc, ed., *Sent into the World*, pp. 156–7.
41. Cf. Peter Manns, 'Zum Vorhaben eines "katholischen Anerkennung der Confessio Augustana": Ökumene auf Kosten Martin Luthers?' *Ökumenische Rundschau* 26 (1977), pp. 426–50 and Vinzenz Pfnür, 'Ökumene auf Kosten Martin Luthers?' *Ökum. Rundschau* 27 (1977), pp. 36–47.
42. For references in Luther see Pfnür, p. 43 and Gottfried Krodel's editorial note in *LW*, 49:345–7.
43. *WA* 30/3, 278:17–279, 7 (*Warnung an seine lieben Deutschen*, 1531). Here Luther contrasts the violent behaviour of 'the papists' at Augsburg and elsewhere, as well as that of Müntzer and his followers previously, with the peaceful conduct of his followers at the Diet. Christian history, he says, has seldom seen 'such a confession, such humility and such patience' as the Lutherans showed at Augsburg; 278:33–5.
44. See the essays by V. Pfnür and Heinz Schütte in Joseph Burgess, ed., *The Role of the Augsburg Confession: Catholic and Lutheran Views* (Philadelphia, Fortress, 1980), pp. 8–9 and 52. This is clearly the case in Luther's letter of May 15, 1530 to his Elector, *WA* Br 5, 319:5–9; *LW*, 49:297–8. For the more difficult letter of Luther to Justus Jonas of July 21, 1530, *WA* Br 5, 495:6–12, see Pfnür, 'Ökumene', pp. 42–3.
45. *WA* 8, 485:19–21; 527:16–18; *LW*, 36:137 and 186 (*On the Misuse of the Mass,*

1521). Cf. *WA* 8, 413:17–20; 449:17–18.

46. *Corp. Ref.* 11:728–9.

47. ibid., 728.

48. Cf. *One Baptism, One Eucharist and a Mutually Recognized Ministry*: Three Agreed Statements. Faith and Order Paper No. 73, Geneva, World Council of Churches, 1975 and *Baptism, Eucharist and Ministry*. Faith and Order Paper No. 111, Geneva, World Council of Churches, 1982.

49. This story has been told by several authors, among them Ernst W. Zeeden, *Martin Luther und die Reformation im Urteil des deutschen Luthertums*, vol. I, Freiburg, Herder, 1950. This study and its accompanying volume of further documentation can still be read with profit without subscribing to the author's view, popular then with Roman Catholics *and* liberal Protestants, that there are in Luther two unintegrated principles, an objective one, that of the traditional orthodox faith, and a subjective one, that of the authority of the critical, free conscience, the latter being responsible for the rise of liberal Protestantism. See the important critique by Ernst Wolf, 'Martin Luther und die Prinzipien des Protestantismus in katholischer Sicht', *Theologische Literaturzeitung* 76 (1951), 271–6. See also the chapter on the history of Luther interpretation of Lohse, pp. 209–46 (note 11 above).

50. *WA* 18, 603:11–12 and the entire context, 603–5 (On the Unfree Will, 1525).

51. *WA* 27, 52:15–22 (Sermon on Sexagesima Sunday afternoon, February 16, 1528). For similar texts see Althaus, *Die Theologie Martin Luthers* (Gütersloh, Mohn, 1962), pp. 307–9; English ed. pp. 359–61.

52. *WA* 26, 155:29–35; 168:40–169, 2; *LW*, 40:241 and 257 (Concerning Rebaptism, 1528). In the same work, 167:19–35; *LW*, 40:255, Luther argues similarly that the universal reception of the Apostles' Creed as well as of the Bible itself points to God's preservative action. See Jaroslav Pelikan, *Spirit Versus Structure* (New York, Harper & Row, 1968), pp. 87–93 and 'Luther's Defence of Infant Baptism', in: C. S. Meyer, ed., *Luther for an Ecumenical Age* (St. Louis, Concordia, 1967), pp. 209–12. That the 'faith of a child' used in *LW*, 40:255 to translate 'den kinder glauben' of *WA* 26, 167:29 more likely should be translated as 'the Apostles' Creed' is clear from such references as *WA* 41, 156:26–30; 51, 513:5 and *LW*, 13:296, note 59 by Pelikan.

53. *WA* 30/3, 552:3–553, 10 (*Sendschreiben an Herzog Albrecht von Preußen*, 1532). Althaus, *Die Theologie*, p. 362 offers other texts relating to the Eucharist which show that 'articles of faith' not only are grounded in the Scriptures and confirmed by the universal reception of the church, but also serve to guide our reading of Scripture – even to the point of allowing us to depart from the simple and direct meaning of the words of a biblical text. Luther's critical, biblical principle was thus not an anti-dogmatic principle as Roman Catholics – and 'neo-Lutherans' – before and since Harnack have thought. In view of the texts to which we have drawn attention, it would seem to be perfectly Lutheran and Protestant, as well as Catholic to see the reception of 'articles of faith', and, indeed, of the 'Biblia' itself by the Eastern and Western churches as a sign of God's preservative action in his 'Holy Christian Church' which 'cannot err': *WA* 51, 515:11 and 30; 518:13–17, 30–4; *LW*, 41:215 and 217 (*Against Hanswurst*, 1541). The context of the latter set of references (*WA*, 51:510–19, esp. 512:17–513, 12; *LW*, 41:212–9) and also the text of *WA* 30/3, 351:1–16 (*Glosse auf das vermeinte kaiserliche Edikt*, 1531) show that Luther can argue from the inerrancy of 'die heilige kirche', which teaches the Word of God, and from the practice of the universal church – 'der gantzen Christlichen kirchen' – against erroneous practices or teachings of a particular church. – These Luther references as well as those in the previous two notes are simply not taken into account by Gerhard Ebeling, *Dogmatik des christlichen Glaubens*, vol. I

(Tübingen, Mohr, 1979), pp. 30–2 when the undervalues the role played by the articles of faith and ecclesial infallibility in reformation theology.

54. Similar view can be found in Calvin, sixteenth century English and Scottish divines, as well as in Balthasar Hubmaier's *Catechism*.

55. Similar to Ebeling (see note 53), Walther von Loewenich, Luther *und der Neuprotestantismus* (Witten, Luther-Verlag, 1963), pp. 404 and 429 muffles the voice of Luther that we have heard concerning ecclesial innerancy when he says, with reference to the traditional Christological and Trinitarian dogmas, for Luther, the thought of their centuries-long ecclesial acceptance had 'only a secondary importance'.

56. Councils, for Luther, are 'the highest judges and the greatest bishops under Christ' for defending 'the ancient faith and the ancient good works in conformity with Scripture.' *WA* 50, 606:3–7; *LW*, 41:121–2.

57. See note 2 above.

58. Cardinal Willebrands, in his Evian address, p. 63 (see note 16) asked: 'Is it not true that the Second Vatican Council has even implemented requests which were first expressed by Martin Luther . . .?' Cf. O. Pesch, *Hinführung*, pp. 151–3 and 217–21. For some of the ways Vatican II modified the Vatican I teaching about papal primacy and infallibility see my essay, 'Some Forgotten Truths About the Petrine Ministry', *Journal of Ecumenical Studies* 11 (1974), pp. 208–36.

59. See my essay mentioned in the preceding note, pp. 234–6.

60. 'Das Wormser Memorandum' in: *Luther in Worms*, p. 183, and note 7.

61. *WA* 7, 69:26–31; 70:3–7; *LW*, 31:372. That Luther constantly and not just in an allegedly later 'neo-papist' period – lamented that his followers confused Christian liberty and carnal liberty is documented by W. von Loewenich, 'Die Selbstkritik der Reformation in Luthers Großem Katechismus' in: *Von Augustin zu Luther* (Witten, Luther-Verlag, 1959), pp. 269–93.

62. Cf. *WA* Br 5, 529:1–3 (enclosure to a letter to Melanchthon, August 3, 1530) and the related correspondence.

63. *WA* 32, 402:3–11 (Sermon on Mount. 5, 4, 1532).

64. Cf. 1 Corinthians 16:13–14 and 22; 2 Timothy 4:2.

65. *S. Thomae Aquinatis Super Epistolas S. Pauli Lectura*, ed. R. Cai, vol. II (Rome, Marietti, 1953), p. 161, note 193 on Colossians 4:17. For other examples see my essay mentioned in note 58, pp. 216–17.

AN EVERYDAY THEOLOGY

John M. Todd

At his boarding school in Eisenach, it was the chant and the poetry of the psalms that spoke to young Martin Luther. He was the protégé of respectable relations and their friends who ran a Church charity for old people. In this 'good old town' which in another later mood he called a 'den of priests' Martin was in and out of church and contracted a deep affection for the ritual. Till the end of his life he never tired of adapting the tunes and the Latin words in new arrangements in German. At Erfurt where he was an under-graduate the great new cathedral, and the older church beside it, dominated the town. Church ceremonies lay at the heart of the town life and that of the university. On graduation day the torches shone high and they remained a perpetual symbol to Luther: 'What majesty and splendour there was when one received his master's degree. They brought torches to him and presented them. I think that no earthly joy could be compared with it.'

It was nothing at all unusual a few months later when the young graduate opted for the life of a friar, the life of 'perfection'. He yearned for heavenly joys. He took to the discipline with delight, the silence, the devotion, the regularity. His superiors encouraged his idealism. He wanted to do everything perfectly. He prayed to every saint there was, each with his or her special area of concern. He availed himself of every channel of grace, every sacrament, every sacramental, and there were many of these, devotions to Mary, to the saints, to relics, to the cross, myriads of special prayers and devotions, and all earning spiritual merit for the one who took part in them.

But there was something wrong. Young Luther felt he could never come within sight of the perfection he aimed at. And once ordained, anything less than perfection was liable to become 'mortal sin' where the celebration of Mass was concerned. The great 'liberty' of the sons of God suddenly seemed to be turned into a threatening abyss, a great trap for the unwary. And the fear of sin, the devil, hell, punishment, which had been part of his experience of religion from the beginning began to loom large. The arms of Jesus on the cross 'seemed to threaten me'. The late medieval devotion to Jesus suffering on the cross paled before the threat of sin. Luther began to rebel inwardly.

Luther's spiritual superior had a case on his hands. Fr Staupitz was a typically spiritual and 'liberated' churchman of the time. He did not take the rigmaroles about sin and merit too seriously, pointing rather to the inner heart of the gospel, love and goodness. His attitude to Luther was tolerant, fatherly, kind and within limits perceptive. His spirituality owed something to Rhineland mysticism and something to renaissance humanism, and a lot to his own experience. This new enlightened practice of religion did not fit properly with the mechanistic theology of grace and the canonical legalisms which surrounded its practice. In effect Staupitz shrugged his shoulders at the incompatability. But Luther did not. Great sensitivity, and a demanding intellect, combined to push him forward relentlessly, to enquire further, to sort out the disparities. Intense depression fed on the threatening theology and provided further motivation for a search for an answer.

What exactly was this love and goodness at the heart of the gospel? Who was Jesus? Who is Jesus? What did the Bible actually teach? As Professor of Bible at Wittenberg (having been rapidly advanced thither by Staupitz so that he could himself resign), Luther had precisely the task of studying this. And so it was he began to use the Bible as the locus where his problem might be solved; and the search continued to have as its context the weekly recitation of the whole Psalter in choir. Luther had the psalms off by heart now and was ever deepening that attraction which had been born in him at home and at school. Then in 1513 in his thirtieth year his first university lectures were on the Psalms. When Luther's intellectual and spiritual breakthrough came in the following years, it was cited in St Paul's Letter to the Romans. But the faith to which St Paul made reference there was the primitive Faith and Trust of Abraham, that same utter reliance on Yahweh, the trust which rings through the Psalms, in 'Yahweh ... my refuge . . . my shelter . . . my rock . . . my castle . . . my Jerusalem'. Luther's spirituality became, as has been said, in theory as sublimely simple as that of St Thérèse of Lisieux, an attitude of pure and total faith, an abandonment of oneself to God. But simple as it was at heart, in practice this spirituality was the complicated, contradictory, anguished faith of the psalms. Always coming back to faith and hope, always rooted in longing for God and utter trust in him, the Psalmist also voices bitterness, resentment, anger, despair, disillusion, a counterpoint to and stimulant of the prayer of Faith. The second book that Luther published, in the spring of 1517, was a translation of the Seven Penitential Psalms including the famous Psalm 139: 'Out of depths have I called unto thee . . . From the morning watch until the evening let Israel hope in the Lord . . . Lord if thou shouldst mark iniquities, Lord who could stand?' His educated friends complained that he had sent them no complimentary copies and he replied that this was not a book of *bonae litterae*, the kind of renaissance literature they would appreciate, it was old fashioned piety for ordinary Wittenbergers.

As Luther expressed and developed his new found theology of faith alone, he did not turn to the silvered prose of the avant garde scholars but began to wrench the forms of late medieval piety, the religious vocabulary he had learnt, into its service. One of these cultural forms was the devotion to relics, to pieces of bone or clothing of Saints, the passion for the very thing itself, half pagan, powered strongly by curiosity, in its most vulgar form. A primary place among these objects was taken by pieces of the 'true' cross, the wooden beams which had formed the cross on which Jesus was crucified. If one saw, even touched, these things, surely one's troubles would vanish. The Church validated the practice, lifting what was practically a superstition into a sacramental, a kind of witness to the enfleshing of the Word; Indulgences were granted for prayers said in their presence. It did not at first occur to Luther simply to reject these practices. Instead he spiritualised them.

In a sermon in mid-Lent, 1518, Luther said that whilst it was acceptable to venerate relics, 'to encase the bones of saints in silver', yet 'it is the inward relic we must seek . . . for what Jesus sends to his devout children is not the wood, stone or clothing which he touched but rather the suffering, the cross'. He went on in angry tones to accuse the Bishops of being unwilling to accept these inward relics of suffering which came to them in the form of public criticism. Luther held them up to ridicule for their reaction to such criticism, sending banning letters 'flying about like bats', claiming they had a duty to defend the patrimony of Christ and St Peter, 'Oh, you poor Christ. Oh, you wretched Peter. If you have no inheritance but wood and stone and silver and gold, you are of all people the most needy'. This led on to a quotation from Isaiah, where the prophet denounces the materialistic view, contrasting it with the spiritual heart of religion:

> *What house could you build me,*
> *What place could you make for my rest?*
> *All of this was made by my hand*
> *and all of this is mine—it is Yahweh who speaks.*
> *But my eyes are drawn to the man*
> *of humble and contrite spirit,*
> *who trembles at my word.*

By 1522 it had become second nature for Luther to use the word 'relic' as a kind of spiritual shorthand or code. In March of that year he sent a famous letter to the Elector of Saxony, at a moment of high crisis, in which the idea of the spiritual relic is used with characteristic Lutheran irony and with the kind of brio he sometimes used when he sensed that he had a prophetic word to say. He had decided to break out of protective custody and he knew the Elector would be both annoyed and frightened and that it would be another severe trouble for him. After an unusually brief address he wrote: '*Personal.* Jesus. Grace and joy from God the Father on the acquisition of a new relic! I put this greeting in place of my assurances of respect. For many years your Grace has been collecting relics from every land, but God has now heard your Grace's request and has sent your Grace without cost or effort a whole cross, together with nails, spear and scourges. I say again: grace and joy from God on the acquisition of a new relic! Your grace should not be terrified by it; stretch out your arms confidently and let the nails go deep'.

The Theology of the Cross is a rather pompous phrase for this simple spirituality, with its New Testament pedigree, going back to such words as 'Take up your cross' and Paul's 'I am crucified to the world'. The Christian identified himself with the crucified. Luther claimed that the troubles of life virtually disappeared if seen as a 'cross', if identified as a blessed 'relic' of the suffering of Jesus, and welcomed. They were absorbed in the suffering of the God-man, Jesus of Nazareth. Luther had a shorthand phrase for this process, which he used regularly by the time of the 95 Theses. The 93rd thesis read 'All those prophets do well who say to the people of Christ "cross, cross", and there is no cross'. As is clear from phrases in his letters of this time this is simply a code phrase proclaiming that to welcome the 'Cross' in one's life is to enable it to disappear.

Immediately prior to that thesis, the 92nd thesis quoted the analogous words of Jeremiah which had been making patterns in Luther's mind for some years and which he used to make an ironic contrast with the 93rd thesis. 'Away with all those prophets who say to the people of Christ "Peace, peace", and there is no peace.' Luther longed for peace in his own being, and in the world, and identified its absence with a special anguish. As District Vicar in 1516 he wrote to depose a Prior, Michael Dressel, because his Community was not at peace: 'Life without peace is dangerous because it is life without Christ, and it is death rather than life . . . It is not enough that a man be good and pious by himself. Peace and harmony with those around him are also necessary.' Luther saw Jeremiah's prophecies as quite relevant to the present times, as he identified self-indulgence and lack of true peace throughout the Church. Jeremiah's words which lead up to the specific reference to peace read:

> *For thus says Yahweh Sabaoth*
> *'Be warned, Jerusalem,*
> *lest I should turn away from you,*
> *and reduce you to a desert,*
> *a land without people.'*

> *Plainly the Word of Yahweh is for them something*
>   *contemptible,*
> *they have no taste for it.*
> *But I am full of the wrath of Yahweh,*
> *I am weary of holding it in.*

For all, least no less than greatest,
all are out for dishonest gain;
prophet no less than priest,
all practise fraud.
They dress my people's wound
without concern: 'Peace, peace', they say,
but there is no peace.

Luther knew well that this true 'peace' was the vibrant harmony, divine and human, identified in the Hebrew word *Shalom*, not at all the mere absence of conflict. It was towards this peace that the Church directed his mind each year, as Advent and Christmas approached, in the words of the Introit for the last Sunday in the Church's year, words again from Jeremiah, set to an exceptionally beautiful Gregorian chant: *Ego cogito cogitàtiones pacis et non afflictionis*—Jeremiah was addressing those in exile, encouraging them to live a normal life and eventually they would return. The Introit has, for the Psalm verse, the Vulgate version of Psalm 84 (85 today): *Benedixisti, Domine, terram tuam: avertisti captivitatem Jacob.*

Luther eventually found peace in his relationship to Christ. The theology of faith was increasingly focused on Christ. Christ alone, 'nudus'. The single Latin word 'nudus', with its Rhineland resonance, though without the ecstatic connotation, Luther used in his key Commentary on Romans. Man can hope in God alone (*Deus nudus*). 'He who depends on the true God has put aside all tangible things and lives by naked hope' (*nuda spe vivit*). And this peace was stripped and bare, because it had no other basis than Christ himself. 'The rule of Christ is in the midst of his enemies as the Psalm puts it. Why then do you imagine that you are among friends?' he wrote to Father George Spenlein in 1516. Luther had already had experience both of spiritual isolation and of terror, and fear of death.

The moment of the thunderbolt when he had vowed to become a monk he once described as a moment when he was 'walled in by terror and death'. Then again when contemplating his own spiritual failure he spoke in utterly anguished terms of a moment when he felt as though he would have been obliterated by it, if an experience of terror and nothingness had continued for another five minutes. Luther's life was deeply marked by the kind of nightmare terror, now sometimes being identified by psychologists as birth or pre-natal trauma. Insight into the psychological identity of Luther's experience enhances rather than cancels out our perception of Luther's experience. He was a man of the sharpest sensitivity, ever on the alert. Another symbol he came to use for man's natural but essentially absurd terror and fright was that of the man terrified by a rustling leaf. A horse will sometimes shy at the slightest movement or the slightest sound, and men may jump at nothing too. A passage in Leviticus had started Luther off on this. The writer describes the effect of Yahweh's actions on the sons of Israel if they did not observe the Law: 'I will scatter you among the nations . . . Then the land will observe its sabbaths indeed, lying desolate there . . . as it never did in your sabbaths when you lived on it. Then I will strike fear into the hearts of those of you that are left—in the land of your enemies the sound of a falling leaf shall send them fleeing as men flee from the sword, and they shall fall though there is no one pursuing them.' In 1525 in a particularly desperate piece denouncing the reformers on the left *Against the Heavenly Prophets* Luther wrote that God was concealed from such false prophets and they, 'dejected, stupid, despairing and anxious spirits tremble at the rustling of a leaf'. Men without God, unjustified men, were subject to every kind of terror, and unable to accept it with joy.

Suffering is unavoidable, but the proper understanding of it, and an ability to welcome and use it spiritually, was the acid test of sincerity and true godliness. When Melanchthon wrote in bewilderment to Luther at the Wartburg, asking him what he thought about the self-styled prophets who had arrived from Zwickau declaring that they relied solely on the Spirit, Luther wrote—'Do not listen if they speak of the glorified Jesus, unless you have first heard of the crucified Jesus . . . You should enquire whether they have suffered spiritual distress and the divine birth, death and hell'.

Death, a common locus for the popular spirituality of medieval preachers, is often the starting point of Luther's own thought. The great Wittenberg sermons start with what may seem a cliché and was certainly part of a well worked vocabulary for those who listened. Luther's genius was to transform and deepen the forms he inherited: 'The Summons of death comes to us all, and no one can die for another. Every one must fight his own battle with death by himself. We can shout into another's ear, but everyone must himself be prepared for the time of death ... It will be a testing moment and one should prepare for it.' The words seem strangely ordinary but they were uttered with Luther's special brand of quiet and urgent intensity. Leading on that occasion, surprisingly, to a doctrine of tolerance and moderation, such insights formed part of a completely revivified traditional spirituality. 'Death' came round regularly in the liturgy each Lent. As the season of Lent approached the Introit for Septuagesima Sunday picked up the Psalmist's words, from the Vulgate for Psalm 17(18) (verses 5, 6, 7) again in a specially moving and plaintive cantus: *Circumdederunt me gemitus mortis, dolores inferni circumdederunt me.*

In the face of actual death, Luther was the pious pastor of the late medieval church. His letters to his father, and a little later to his mother, when one after the other they fell seriously ill, dying shortly afterwards, set forth the best of this central Christian tradition. To his father Luther offered the usual sentiments, but presented with the faithful simplicity of his theology of the cross. His spirituality is a usable everyday tool, it is biblical, yet blunt and contemporary. With allowances made, it can hardly be said to date. It might seem overly pious or overly individualistic, but in fact it sprang from the local community, and suited the needs of the individual person who is never so isolated as in a final illness and death.

Luther wrote: 'I pray from the bottom of my heart that the Father who has made you my father and given you to me, will strengthen you according to his immeasurable kindness, and enlighten and preserve you with his Spirit, so that you may perceive with joy and thanksgiving the blessed teaching concerning his son, our Lord Jesus Christ to which you have been called ... because of me you, together with all of us, have suffered much slander, disgrace, scorn, mockery, contempt, hatred, hostility, and even danger. These are but the true marks with which we have to become identical to our Lord Christ, as St Paul says, so that we may also become identified with his future glory ... His power over death and sin is too great for them to harm us.

He is so wholeheartedly faithful and righteous that he cannot forsake us nor would he wish to do so . . . "Ask and it will be given you; seek and you will find, knock and it will be opened to you", And: "All who call on the name of the Lord shall be saved". The whole Psalter is full of such comforting promises, especially Psalm 91, which is particularly good to be read by all who are sick . . . you are not permitted to worry about or be concerned for anything except keeping your heart strong and reliant on his Word and faith. If you do this, let him care for the rest. He will see to it that everything turns out well . . . we shall shortly see each other again in the presence of Christ. For departure from this life is a smaller thing to God than if I moved from you in Mansfeld to here . . . it is only a matter of an hour's sleep and all will be different.'

For his mother also the traditional pastoral comfort and teaching was transformed into newly minted but essential 'gospel' spiritual theology. '. . . dear Mother . . . you well know by now that this sickness of yours is God's fatherly gracious chastisement . . . you should accept it with thankfulness as being sent by God's grace . . . how slight a suffering it is—even if it be a sickness unto death—compared with the sufferings of his one dear Son, our Lord Jesus Christ, who did not have to suffer on behalf of himself, as we have to do, but who suffered for us and for our sins . . . We may joyfully and cheerfully listen to the sweet words: "Be of good cheer; I have overcome the world" . . . You possess the gospel you hear preached, baptism and the sacrament of the altar, so that you should have no trouble or danger. Only be of good cheer and thank God joyfully for such great grace . . . The Father and God of all consolation grant you, through his holy Word and Spirit, a steadfast, joyful, and grateful faith blessedly to overcome this and all trouble, and finally to taste and experience that what he himself says is true: "Be of good cheer; I have overcome the world". And with this I commend your body and soul to his mercy. Amen. All your children and my Katie pray for you; some weep, others say at dinner; "Grandmother is very ill". God's grace be with us all. Amen'.

This everyday spirituality was down to earth and not lacking in humour. In the letter to his father he wrote: 'This cursed life is nothing but a real vale of tears—nor is there respite, until we are battened down in the grave.' He would suddenly use an unexpected text as a literary conceit when discussing a matter of the utmost seriousness for him: 'Many such things, my reader, you will find in the sacred decretals, and also others, which if you use the nose of the bride overlooking Damascus that is a nose of flesh and blood, you will often be offended by the smell'. It was 1518, Luther was threatened for the first time with a Roman denunciation and turned suddenly to the Song of Songs to find an apt and emphatic image to delineate what seemed to him the outrageous claim of Rome in regard to the Petrine texts:

> *Your eyes, the pool of Heshbon*
> *by the gate of Bat-rabbim.*
> *Your nose the tower of Lebanon,*
> *sentinel facing Damascus.*
> *Your head is held high like Carmel*

A fine nose for a fine smell!

Luther's faith was one 'in the midst of enemies', a faith for someone who often found life intolerable. His life was one of encounter for all of its course. His writing, preaching and lecturing always included critical and aggressive sequences. Well known examples from the early days are his angry references to Aristotle, the rancid philosopher, in the margins of the books he used for his early lectures on Lombard and Augustine, when he was about thirty, and a sharp and crapulous sermon about back-biters three years later. The aggressiveness also appeared in his personal relations, but neither his wife nor his friends and acquaintances seem to have found it a fundamental threat to love and friendship. Yet it is wrong to try to construct a picture of Luther's spirituality without reference to his anger and his aggression which are perhaps too easily forgotten or dismissed. It is not sufficient to do some kind of psychological analysis and then forget it. It was a permanent dimension and was in some sense I think a real defect. But it also provides the opportunity for understanding 'anger' as part of human make-up, like other bitter emotions, part therefore of one's spirituality. The Old Testament authors are not afraid of grumbling against Yahweh, and of giving voice to more extreme emotions. The Christian who recites the Psalms has to find a way of allowing the Psalmist's expression of moods to find its place on his lips, and yet not to lapse into purely negative self pity.

Luther's aggression was projected always towards the Pope, the Turks and, in real anguish, towards those colleagues and reformers who began to challenge not just the style of the Roman Church, its structure and its encouragement to earn spiritual merit through works, but other traditional christian doctrines and his own reforms. Luther's prime theme of the salvation which lies open to man, free, and easy to have, by faith alone and grace alone, through scripture alone, was commonly bracketed with an expression of the converse that it could not be obtained by doing what the Pope encouraged people to do, whether putting on a monk's cowl or obtaining an Indulgence or doing some other 'work'. The thought of such 'works' would often let loose a torrent of abuse, which it must be said, became a cliché. Similar abuse would be poured on the head of Erasmus. In both cases the abuse became habitual, thoughtless, hysterical and foolish. But spirituality is something in a real world not in some fairy world of spiritual reading, untainted by the 'world'. Luther defended his aggressiveness as part of his nature which worked with an axe and a pike as distinct from the delicate work with a handknife undertaken by Melanchthon. And he felt with a special and frightening certainty that the papal church was missing the whole point of Christianity and deserved everything he said about it.

The stormy faith of Luther's twenties, thirties and forties stayed with him till the end, but in middle age it tended increasingly to focus not so much on 'faith' as on the object of faith, the man, Jesus of Nazareth. It became essentially a descriptive christology, centred always on the incarnation, with the incarnation itself centred on the Trinity. Spirituality became itself a theology. The weekly sermons given on Saturdays in Wittenberg parish church 1536–9 present this spiritual theology and the heart of them as always the Man Jesus.

'By faith I am incorporated into the Man from heaven, and He says to me: "You are mine, and I am yours; for I have done these heavenly works for you". This Man brings us the Holy Spirit. Christ lacks nothing; "in Him the whole fullness of deity dwells" (Colossians 2:9). This fullness becomes ours, not in our person, as with Him, but by faith; ... Wherever the Lord is, there the Spirit is: yes there is all.' Luther is lavish with analogies for the unity of

God, the unity of divinity and humanity in Christ, and our union with God through Christ. A favourite image was provided by the German idiom of 'one cake', *ein Kuchen*, used for an entity uniting disparate elements, 'baked together into one cake'. Christ and the Father are 'one cake' in their words and actions towards us. Divinity and humanity are 'one cake' in Christ. Christ and His Christians have been made 'one cake' in order that good fruits may result. 'When you see Me risen from the grave and death, and ascending up into heaven to the Father, and you preach this concerning Me, then you will learn and discover, through the Holy Spirit and your own experience, that I am in the Father and the Father in Me, and moreover I in you. Thus we shall be "one cake" with each other'.

There are occasional phrases describing the indwelling of God in the soul in terms which sound almost mystical: 'God comes to you and makes His dwelling in your heart, converting it into heaven and paradise'. But in fact this is part of a normal presentation of faith. The preceding sentence runs: 'Faith must be a living document, a seal, a signet, a conviction so strong that one is willing to forsake all for it. Then God comes . . .'. The doctrinal and spiritual exposition is always set in the full theology of faith; it is also set in a traditional ecclesiastical setting of ministry and sacraments: 'Christ is our God's letter. Those who believe and lead a Christian life are sealed; that is they have faith, and the Holy Spirit has inscribed the Word in their hearts with the conviction that it is true . . . It is a vibrant letter written into the heart by means of our ministry and the Sacraments, so that the heart is now replete with living letters which are aglow with love. True faith shines forth to condemn all heresy and error and to inscribe the truth in the heart through the preaching ministry of the Holy Spirit, so that it says: "I do not doubt that Jesus Christ is the Son of God and of Mary". This is the import of the words we have written'.

Appropriately in this text on St John he never tires of returning to the incarnate Lord. 'We own a definite Lord, one whom we can touch. He lies in His mother's lap, and He hangs on the cross, as infinite God He became finite man. Our heart can feel in heaven and on earth, before whom angel and devil prostrate themselves, a Lord whom the Father loves as His only-begotten Son.'

Sacramental religion is central: 'In our day, in the time of the New Testament, God has given us Baptism, the Sacrament of the Altar, and absolution to bring Christ very close to us, so that we can have Him not only in our heart but also on our tongue, so that we can feel Him, grasp Him, and touch Him'.

In daily practice Luther was emphatic about the gospel spirituality which sees Christ in others: 'When God wants to speak and deal with us, He does not avail Himself of an angel but of parents, and of the pastor, or of my neighbour. This puzzles and blinds me so that I fail to recognise God who is conversing with me through the person of the pastor or father. This prompts the Lord Christ to say in the text: 'If you knew the gift of God, and who it is that is saying to you, "Give me a drink", then I would not be obliged to run after you and beg for a drink'. The paragraph continues later: 'Even if Christ did no more than greet us, it would be a treasure above all treasures; it would be honour and treasure enough. He has another treasure in store for us, however, which He reveals when He brings us forgiveness of sin and redemption from death, devil, and hell, when He transforms us into heavenly people and illumines our hearts'.

Luther's spiritual theology which I see as a theology for every day has its first source in the Psalms. And it is not just a matter of a source, but of dynamic everyday use as private and public prayer. Its second source is the New Testament, and again it is a matter of taking the text for study and meditation. And it is a New Testament rooted in the Torah as part of what we identify today as the Abrahamic tradition. More important to Luther than all the controversies, in which he was impelled to engage, was his commitment to and exposition of the vibrant Word, the living waters of the great spiritual tradition.

LUTHER AND THE CATHOLIC PREACHERS OF HIS YOUTH

Ian D. K. Siggins

Martin Luther liked to claim that he was a real peasant, but on his mother Hanna's side, Luther sprang from a highly educated urban patrician family.[1] The Lindemanns of Eisenach, Luther's maternal cousins, supplied Saxony with an impressive number of professional people – doctors, lawyers, mayors, magistrates, and teachers. Martin himself was sent away to Eisenach as a teenager to study under the supervision of his mother's family with the prospect of such a career in public life. His uncle, Heinrich Lindemann, was mayor of Eisenach when Martin arrived there in 1497 at the age of thirteen.

But the Lindemanns were also a godly family. The devout leading citizens of Eisenach had formed a religious fellowship, headed by Martin's host, Heinrich Schalbe. Schalbe was his uncle Heinrich's fellow councillor for over twenty years, and he and his household were intimates and devotees of the local Observant Franciscans – 'almost their captive and slave,' Luther said later.[2] The Observants, the strict faction of the Minorites, had a cloister within the city of Eisenach and a retreat house outside it (the hostel of St Elizabeth of Hungary at the foot of the Wartburg). At the time of his first mass in 1507, Martin Luther wrote to Johann Braun in Eisenach expressing his profound gratitude for the influence of that pious fellowship upon him.[3]

Part of that influence was certainly the preaching young Martin heard in the churches of Eisenach, that 'nest of priests'. As Vincenz Hasak has pointed out, there was at least as much preaching at the end of the fifteenth century as there is now, and attendance at sermons was regarded as a Christian's most solemn duty.[4] In the decades before the Reformation, the pulpit was a focal feature of the religious culture for the laity of the imperial cities. We shall not begin to understand Luther's relation to the

Catholicism of his day until we know what beliefs and practices were inculcated by the preachers. Without this indispensible background we shall understand neither Luther's own progress towards reform, nor the reception of his ideas by the burghers who became Lutherans.

Before I turn to the evident impact of this late medieval preaching on the young Martin Luther, it would be well to sketch the sources and the character of the sermonic literature.

Because attendance at sermons was regarded as such a pious duty, the fifteenth century was a period of vigorous homiletic effort in the cities of northern Europe. The significance of this effort has been overlooked for a number of reasons. In the first place, there was as yet little sign of any fresh or innovative oratory to match the new classically inspired pulpit styles that emerged during this time in Renaissance Italy.[5] Instead, the northern rhetoric adhered closely to the traditional patterns of the scholarly manuals of preaching method, the *artes praedicandi*, complete with authorities, *exordia*, numbered points and subpoints, distinctions, mnemonic devices, and *exempla*. Not only in style, but also in content, the fifteenth century sermon books seem at first a mere compilation or repetition of materials and themes familiar for centuries. It is not simply that the same ancient *catenae* of images or patristic authorities are drawn upon, or that the reworking of old outlines is an acceptable (indeed, preferred) method, but entire sections of sermons composed centuries apart may be stitched together into a new outline without any sense of anachronism. (The pseudonymous editor of the *Postil of Guillermus Parisiensis*, for example, in 1470 simply interspersed sermon outlines from the thirteenth century preacher Hugo de Prato into an expository manuscript of 1437 attributed to Johann Herolt, and plainly perceived no unevenness.) There are external grounds, too, on which fifteenth century preaching has been discounted – not least the disdain of the Reformation preachers for their predecessors, and the place of a new biblical preaching at the heart of the reform movement.

Whatever the causes, it seems to have been assumed that parochial preaching was an insignificant contributor to the Reformation's genesis. But there are the strongest reasons for believing otherwise.

The first is the sheer extent of the homiletic enterprise. Each half of the fifteenth century made its contribution to the spread of preaching materials, the first half by a creative new attention to sermonic aids, and the second by their wide dissemination in print.

In the early decades, the growing strength of the Observant movement in the preaching orders combined with conciliar conviction and the widespread piety of the *devotio moderna* to encourage a renewed commitment to the preacher's task, and the result was a spate of sermon-books, circulating widely in manuscript, that contained model sermons and outlines, collections of exemplary stories, catechetical series, and festal homilies intended to be intelligible, practical, and complete, and above all directed to the ordinary parish congregation. However much they derived from earlier tradition, these collections have a characteristic tone that to the practised ear soon distinguishes them from sermons of the preceding centuries.

Then, after the invention of printing in mid-century, these same collections became a prized item in the offerings of the printers, and were reissued time after time in the forty years before the Reformation. In printed form, the sermon-books achieved a vastly increased circulation and a far wider sphere of influence. The marginal annotation and the rubrication of many exemplars still extant indicate clearly that these homiletic aids were not only bought in large numbers but actively used in the pulpits.

To illustrate the extent of this circulation, let me give figures for just a few of the most popular sermon-books. Around 1430, the Franciscan Johann Gritsch wrote *a Quadragesimale* (a complete series of lenten sermons) which could be adapted for year-round use by means of an index: it was printed twenty-four times in Germany, and five times elsewhere, between 1475 and 1500.[6] Another Franciscan, Johann of Werden (d. 1437), composed one of the most popular and appealing annual collections, the *Sermones dormi secure*: it was printed thirty-four times before 1500, and nearly sixty times more in the following fifty years.[7] The anonymous mid-century collection, *Sermones thesauri novi*, was valued for its thoroughness, and enjoyed twenty-nine editions in the fourteen years 1483–1497.[8] The pseudonymous *Postil* mentioned above, and attributed in its first printed edition to the non-existent 'Guillermus Parisiensis', was the most popular homiletic aid of all, and went through the startling figure of 110 or 111 incunabular editions.[9] The most systematic, comprehensive, and accessible sermon-writer of the period was the Nurnberger Dominican Johann Herolt (d. 1468), who in a long project beginning during Constance and spanning three decades produced a whole library of sermon-books – catecheses, lenten and advent series, multiple models for each Sunday and feast day, and two marvellous sets of *exempla*. Various of these volumes saw at least sixty-four editions between 1470 and 1500, and many more thereafter.[10] And there are sixty or seventy more fifteenth century sermonists whom the humanist Johannes Trithemius (Tritheim) listed in his *De scriptoribus ecclesiasticis* in 1492: he personally knew of thirty who had composed sets for the entire church year.[11]

Not all the notable preaching was of the parochial sort, of course. The most famous preachments were the often histrionic itinerant sermons of mendicant missioners. An elite of learned preachers was highly honoured in the academies and the churches of the nobility. Within the monastic cloisters themselves, there was a continuing tradition of deeply devotional, contemplative and sometimes mystical preaching. But far and away the largest and most influential body of preaching was represented in the sermon-books designed for parish use in the cities. The books that were in greatest demand and constantly reissued were those directed to the needs of parochial preachers, and dealing with the daily concerns of pastoral care. Since that was their goal, they self-consciously adopted a simplicity of approach that would make the sermons useful to unassuming preachers and intelligible to ordinary urban congregations. Herolt declared that it is 'better for simple preachers to preach simple things' rather than the profound opinions and cultivated rhetoric of the 'illustrious doctors';[12] and Werden called his collection *Dormi secure* – 'Sleep Soundly!' – precisely to indicate that they could be readily adapted for preaching to the laity 'without great study'.[13]

What image of Christian life and divine grace would an impressionable teenager like Martin Luther gain from the sermons he heard?

Since the deliberate intent of the sermonists was to cover every contingency of topic and occasion, the subject-matter of particular sermons covered an immense range: the proprieties of food, drink, and dress; almsgiving and the status of the poor; the spiritual significance of wind and weather; Christ's coming to judgment; the nine circles of the angels; salutary and unsalutary grief; veneration of the Blessed Virgin; worthy communion; marriage; prayer and self-discipline; Christians most liable to backslide; the example of the saints; purgatory; the virtues; the works of holy mercy, physical and spiritual; the status of women; alien sins; illicit magic; the Jews; and so on across the entire spectrum of doctrine, morality, church law and social regulation. Sometimes a topic occupied several sermons in a row; more often, a single sermon touched two or three related themes. In style, many fifteenth century preachers adopted a didactic and explanatory approach, literal in its use of proof texts and authorities, and illustrated by cautionary and exemplary stories; other preachers adopted a more persuasive and evocative style, rich in tropological allegories, biblical imagery, and visually allusive symbols drawn from nature and the bestiaries. But whatever the diversities of subject, style, and (it must be said) skill, there was a remarkable unanimity amongst the sermonists on the basic shape of the way of salvation. The central message could not have been lost on an attentive hearer.

First of all, there was an implicit (and occasionally explicit) multiple standard applied to Christians in what was expected of them. Perhaps as an accommodation to pastoral experience, preachers subdivided their potential audience into classes of responsiveness, and addressed various sorts of appeal to each. The great mass of people in occasional conformity with the church encompassed many 'bad Christians', whose lukewarm, negligent and wordly attitudes demanded constant rebuke, and whose dissolute and avaritious lives deserved fearful warnings of hell – 'true Christian life' was very rare in the world.[14] Nevertheless, an important part of the preacher's responsibility lay in the instruction of ordinary, well-meaning laypeople who intended to be good, and accepted church discipline, but could never be sure whether their merits outweighed their sins: much standard parochial sermonizing was directed to them in moral instruction, fervent appeals for sincerity, and exhortations to true contrition. From amongst these people, an occasional soul – 'perhaps one in thirty thousand', a preacher guessed – understood the true call to godliness and entered wholeheartedly upon the path of holiness. Even on that path, the Holy Spirit conferred different graces upon beginners, proficients, and *perfecti*.[15] For this minority who intended to live in grace, the preachers held out the theoretical possibility of a life of sanctity in the midst of the world – austerity amid plenty, celibacy within marriage, humility despite power – and spelt out in the disciplines of harsh clothing, hard beds, prayers, prostrations, bodily castigations, and abstinence that were its characteristic marks. Yet a secular life of such asperity was so rare and so difficult of perseverance that two other expressions of commitment seemed more realistic. One was a pious life regularly punctuated by such spiritual exercises, whether as penance or self-denial, and dedicated to works of mercy, membership in religious brotherhoods, imitation of Christ, hearing mass, and attendance at sermons. The other way, and to the mendicant preacher the best and safest way of all, was conversion to the religious life: there at least the means of grace were always to hand, the virtues of humility and obedience could flourish, and the disciplines of self-abnegation were built into the fabric of day and night. The appeal of this commitment was offered to devout young people as a Christian ideal and a source of special graces.

Because the parish congregation contained all these different audiences, with all their diversities of understanding and openness, the logic of the preachers' persuasions was also various. And here, as we shall see, some of the confusion about the way of salvation took rise. The declaration of God's sheer mercy stood alongside a crasser calculus of sins and merits. The appeal to pure heartfelt contrition was lumped together with blatant exploitation of the fear of death, the terrors of hellish punishment, and the enticements of heavenly reward. Calls to transformation of life accompanied the promotion of outward observances – relics, indulgences, suffrages, pilgrimages, vows – that seemed to offer an automatic dispensing of the storehouse of grace.

And yet, as I have said, the basic shape of the way of salvation was repeatedly stated for the earnest seeker. Amongst this flood of topics, two or three themes sounded insistently. God always stood ready to forgive the sinner, even *in extremis*. All that was needed to receive that mercy was for the sinner to do the one thing that lay within his capacity – to be contrite for his sins:

> It is a greater miracle for God to receive sinners to grace than to make a new earth. For God created the world without help and without assistance; but according to his justice he cannot accept sinful man to grace without the help of the sinner. Yet the help of the sinner is only to say these four words with contrition of heart: *Peccavi, Domine, miserere mei.*[16]

The focus of the pastoral message was the urgent need for true contrition. It is not too much to say that the preachers taught a doctrine of justification by contrition alone.

Many academic theologians and writers of confessors' manuals in this period placed increasing emphasis on the pastoral efficacy of the priest's role in penance, sacramentally effecting absolution in spite of any initial inadequacy of a penitent's sorrow.[17] In this they followed a Scotist tendency; but with striking unanimity the parochial sermonists instead maintained an older tradition, flowing from Peter Lombard and Thomas Aquinas, which located the efficacy of penance in the prior sincerity of the contrite heart. Heartfelt grief for one's sinful estate, and for actual sins, secured God's mercy and grace before and apart from the outward acts of confession and satisfaction, provided only that the penitent firmly intended to do sacramental penance as an outward sign of his sincerity, and as an act of filial obedience to church discipline. The implication was plain: the pastoral goal was successfully attained only when the sinner was led through humble self-examination to a place of utter sincerity.

To evoke that sincerity, the preachers devoted their most intense energies and most exigent rhetoric to expounding the inducements to penance. Gritsch listed five inducements: consideration of future bliss; the severity of final judgment; the present opportunity for grace; uncertainty of one's standing before God; and the inescapable certainty of death. Awareness of death, above all, was the pervasive context for the call to repentance:

Our life is a headlong rush towards death: in it we are never allowed to stand still for a moment, or even to slow down . . . And since the sinner is hurtling towards death like this, the Lord comes often to meet him and tells him through inspiration to reflect how he has been judged worthy of an eternal punishment, and is being driven to it without pause. The Lord says, 'Grieve that you have committed sin and slain your own soul'. If then the sinner will say, 'I grieve from my heart', immediately he is freed by the Lord from hanging in hell and is reconciled to God . . . See, the sentence of death is repealed![18]

Herolt agreed: 'We must all die,' he declared, quoting Solomon, Augustine, Gregory, and Jerome on the salutary importance of meditation on death. 'He who remembers daily that he will die despises the present and hastens to the future.'[19] Seven reflections fitting for a dying person were these: he passes hence alone, with no help but God; he leaves naked, is buried and eaten by worms; his sins follow him unless he has repented here, and if he has not repented, God condemns him, the angels separate him from the good, and the demons torture him perpetually in hell; the demons therefore gather like vultures about a man's death struggle to await their due; he goes hence to a region totally unknown to him, knowing nothing of what awaits him, or whether he will spend his first night in heaven, purgatory, or hell; the time of grace and negotiation is lost to him forever; and death deprives him of all the joys of the world – 'so leave them now for those merits that last!'[20]

The Franciscan Werden, one of the most graphic preachers of the *memoria mortis*, made the parable of the sower into an elaborate allegory of the ploughing of the Christian's heart by contrition and confession, followed by fertilizing with the 'manure of the memory of death' so that it would bear fruit:

You must keep these things in mind constantly . . . Death does not tarry. Let a man think of the deaths of our predecessors when they were strong – Absalom at his most beauteous, David at his boldest, Solomon at his wisest, Samson at his strongest. They all passed and reverted to earth.[21]

All the fifteenth century preachers repeat and add to the catalogue of warnings from Gregory, Bede, Isidor, and – most eloquently – Bernard on the inevitability and yet unpredictability of death. 'I say,' Werden declared, 'that a man must be converted on account of the uncertainty of death; whence Bernard: "Nothing is more certain than death and nothing more uncertain than the hour of death." '[22] Not only did it come on people unawares, but all men inexorably received its sentence, the horrible vision of demons accompanied it, and the fearful examination of judgment followed it with no remaining hope of repentance.[23] The preachers made much of the corruption of the body and the dissolution of all its members in death, gruesomely picturing the serpents, toads, and worms that gnawed it in the grave, but even more gruesomely describing each successive groan and rattle of the body's death agony, with spiritual analogies for each stage of that struggle.

The fear and horror of physical and spiritual death was the most urgent spur to repentance, and the most potent means of mobilizing the grief of contrition in tender consciences. The rightful intensity of that humiliation and grief was also spelt out in sermon after sermon.

'There is no justification without fear,' warned the compiler of the *Sermones thesauri novi*. Shame 'is the greatest part of penitence,' and grief 'is the way a man must needs turn back to his own heart morning and evening, to harrow his conscience and expunge his sin.'[24] What cleansed the soul, said Herolt, was frequent outpourings of tears.[25] This harrowing grief over sins was the work of the Holy Spirit in the souls of beginners.[26]

The paths of contrition led sinners through the wilderness of penitence, Werden preached. The paths were these: contrition must be so bitter that one recalled every season of one's whole life in bitterness, 'all the days and all the years so uselessly wasted'; again it must be universal, so that like David one perceived how great and pervasive was one's sin; it must be specific and deal in turn with each individual sin causing sorrow; and it must be continual with every single recollection of past sins evoking a renewed act of contrition.[27] Though a suicidal grief of the appetites might well prove excessive, Gritsch thought, the grief of the will repudiating its sin could never be too great.[28]

What we hear in this preaching is the doctrine and the spirituality that drove young Martin Luther to abandon his legal studies at Erfurt (and with them his family's ambitions for him) to seek the mercy of God in a life of devotion and penitence.

He had received his grounding in piety from a mother who – according to Melanchthon and Schneidewein – was God-fearing, prayerful, saintly and wise.[29] The boy was introduced 'by diligent instruction at home' to the knowledge and fear of God,[30] and this formation was continued with a special intensity in the turbulent, impressionable years of adolescence among his devout maternal relatives in Eisenach. All his later life gave testimony that he was by nature passionate, labile, and ardently committed, and in such a youth the preachers' appeal for harsh self-judgment and grief over sin took deepest root.

There is no way of knowing by what stages this seed grew to fruition, and brought Martin to seek solace from his inner turmoil in the special graces of monasticism. But we do know that the awareness of death – the preachers' classic occasion for such conversion – was sharply present to him at the time of his sudden entrance. This was Melanchthon's account of that decision: Luther had told him that when he thought earnestly about the wrath of God or about extraordinary instances of divine punishment 'he sometimes was suddenly smitten by such terrors that he almost expired . . . He felt these terrors either for the first time (or at any rate most sharply) in that year, when he lost a friend who died from I know not what cause.'[31]

At some time earlier, Luther himself had come perilously close to death. As he set out to walk home from Erfurt to Mansfeld, his sword slipped out and slashed an artery in his leg, and he was near death from loss of blood before a doctor arrived to dress the wound:

> As he waited, he was in danger of dying, and cried, 'O Mary, help!' ('I would have died there upon Mary!' he said.) Later that night, in bed, the wound haemorrhaged again: as he faded, again he invoked Mary.[32]

And there was a parallel account of a similar accident befalling one of his brothers.[33]

The immediate catalyst for his entrance into the Augustinian cloister was yet another, and most famous, close encounter with death – the thunderstorm at Stottenheim. Terrified by a bolt of lightning he cried out in terror, and vowed, 'Help me, St Anna, and I will become a monk!'[34]

Atmospheric disturbances, he would have heard from the pulpit, were special messengers from God to remind human beings of sudden death:

> God sends storms so that he may smite sinners with terror, and thus at last they may be converted ... Why are the church bells rung against the tempestuousness of the air? ... so that men, hearing their peals, may be aroused to call upon God lest he drown us on account of our sins as he drowned the whole world when the flood came. So when men hear the pealing of the bells against the storms of the sky, whether by day or night, they must fear for themselves, and humbly call on God to deal mercifully with us.[35]

If the terror of death was the catalyst for decision, the goal of Martin's quest was that pure and sincere contrition that would lead to peace with God:

> I was never able to be consoled about my baptism. 'How (I thought) can a person become pious even once?' And so I became a monk.[36]

But as a monk, the more he struggled to harrow his own heart as the preachers had enjoined, the more he discovered how unattainable was the contrition they demanded – an unalloyed sorrow, purged even of the fear of loss but evoked only by desire for God. Only God could infuse such contrition, and because he could not find surcease Brother Martin hated God for not doing so. The wise counsel of his mentor, Johann von Staupitz, at length broke the loop. Staupitz convinced him that he was trying to do far more than lay within him, and that he was looking for the sign of God's mercy in the wrong place: forgiveness was to be found in the sweet wounds of Christ.

The result was a new freedom of conscience, and a new

experience of what repentance meant. This freedom released in him a freshness, and confidence, and a vitality of expression that presaged the theological innovations of years to come. yet that freedom of spirit was not yet the source of a new doctrine; rather, the very doctrine of contrition that he had heard from the pulpits of his youth, now purged of its confusions, was reclaimed by him as a source not of oppression but of joy.

For Luther soon became a preacher himself, and a biblical expositor, and a pastor to both monks and townspeople. As he became more and more active as a pastor, he grew passionately aware of the ambiguity of the message reaching the people. On one hand they were told that true contrition was their 'spiritual conception'; on the other they were offered indulgences and relics which shortcircuited both the sorrow and the joy of self-examination. On one hand, they were told that their repentance must spring from grace and love and never from fear, or else it would be worthless; on the other, the uncertainty and terror of death, judgment, demons, and a grotesque vision of hell was the indiscriminate goad to spur laypeople to penance. On one hand, the preachers taught that forgiveness was a response to the heart's sincerity before and apart from sacramental penance; on the other, priestly confession and satisfaction were the most stringently guarded instrument of clerical control. On one hand the doctrine was plain that hope sprang only from God's abundant mercy, and indeed was available to faith alone;[37] on the other, the calculus of merits and sins, rewards and satisfactions, was embedded in every facet of popular religious culture, and confirmed by the special graces claimed by the priests and monks for their sanctity. The multiple standards of spirituality, poignantly intended to make a ministry accessible to all, had instead confused and destroyed the laity's chance to solve the 'really knotty problems' of penitence Luther had wrestled with in the cloister. The Reformation, in its earliest and simplest form, was a protest against the present state of penitential practice.

That, after all, is what the *Ninety-Five Theses* were about:

1. When our Lord and Master Jesus Christ said, 'Do penance,' he wanted the whole life of believers to be penance.

2. That word cannot be understood of sacramental penance (that is, confession and satisfaction, celebrated by the ministry of priests).[38]

Luther wanted first to assault the citadel of priestly authority in sacramental penance, with all its attendant cheapening of grace, empty or trivial satisfactions, and indulgences. Rather, Christians must be 'zealous in following Christ their head through penalties, death, and hell, and so trust rather to enter heaven through many tribulations than through the security of peace.'[39] Contrition's truth seeks for penalties and loves them.[40] Thus in the name of contrition Luther disputed the scholastic theology that shored up the system of penances by assigning the efficacy to priestly authority and churchly grace. And he was acutely aware of the double message that resulted, with its disastrous pastoral consequences:

It is very difficult, even for the most learned theologians, at once to extol before the people both the largesse of indulgences and the truth of contrition.[41]

Against the cheapening of grace, Luther reasserted fervently the need for a rigorous, constant, all-embracing contrition. Yet he did not simply repeat the contritionism of the preachers of his youth, for he also perceived an opposite danger – that people could easily be led to substitute trust in their own sincere contrition for faith in the gospel. 'No-one,' thesis 30 declares, 'is certain of the truth of his own contrition.'[42] In the *Explanations* of the theses, Luther affirmed that the keys were rightly exercised when the people sought and gained absolution in simple faith:

But some sophisticated people try to calm themselves by their own contritions and works and confessions, and achieve nothing but to go from disquiet to disquiet, because they are trusting in themselves and their own efforts, when, if they feel distress of conscience, they should trust in Christ who says: 'Whatever you shall loose on earth shall be loosed in heaven.' But recent theologians contribute all too readily to this evil conscience when they present and teach the

71

sacrament of penance in such a way that the laity learn to believe that they can wipe out their sins themselves by their contritions and satisfactions, which is the vainest presumption ... First, faith in Christ the free bestower of remission must be taught, then despair of one's own contrition and satisfaction must be urged; that so, when trust and joy of heart in Christ's mercy have been firmly rooted, then at last they may gladly hate their sins, be contrite, and make satisfaction.[43]

Luther became a reformer out of urgent pastoral concern. It was not his first intention to begin a theological revolution; it was certainly not his first aim to lead an ecclesial revolt. These steps followed, to be sure, but (as he himself later insisted) they were not yet in view 'when I began that cause.'[44]

Luther's cause is incomprehensible without a clear account of the religious culture from which it sprang. That. of course, seems like a truism until one examines the varieties of 'Catholicism on the eve of reform' that have been offered in explanation of Luther's Reformation.

The standard explanation, I suppose, has been that the Reformation was demanded by the parlous state of the church. In its crasser forms – in undergraduate exam papers, for example – suitable references to 'tensions and weaknesses in the late mediaeval church as reflected in the Great Schism, the Conciliar movement, the emergency of Wyclif and Hus, and the secularization of the Papacy'[45] have been taken as adequate explanation of the break – so long as one pays due regard to Luther's own 'struggle'. In a far more sophisticated and sensitive form, the same thesis is the burden of Joseph Lortz's *How the Reformation Came*.[46] As Reformation scholarship has persisted, however, it has become obvious how broadly these simple generalities are brushed, and how much they are coloured by hindsight and by the rhetoric of the Reformation itself.

Yet I cannot escape the strong impression that some of the corrective emphases of recent research are themselves misleading. For instance, although it has been invaluable to have far more detailed accounts of the theologies of grace canvassed in scholastic circles on the eve of the Reform, it would be extremely misleading to suppose that scholastic theology was the decisive context for Luther's personal evolution, or for the reception of his message by the faithful laity. Yet this is implied by the fashion in combing through all Luther's pre-Reformation utterances for traces of Gabrielist nominalism affirmed or abandoned.

Just as the older historiography implied that the institutional Catholicism of the hierarchy was the decisive context, so this newer fashion implies that the intellectual Catholicism of the universities was all-important. These are both elitist assumptions, which pay too little attention to the popular experience of Catholic religion as a culture – a complex of meanings and injunctions and **practices, a source of aspirations and fears, and mode of social** control, an exercise of public power, and a pervasive graphic definition of human life and death.

It is refreshing to find historians who are now devoting themselves to a far closer view of this religious culture in the cities where the Reformation took root, in the hope of creating, out of a mosaic of close instances, a more authentic and inclusive picture of the whole – a picture that reveals the links between the minutiae of people's lives and the great movements which swept them up.

NOTES

1. For details, see my *Luther and His Mother* (Philadelphia: Fortress Press, 1981).
2. *WA* 30/3, 491:39.
3. *WA* Br, 1, 10–11: #3.
4. Vincenz Hasak, *Dr. M. Luther und die religiose literatur seiner Zeit bis zum Jahre 1520* (Regensburg: Mainz, 1881; reprinted Nieuwkoop: de Graaf, 1967), 27–8.
5. As so excellently described by John O'Malley, *Praise and Blame in Renaissance Rome: Rhetoric, Doctrine and Reform in the Sacred Orators of the Papal Court, c.1450–1521* (Durham, N.C.: Duke University Press, 1979).
6. Hain – Copinger – Reichling, *Repertorium Bibliographicum*, and supplements: Hain 8057–8082; Copinger 2800; Reichling 201, 1221.
7. Hain 15955–15979; Copinger 5971–5978; Reichling 356.
8. Copinger 5409–5438; Reichling 1390, supplement 177.
9. F. R. Goff, 'The Postilla of Guillermus Parisiensis', *Gutenberg Jahrbuch 34* (1959): 73–8.
10. Hain 8473–8522; Copinger 2921–39; Reichling 207, 549, 1223, 1536, 1750.
11. Johannes Trithemius, *De scriptoribus ecclesiasticis* (Basel: Amerbach, 1494). Hain – Copinger 15613.
12. Johann Herolt, O.P. ('Discipulus'), *Sermones de sanctis* (1434), prologue. The edition I have used here was printed by M. Flach: Strassburg, 1492, M1r.

LUTHER

13. Johann of Werden, O.M., *Sermones dormi secure*, preface. The edition I have used here was printed by A. Koberger: Nurnberg, 1498.
14. Herolt, *Sermones de tempore*, 97:2; *Epistolae*, 41:3.
15. Herolt, *Sermones de tempore*, 71:3 and 102:2.
16. Werden, *Sermones dormi secure de tempore*, 6:2.
17. See Thomas Tentler, *Sin and Confession on the Eve of the Reformation* (Princeton: Princeton University Press, 1977).
18. Johann Gritsch, *Quadragesimale*, 10. The edition I have used here was printed at Ulm: Joh. Sainer, 1475 (Hain 8063), viii, O.
19. Herolt, *sermones de tempore*, 115:0.
20. ibid., 115:1–7.
21. Werden, *Sermones dormi secure de tempore*, 11:2.
22. ibid., 15:3.
23. *Sermones thesauri novi*, 24:0. Werden, *Sermones dormi secure de tempore*, 57:1.
24. *Sermones thesauri novi*, 134, D–E.
25. Herolt, *Sermones de tempore*, 102:2.
26. ibid., 71:3.
27. Werden, *Sermones dormi secure de tempore*, 17:1–2.
28. Gritsch, *Quadragesimale*, Monday in Holy Week, xl, N.
29. *Corpus Reformatorum* 6, 156; *Scriptorum publice propositorum a gubernatoribus studiorum in Academia VVittenbergensi Tomus Tertius, Complectens annum 1556 et tres sequentes* (Wittenberg, 1559), 190[b].
30. *CR*, 6:156.
31. *CR*, 6:158.
32. *WA* Tr, 1, 46: #119 and notes.
33. *WA* 40/1, 315:2.
34. *WA* Tr 4, 440: #4707.
35. Herolt, *Sermones de tempore*, 108:2.
36. *WA* 37, 274:14.
37. Herolt, *Sermones de tempore*, 97:3; Heinrich Herp, O.M., *Sermones de tempore*, 1:7.
38. *WA* 1, 233:10.
39. *WA* 1, 238:17.
40. *WA* 1, 235:16.
41. *WA* 1, 235:14.
42. *WA* 1, 235:35.
43. *WA* 1, 542:29.
44. *WA*, 54:179.
45. From a course outline in a history curriculum handbook from Victoria, Australia (1980).
46. Herder and Herder, 1966.

MILES EMERITUS? CONTINUITY AND DISCONTINUITY BETWEEN THE YOUNG AND THE OLD LUTHER

Gordon Rupp

It is natural that a great deal of the attention of modern scholarship has been devoted to the Young Luther, and to the investigation of those intriguing documents which have been edited and published in this century, which show the young Martin of Wittenberg as a scholastic theologian, and imbedded in which documents must surely lie the answer to many questions still far from being settled, and so almost justifying the conveyor belt procession of dissertations and monographs. For most students, too, the events from 1517–22 and the documents they evoked, are the exciting things. There is so much that is dramàtic, poignant and at times enthralling in the confrontations of Luther at Augsburg, Leipzig, and Worms, in the months of hiding on the Wartburg, and the sudden return to Wittenberg, in March 1522. During that time of immense and creative mental ferment he produced some of his most memorable writings, commentaries, works of edification, manifestos, and the beginnings of the great German Bible.

If we go on to 1525 which was in some ways the watershed year, with his marriage, with the Peasant War, with the debate with Erasmus it might be argued that the rest of his career was in some ways an anti-climax, that the great pioneer, lonely figure was now swallowed up in a great movement, ever widening, throwing up new leaders and a new diversity amid which his own pattern of salvation was but one. So much so that when he died, in 1546 the surface of history seemed barely ruffled by the event.

Heinrich Bronkamm's fine, luminous and sadly unfinished study of Luther's Middle Years has taken the story to the Diet of Augsburg. But what of the Old Luther? It is often assumed that his last years were racked with illness and exhaustion, and the symptoms of old age: that pessimism and intolerance provoked him into outrageous polemic and made him the scorn of his enemies, and a trial to his friends. I believe this to be a quite exaggerated impression. 'Miles Emeritus' he might indeed sigh to be, but the old war horse was never put out to grass.

Nor in his thought and in the quality of his writing, and in the depths of his achievement is it permissible to drive a wedge between the Young and the Old Luther. There were great and important and lasting continuities. Not that there were no changes. It seems to us no great compliment when disciples of Calvin emphasise his claim never to have changed his mind and more preferable to follow Newman's slogan 'Growth is the only evidence of life'. We must not shirk the ultimate question – 'but had he ceased then to grow'? as long as we remember that he was an old man, and that there must always be an ambivalence between the outward frame so evidently perishing, and that inward man, 'sola fide perceptibilis', as Luther would say, which is renewed day by day.

There is another consideration at least as important to be borne in mind as the contrast between a man at the height of his powers and a man of waning energies, and that is the difference in the historical setting, a difference to which he had himself contributed and to an astonishing degree provoked.

For Martin Luther was not, like Napoleon, a 'Man of Destiny' – he did not set out to shape events to his own liking. 'God has led me like an old blind horse' he truly said, and hence the occasional nature of his writings, wrung from him by the pressure of events. Nothing in the events of that last decade 1537–46 can compare with those which began with the Indulgence controversy. In the early 1520s it really seemed that the Word might triumphantly reform the church, and that 'Popery' might once for all have been defeated. By 1545, though the Reformation movement had spread widely and irrevocably through much of north western Europe, it was clear that the Papacy was by no means done for, and as Titian's foxy popes succeeded Raphael's urbane pontiffs, it seemed that the Papal council so long scorned, must formidably meet, while, old enmities put aside, the Emperor, as 'miles papae', was able to summon up a combination of military powers which was to burst triumphantly into Germany within months of Luther's death.

And if, facing them there was a coherent association of Protestant princes, they were such that Luther could not view them without misgivings. When he said at this time that 'The devil has gone from Thomas Müntzer and into the Princes' he was aware that the confrontation was no longer the open and shut Catholic–Protestant dilemma as at Augsburg, but that now dynastic and family considerations and an intricate network of noble relationships, might disastrously bedevil the situation. This is apparent in one of Luther's last writings: his memorandum to the Elector and the Protestant princes on how they should treat their captive Henry of Brunswick, who had succeeded Duke George of Saxony and Albert of Mainz as Luther's Public enemy no. 1.[1]

Luther let events come to him. One result was that he became more and more imbedded in the Saxon setting and in the life of Wittenberg. In 1525 all Christendom was his parish, but in 1546 he seemed most concerned with the parish pump. It is true that his last correspondence dealt with church problems over a great area from Scandinavia to Hungary and Venice. It is impressive to note the numbers of influential men and women who turned to him for political advice and pastoral counsel – and historians have underestimated the importance of such people, the officials of the cities, and those smaller gentry who were rather like the 'lairds' in Scotland and to whom he dedicated so many of his writings. But we have not the sense that we have in reading the correspondence of Calvin or even Bullinger, of one keeping his finger on the pulse of distant events, guiding the advance and progress of his pattern of Reformation. To use the crudest of illustrations, Luther who had begun as a striker was ending as a goalkeeper. But if he concentrated on the day to day duties in the place where God had put him, there to he stood because he could do no other. The God who had commanded him to go to Worms now guided his footsteps daily to his classroom or the parish church, to preachments before small congregations of little people most of whom he knew by sight and name. This was the setting in which he worked out his salvation with fear and trembling until the moment of dismissal came. The absence of the great sights and sounds and immense publicities does not mean that Luther's last years are about decline and fall.

Despite changes of emphasis, and a way of picking on a phrase like 'Christ's strange work' or 'gratia' and 'donum' or the thought of the Pope as a Werewolf, which he uses for a time, and then drops, and despite the fact that he was no systematizer, there is an inner coherence and consistency in Luther's thought. This is most evident in the firmness with which he held to the doctrine of Justification 'sola fide' and 'solo Christo'. The Schmalkaldic articles which he drew up in 1537 for presentation to the gathering of Reformers in face of a Papal Council have his own personal flavour. It was his own serious and almost fatal illness which removed him from the deliberations, giving place to Melanchthon's much smoother statements. But Luther's statement has remained a classic statement of his mature views and among its memorable phrases is his affirmation about justification by faith alone 'From this article there can be no surrender or compromise, though heaven and earth shall fall and whatever else may not remain'.[2]

In one of his last 'set piece' sermons at the Baptism of the infant Prince Bernhard of Anhalt he not only repeats the doctrine of his fine sermon of 1519, but he explains it in terms of his theology of the Cross and invokes that 'sacrum commercium' the exchange between Christ and the believer which as a young man he had first learned from Augustine and perhaps from Staupitz. 'Through this blessed exchange in which Christ changes place with us (something the heart can grasp only in faith) and through nothing else are we freed from sin and death and given his righteousness and life as our own'.[3] In his early writings, from the luminous 'Sermon on Good Works' as in his 'Preface to the Romans' Luther had made clear that he did not leave Christian ethics hanging in the air, and that faith must bring forth the fruits of a new life. For him the dialectic of Law and Gospel was always of first importance, and was reinforced in 1537 when during his absence at Schmalkald, his colleague and guest Agricola (Luther had taken him and his large family in) circulated propositions behind Luther's back, which launched what became known as the Antinomian controversy. Luther was angry and bitter not only to find that his foes were those of his own household but at the scandalous implications of Agricola's insistence on abandoning the Law. But if he wrote in the margin of the propositions – 'Yes, you understand that very well, you great fool'[4] we may remember that the very first writings we have from him consist of marginal jottings which include such phrases as 'Lousy' 'Rancid!' and 'O Sow theologians'.

Similarly with Luther's doctrine of the Church. K. Holl's statement that the whole of Luther's doctrine of the church is to be found in his first lectures on the Psalms has been but little modified by modern research, and despite statements to the contrary there is, as Holl asserted a link between his ecclesiology and his doctrine of justification.[5] But that the church like its Master appears on earth under contrary species, and is 'sola fide perceptibilis' is a doctrine which binds the Old with the young Luther, in two of his most luminous sayings, the first from the Schmalkaldic articles – Thank God a child of seven years knows what the church is, namely the holy believers and the lambs who hear their shepherd's voice' and in his 'Wider Hans Worst' (1540) 'Oh, it is a high, deep, hidden thing is the Church which nobody may perceive or see, but can only grasp by faith in Baptism, Word and Sacrament'.[6]

It is true that Luther himself became more and more involved in the visible church, and in the Landeskirche of Saxony. But there is no inconsistency between such concern and his thought that the essential nature of the church is known only by faith, which alone can grasp the true significance of the outward signs which attest its presence. And in his great initial emphasis on the Word, from which the church is born, and the great primary sacraments, so often expounded in his early Reformation writings there are affirmations which are supplemented but not contradicted in his last two great treatises on the subject, 'Von Konziliis und Kirchen' (1539) and 'Wider Hans Worst'. (1540). In the first, he maintains that the evangelicals have no need of a reforming council, and affirms them to be the true old church, a point he had already stressed in his writings of 1530. And in both he lists the notes of the true church:

1. The Preaching of the Word.
2. The Sacrament of Baptism.
3. The Sacrament of the Altar.

4. The Keys of Christian discipline.
5. A called and consecrated Christian ministry.
6. Public thanksgiving and the worship of God.
7. Suffering, the possession of the Holy Cross.

We have seen how he continued to express his faith in the doctrine of Holy Baptism in his later sermons. His doctrine of the eucharist he had maintained unchanged since his great treatise in 1528, and about it he was not prepared to compromise despite the agreements reached at the Wittenberg Concord of 1536. But when in 1539 he consented to the abolition of the Elevation, it was rumoured that he was abandoning his eucharistic doctrine too and the result was a violent treatise in which he attacked the doctrines of the long dead Zwingli with a vehemence which made Bucer and Bullinger gasp. He was also violently opposed to the doctrines of the Silesian nobleman Caspar Schwenckfeld whose doctrine of the glorified body of Christ had eucharistic implications. Indeed in his last writings and sermons Luther still kept up his warfare on two fronts. The Schmalkaldic articles dealt with the Mass at some length, while Luther never ceased to attack the opinions of the various 'Schwärmer' who continued to spread. This is part of the reason why in his last decade he devoted a good deal of time to preaching and expounding the doctrines of the Trinity and Incarnation, for as Kooiman demonstrated some years ago, the first generation of Reformers generally did not question the classic definitions of the Early Church in those great doctrines. And although in connection with the eucharistic debate his use of the 'communicatio idiomatum' was charged with Eutychianism, he himself regarded the doctrines of the Person and Work of Christ as of fundamental importance. His later anti-semitic writings, were in some part Christologically conditioned, as may be seen in some fine passages in his exposition of the 'Last Words of David' (1544). Imbedded in the unpleasant 'Schem Hamphoras' (1543) there is a lively and extremely able defence of the Incarnation against Gnostic and Cabbalistic interpretations of the Tetragrammaton.
About Luther's teaching on Temporal Government and his teaching of the Two Kingdoms notably expounded in 1523 there has been continuing debate, much of it less concerned with

problems and inconsistencies of Luther himself than with problems of later Lutheranism, and indeed of questions raised during the Church struggle under the Nazis. Luther's own firm acceptance of Romans XIII as a classic statement of the Christian attitude towards civil government, never wavered, and he did not recant his own 'Leiden, Leiden, Creuz, Creuz' against the violence of Thomas Müntzer's liberation theology. At the Diet of Augsburg, and thereafter, he and his Protestant Princes were faced with the ominous threat of armed intervention by the Emperor and the Catholic Princes. While the city of Nuremberg held to Luther's earlier teaching which allowed only passive resistance, the Wittenberg theologians, Luther among them were persuaded by the lawyers that the very constitution of the Empire allowed armed defence and Luther signed memoranda supporting this view, though he always disliked violence and never sanctioned pre-emptive strikes of the kind to which Philip of Hesse was prone. Nor despite my old friend, Professor Cargill Thompson, do I think Luther came within a thousand miles of supporting the kind of attitudes and policies of John Knox.

The attempts to clarify and perhaps smooth out the doctrine of the Two Kingdoms belong to Luther's middle years and do not here concern us. But it is important to note that in his later years he came to speak more and more of the 'Three Hierarchies' of civil, spiritual and domestic government and found abundant illustrations of them in his final course of lectures on Genesis. Of interest and importance are the famous 'Circular Disputation' theses of 1539, as brilliant in their contriving as those of 1517. In this set of 83 theses he asserted that the Pope belonged to no lawful authority since he transgressed all three forms of God given authority. He is therefore a monster, a rabid werewolf. And he who supports the Pope like the Emperor, is a 'miles papae' and is therefore also to be resisted. The relation of Luther's teaching about the Kingdoms and the hierarchies, to the overall command of love, and Luther's view of law generally has been the centre of a lively and intricate debate provoked by the publication in 1955 of the lawyer Johannes Heckel's 'Lex Charitatis'.[7]

The violence of Luther's later anti-Jewish treatises has offended all Luther's friends, and must strike harshly on an age which has only too much reason to be sensitive about anti-semitism, and a twentieth century which bears more guilt than all the Christians of the Middle ages and of the sixteenth century put together. But Luther's anti-semitism was not simply mediaeval racism, but it was bound up with his own evangelical beliefs about Christ and the gospel. Nor were they some aberration of his later years. In 1514 when Reuchlin was involved in the great controversy, Luther wrote to Spalatin supporting Reuchlin it is true, but not on humanist grounds and affirming the blasphemy of the Jews. It is true that as Lewin demonstrated, Luther in the early years of the Reformation movement thought that the Jews might be won over by kinder treatment, but he was soon disillusioned and was incensed when at the end of the 1530s it seemed that so far from Jews becoming Christians, radical Christians were initiating a kind of Christian Judaism.

For much of the violence of Luther's pamphlets of the 1540s there can be no defence, with their dreadful programme for the exercise of 'sharp compassion' a programme hardly different sadly enough, from that advocated by Martin Bucer but on different theological premises. Luther believed that when one had appealed in vain, then one could only denounce, since otherwise one became a partaker of the sins of the unrepentant. This is the theme of that last, sad sermon which he preached within hours of his death – 'they must be invited to turn to the Messiah . . . if not we must not suffer them to remain for they daily abuse and blaspheme Christ'.[8]

It was well for Luther and for many others, that he did not persist in his original intention to become a lawyer, for he was as Hans Leiermann has said a most 'unlawyer like' person. He detested legalism and loved to praise those who in his opinion had a natural flair and were 'born' rather than text book lawyers. From all periods of his life his interest in Equity – 'epieikia', can be attested. But he also hated canon law, for supporting Papal claims, and by which he was condemned as an apostate monk who had married a nun. The result was his growing estrangement from his old ally, the Professor of Law, Jerome Schürpf, who accepted much of the older law and was not willing to surrender to Luther's view that the Bible and the practice of the new evangelical church provided new material for church law. The division became apparent in relation to the controversial marriage laws, and to the question of secret engagements, and the relative authority of the consent of parents.

Luther's antagonism to secret engagements was rooted in his early pastoral experience, and what happened to him as a young Confessor became important in 1544 when, as on other occasions he intervened on behalf of a young couple, one of whom was a student. The matter erupted in a series of polemical sermons which Luther preached during Epiphany 1544, when he publicly attacked the methods of the lawyers and formally consigned them to perdition.[9] But he won his case, and a meeting at his Prince's orders with the lawyers of University and court showed their deference for the old man, whose Churchillian qualities were recognized.

Some writers speak of the 'Weltpessimismus' of the later Luther, and it is true that the Doomwatch quality of his comments are notable. It found striking expression in a dedication to John Frederick in March 1530 – 'the world is cracking to pieces . . . it seems to me this is the end, as when a light or straw which is almost burned out suddenly lights up once more as though it had just been set alight, and in that very moment goes out – '[10]

And it is true that in his last years apocalyptic became more important. This too is not to be exaggerated, for his correspondence shows how important for him 1520–1 was the thought that the Pope must be Anti Christ as Huss and other late mediaeval reformers had asserted. His early dismissal of the Book of Revelation did not mean that he had no use for it and in his last years both the time schedule of Daniel and the events of Revelation continued to intrigue him. He spent and probably wasted a great deal of time constructing a probable chronology of the history of the world and of the church. And in these last years too, his enemies became apocalyptic figures, notably the Pope, the Turk, the epicureans and sophists, the Schwärmer and his most old and intimate enemy, the Devil. About the Pope he wrote in terms of righteous fury, and though there is hardly an expression of Luther in his last polemic[11] which cannot be paralleled in the writings of the young reformer, his vehemence displeased his friends, though perhaps significantly often pleasing his Prince.

He is not to blame for Lukas Cranach's obscene illustrations to which he reacted in an almost old maidish way. Indeed his concern for moral standards was generally of an old fashioned kind, and is shown in the outspoken way in which in the last years he attacked the vices of the court, and notably gluttony and drunkenness.[12] While his attempt to leave Wittenberg for ever, on the ground that its moral level was no better but ungratefully worsening is not to be written off as a senile gesture.

In his last years Luther exercised his three-fold vocation as a 'professor, a preacher of the Word and a pastor'. Those last lectures of his upon the book of Genesis are unlike any lectures which he gave in his youth, but they are none the less masterly and impressive and it is no wonder that many of the most famous quotations cited in the monographs of the last fifty years come from their pages. 'Ripeness is all.' Into them he crammed the experience of a life time and the great affirmations about the gospel of grace, while his series of portraits of the Patriarchs have a marvellous life which recalls Michelangelo's Sistine prophets.

Though by the end of them he was exhausted, and though they break off suddenly, they are one of the most impressive of his theological feats. It is no wonder that during them Melanchthon prompted the students to stand when he entered the lecture room. Bad health, fainting fits, bronchitis, often stopped his preaching for long periods, but if some of his last sermons are tired and repetitive – for he had no arguments to add against the Schwärmer or the Papists, there are some splendid passages and high moments. And this preaching went hand in hand with his pastoral care. It was in 1542 that he induced Bugenhagen to let him add an appendix to an edifying work, 'To comfort Women who have had a miscarriage'.[13] When Jerome Baumgartner of Nuremberg was hi-jacked on his way from the Diet of Speyer in 1544 Luther wrote a letter to his wife which she handed to her husband when at last he came home, and both of them dissolved in tears at such loving concern. And when his old friend George Spalatin made an ass of himself by marrying a man to his step mother, Luther wrote him a wonderful letter of absolution and comfort, a letter which was copied and circulated with the comment of Myconius of Githa that Luther is 'that most expert of all expert doctors in all which pertains to morbid, afflicted and dead consciences'.[14]

It was his loving concern for his home country and his own particular 'Obrigkeit' which led him to that last wearisome journey back to Eisleben to settle the quarrel between his two young princes, in the depth of a cruel winter, a bourne from which he did not return. Of course there are many signs of his age and weakness. His friends found him much of a trial, but if Luther was an old man, Melanchthon was more than a bit of an old woman. And certainly right to the end his princes and their very canny civil servants looked for and valued his advice – he was by no means written off as 'past it'. And it is interesting how many of the most valuable stories of the young Luther come to us from his lectures and sermons of these last years, including the most important single document of all, his own autobiographical reminiscences of his beginnings, written in 1545. And right to the end, he was the lynch pin of the Lutheran Reformation. How much he had counted and how many tensions had been held together in his heart and mind can best be judged by what happened after his death, by the disastrous political and military manoeuvrings for which Philip of Hesse was much to blame, and for the splitting asunder of his disciples, Melanchthon on the one side, Amsdorf on the other, in a series of growing theological schisms, each claiming to be followers of the authentic Lutheran teaching, and none of them without some plausibility. It is true, as we have said, that at his death, the man who in his youth and in his prime had shaken kings and nations, disturbed hardly at all the European pattern. But if we pay attention not to the Luther macrocosm but to the microcosm, the pilgrimage within, then Luther's progress to the Diet of Worms seems to have continued on much the same path, and he himself continued to fight manfully the good fight of faith, until his journey's end.

NOTES

1. *LW*, 43:258 ff.
2. H. Volz, *Urkunden u. Aktenstücke zur Geschichte von Martin Luthers Schmalkaldischen Artikeln*. (1536–74), Berlin, 1937, p. 38.
3. *LW*, vol. 51. Sermons, (April, 1540), p. 316. D. Steinmetz, *Luther and Staupitz*; Duke University, 1950.
4. *W.* 60; 234.
5. Modern study has investigated the relation between Luther's view of church and synagogue and the implications of his hermeneutic. Cf. J. Vercruysse, *Fidelis populus*, Wiesbaden, 1968 and S. H. Hendrix, Leiden, 1974.

6. *W*, 51:507; 9 ff.
7. For a useful summary of this debate, with texts, *Luther und die Obrigkeit*, ed. G. Wolf 1972, and H. Sheible, *Das Widerstandsrecht als Problem der deutschen Protestanten 1523–46*.
8. E. G. Rupp, *Martin Luther and the Jews*, London, 1972. W. Maurer in *Kirche und Synagoge* ed. Rengstorf, Bd. 1, 1968, Ch. 5. J. Brosseder, *Luthers Stellung zu den Juden im Spiegel seiner Interpreten*, Munich, 1972. C. B. Sucher, *Luthers Stellung zu den Juden*, Niewcoop, 1977.
9. H. Dörries, *Wort und Stunde*, Bd. 3, Göttingen, 1970, 271:326.
10. *W*, DB, 11:2, 380.
11. *Against the Roman Papacy. Instituted by the Devil*; *LW*, 41:256 ff.
12. *LW*, 51:291. *Sermon on Soberness, Moderation* (1539). There are many statements of this kind in the 'Table Talk'.
13. *LW*, 43:2, 245 ff.
14. I. Höss, G. Spalatin, 418 ff.

LUTHER'S UNDERSTANDING OF JUSTIFICATION BY GRACE ALONE IN TERMS OF CATHOLIC CHRISTOLOGY

George Yule

When one studies Luther's works chronologically, it becomes apparent that more and more he discussed justification by grace alone in terms of the traditional Christology of the Church. The originality of Luther's theology is in the way he interwove its anti-Pelagian slant with the central affirmation of the Christian faith, that Jesus Christ, though of one nature with God the Father, became our brother man. His whole discussion took on a fresh and personal approach which was often lacking in the later Mediaeval theologians whose works on this subject often read like a text book on symbolic logic.

By the fifteen thirties, though I think it began in 1518 or 1519, his new way of stating the matter has become almost invariable. 'For if this foundation stands and is ours by faith – that Christ is both God's Son and the Virgin's Son in one person, though of two different natures, of the divine nature from eternity through the Father, of the human nature through His birth from Mary – then I have all that is necessary, and it is superfluous to let my thoughts flit heavenward and explore God's will and plan. Then I am spared all the disputations of the Jews, Turks, heathen and all the world about God, how He is to be sought and encountered, or how He is to be served and pleased. And I am relieved of all fear and anxiety of my own heart'.[1]

In his sermons on John of this period he explicitly linked Christology with his new insights into the righteousness of God. In commenting on John 16:10 – 'of righteousness because I go to the Father', he wrote, 'He is speaking here of a righteousness recognised by God, a righteousness far different from that acknowledged by the world ... He identifies it exclusively with

Himself . . . and is related to the words "because I go to the Father and you will see me no more" . . . Christ did not go to the Father for His own sake . . . but just as He came down from heaven for our sakes and became our flesh and blood so He also ascended to heaven for our sakes after conquering sin, death and hell and entering into His dominion . . . Such is the nature of His reign that His kingdom is called and is "righteousness".[2] . . . It is entirely outside and above us; it is Christ going to the Father, that is, His suffering, resurrection and ascension . . . The only way it can be grasped is by faith in the Word preached about Him which tells us that He himself is our righteousness . . . in order that before God we may boast not of ourselves but solely of the Lord'.[3] Christ our righteousness is now the clue to his understanding of justification. Notice how entirely Christocentric this discussion of righteousness has now become, compared to his discussion in his *Commentary on Romans* of 1:17 in 1516.

Luther's mind was saturated with the Bible so it is little wonder that when he came to his new understanding of the righteousness of God as Christ our righteousness he should not only express this in the existential and historical terms of the Bible rather than those of Mediaeval theology or even of mysticism, but also that as the Bible never makes an abstract distinction between the person of Christ and His work of salvation so Luther likewise expressed his clearer understanding of the saving righteousness of God in terms of God's saving presence in Christ. For he now saw in a direct and personal way that the being of God and His saving activity in Christ are identical. Just as Athanasius had seen so clearly that the Arian heresy which denied Christ's deity drove a wedge between the being of God and the love of Christ, so Luther saw that 'this article that Christ is both very God and very man is the rock on which our eternal welfare and salvation are built'.[4] For 'In Christ I have the Father's will and heart'. 'God does not come to punish, but His will in Christ is the only gracious will of the Father'.[5]

In his tower experience he realised with clarity that the *iustitia Dei* and the *iustitia Christi* were identical and given simultaneously, so that the gift of Christ was itself the grace of God. Everything now stemmed from this love of God which, given in Christ, was utterly, dependable. Now the whole emphasis was on Christ, the grace of God Himself and therefore the sole object of faith. Two consequences of immense importance followed.

First he now saw how salvation was entirely bound up with the incarnation. Salvation comes alone from the God who so loved the world as to become our brother man in Jesus Christ, who as God and man is the righteousness of God. The Nicene faith that Jesus Christ is very God and very man entails *sola gratia* – grace alone. From now on, in Lienhard's phrase, his Christology was always 'under the sign of the cross',[6] and whether he was discussing Christ's deity or humanity he set forth the incarnation as the complete expression of the grace of God.

In an extended comment in 1537 on John 14:20, 'in that day you will know I am in my Father and my Father in Me', Luther wrote, 'It is not our intention to debate against the Arians as some of the ancient Fathers have done on the basis of this text, how to view the one undivided divine essence. No, here we want to confine ourselves to practical applications of this doctrine . . . If the devil wants to frighten you with God's wrath and judgement, with death and hell and tells you that God is angry with you . . . tell him . . . "in Christ I have the Father's will and heart". If God is for us, what then is there to harm us? In brief, if you comprehend and see this, you comprehend Christ in the Father and the Father in Christ: then you see no anger, death or hell but sheer grace, compassion, heaven and life'.[7]

Equally, it was essential for Luther's understanding of this righteousness of God bestowed on man as a gift, that Christ be truly man, in order to stand beside man the sinner and to rescue him from law, sin, death and judgement, and as man to render the truly loving obedience to the will of God. In his sermon on Psalm 2:3 of 1532 he wrote: 'But the Gospel only holds up Christ to the soul and the eyes of all and commands all to behold Him alone, to depend on Him alone, to trust and believe only in Him. For having assumed our flesh, in our flesh He conquered Satan, killed death, laid waste and destroyed hell. It proclaims He alone is wise, because He alone knows and does the will of God the Father . . . and communicates this righteousness to all who believe in Him'.[8]

He combined both ideas frequently in his mature works. 'Now I see that God my Lord is not angry with me, for He is my flesh and blood and sits at the right hand of my heavenly Father . . . If he were ill-disposed towards me, he would not have taken on my flesh and blood'.[9] For Luther, the work of Christ was the clue to understanding his person.

But conversely his new insights into the centrality of the incarnation purged his understanding of salvation from every trace of Pelagianism. He had clearly seen in his *Romans commentary* that one must not separate faith from its object, Jesus Christ, but when he saw that the righteousness of God was the gift of Christ our righteousness, truly God and truly man, then he saw that the incarnation meant *sola gratia*, and that the faith he was talking about was 'only that faith which hides under the wings of Christ and glories in his righteousness'.[10]

Luther's deep piety had been re-fashioned when he entered the monastery by both scholastic and mystical theology. The scholastic tradition held that there was in man a spark of the divine which continued despite the fall, which enabled man unerringly to know the basic moral principles and on this the grace of God could build. Luther in his earlier writings assumed something of this notion of *synteresis* but in his *Commentary on Romans* 1515–16, had seen that it easily leads theologians into a Pelagian position.[11] Like Erasmus he had found this scholastic theology spiritually unhelpful, and this partly explains his great appreciation for many of the mystical writers, especially during the years 1516 to 1518 when he was hammering out his theology. For it was during these years that he described Tauler's sermons as 'pure and solid theology' and edited the full text of the *Theologica Germanica*.[12] Luther liked their personal non-scholastic approach and their emphasis on passivity, suffering and self-denial,[13] and he himself in his *Dicta Super Psalterium* of 1513–14 had insisted on the importance of *accusatio sui*, accusing oneself to escape the judgement of God, while in his *Romans* there is frequent emphasis on the necessity of *humilitas* for receiving the grace of God. In a way these played something of the role of *synteresis*, and could bend to the same Pelagian pressure. Luther, in the *Dicta Super Psalterium*, had broken from the usual Mediaeval exegesis of like seeking like, of grace building upon grace, and insisted that as the Psalmist even in his sin relied entirely upon God and received mercy, so it is he who sees himself as even the most vile, who is most beautiful to God', and wrote 'for if we judge ourselves we shall not be judged of the Lord. For we shall not be judged twice for the same thing'.[14] This idea was subsumed in the phrase *humilitas* in his *Romans* commentary.

But in *Romans* Luther also developed in a quite brilliant way the nature of sin as self-idolatry and so the problem of man's response to the Gospel was sharpened to the point of impossibility as it was in St Augustine and St Anselm. Why did St Augustine oppose Pelagius to sharply? Because he saw that the sins which worried Pelagius were merely the manifestations of something much more intractable, namely our turning away from God to idols, many of which were our own ideals as Bernard Shaw so aptly observed. To cure merely the manifestations leads to hypocrisy and self-righteousness. The problem is how does one 'delight to do God's will' because till we delight to do it we are not doing it. Delighting to do God's will cannot be legally imposed. The prescriptions of Pelagius in the face of this dilemma were hopeless. This is why the legalism and moralism of Western Christianity led to an inadequate view of sin and therefore to an inadequate view of grace. When Luther by his careful exegesis of *Romans* discovered the profundity of Paul's understanding of sin, the need for a deeper understanding of grace was forced upon him. And this is what one sees in his *Commentary on Romans*.[15]

He was coming closer and closer to the solution but he still did not fully grasp the significance of what he now knew. Grace was still a religious quality which was indeed given freely, but the idea of some necessary condition, in this case humility, still lingered, so that the final solution eluded him.

But by 1518 he saw that Christ himself was the righteousness of God – 'Christ our righteousness'. God's demand is completely given and fulfilled in the gift of Christ. Any trace of Pelagianism was now impossible.

All parts of the solution except this clear perception of the identification of Christ himself with the righteousness of God were in his hands by the time he was lecturing on Romans, and at times he seems to make even this identification. But he did not understand the significance of all that he had until this identification became central. Then everything fell into place. Salvation was all of grace for it was given in Jesus Christ himself truly God, so that nothing could be added, truly man and so fully identified with lost humanity. From then on the Nicene formulation of the faith took on a completely fresh significance. It spelt out the means and cost of our redemption – *sola gratia*.[16]

In his remarkable little sermon on *Two Kinds of Righteousness*, possibly preached on Palm Sunday 1519 or 1518,[17] these insights are present. It was based, significantly, on the Christological text of Philippians 2:5–6, 'Let this mind be in you which was also in Christ Jesus, who though He was in the form of God, did not count equality with God a thing to be grasped'. First, there is, he insisted, a righteousness given to men by Christ. It is not in themselves but 'given to men in baptism'. This is the great exchange received only in faith—that is, by its nature it cannot be earned for it is *sola gratia*. In this great exchange 'a man can boast in confidence and say "Mine are Christ's living, doing and speaking, his suffering and dying, mine as much as if I had lived, done, spoken, suffered and died as He did'.[18] Immediately he linked this given (or the rather unfortunately phrased 'alien'), righteousness to the incarnation quoting Isaiah 9:6 'For unto us a child is born, to us a Son is given', and saying as Athanasius or Irenaeus or Cyril of Alexandria could have said, 'Where Christ did the most sacred will of the Father and became obedient to Him, and whatsoever He did, He did for us and desired it to be ours'. 'He is entirely ours with all His benefits'. 'Through faith in Christ therefore Christ's righteousness becomes our righteousness and all that He has becomes ours; rather He Himself becomes ours. Therefore the Apostle calls it the righteousness of God (Romans 1:17). For in the Gospel 'the righteousness of God is revealed . . .' as it is written, 'the righteous shall live by faith. This is an infinite righteousness and one which swallows up sin in a moment, for it is impossible that sin should exist in Christ. On the contrary he who trusts in Christ exists in Christ, he is one with Christ having the same rightousness as He'.[19]

This is the primary righteousness of a Christian. The second kind of righteousness is now what a Christian performs out of gratitude and 'is a product of the first type of righteousness', and follows the example of Christ.[20]

In illustrating the example of Christ, Luther again made a profound Christological statement. In his controversy with Arius, Athanasius had said that at one time he used to say that at the incarnation the Logos of God entered into a man Jesus, but that he came to see that this did not do full justice to the understanding of the incarnation and that one had to say that 'The Son of God became this man Jesus',[21] so that Christ was both truly God by nature and truly the man whom He became. And here Luther made the very point in commenting on the next part of the text that 'though He was in the form of God He did not count equality with God a thing to be grasped but emptied Himself taking the form of a slave'. 'The term "form of God",' said Luther, 'here does not mean "essence of God" because Christ never emptied Himself of this' but as the incarnate one, in His human nature, He did not act in the way which His divine nature entitled Him to, but renounced this divine entitlement and 'did not please Himself' and unlike the Pharisee did not say "God I thank Thee that I am not like other men",' for he was 'unwilling to use His rank against us, unwilling to be different from us. Moreover for our sakes he became as one of us and took the form of a servant, that is, subjected Himself to all evils, which were ours and lived as if they were actually His own'.[22] The way Luther uses the technical language of person, form, essence in his writings of 1518 to 1530 needs much closer analysis.

It was our fallen enslaved humanity which was freely assumed at the incarnation, and Christ, continuously in His obedience to the Father, placed Himself under the misery which is the lot of sinful man, though in 'the form of God', He could have been free from this but for our sakes fully assumed the consequences of man's evil. But more importantly this saved Luther from expressing the incarnation in an Apollinarian or monophysite way (which denied Christ's full humanity). The true humanity of Christ was as essential to Luther as it was to Athanasius and Cyril of Alexandria.[23] And it is noteworthy that in this sermon he stated his understanding of the deity of Christ in a similar way to Athanasius, although I think he was at this time unaware of the fact and had arrived at this position solely from his study of the Bible, St Augustine and *The Sentences of Peter Lombard*, the text book of Mediaeval theology on which Luther had lectured, though he would also have had collections of sayings of the Fathers.

Luther's insistence in this sermon that Christ truly took the form of a servant meant that His deity was hidden. The one who suffered, who hung on the cross and was derided, was indeed truly a man and appeared to all as such. But the eye of faith, aroused by the Word of God, could see He was also *vere Deus* – truly god. This is one way in which Luther, from an Alexandrian Christology, escapes from any monophysite tendency. God is really present in this man in the person of His Son. But there is no confusion of the two natures, no divinising of Christ's humanity. The humanity conceals the divinity and this is why the Word and faith are necessary to see this.[24]

The insights expressed in this brief sermon were clarified by Luther in the next two decades of his life in his eucharistic writings, and especially in his sermons on the Psalms and St John's Gospel. The manner in which he expressed this new insistence on the centrality of Christology broke right away from the common Mediaeval formulations in several ways.

During his exile in the Wartburg in 1522 Luther began to write his *Postils*, sermon outlines for preachers which were, he said, what one should seek and expect in the Gospels. Because they are expounding the Bible the themes are couched in the direct and personal language of the Bible and this is a feature of Luther's Christological statements. Gone is the abstract impersonal scholastic terminology, the abstract distinction between Christ's person and His saving work. The great themes of the Trinity and the incarnation are woven into the texture of salvation. 'What does it avail', he wrote, 'that we condemn such heresy' (such as those who denied Christ's divinity) 'with our mouths and know Christ correctly, if nevertheless our hearts do not consider Him differently from the way they do? I do not see what they might point as the reason for the need of Christ if I am able to attain God's grace through my own works. It is not necessary for Him to be God and become man; in short, nothing written concerning Him is necessary. It would be sufficient to preach God as a person as the Israelites believe and then I would obtain His grace by my works.[25]

He now clarified the relationship of faith and good works in a most felicitious manner. In his early writings on the Psalms he had used the expression concerning Christ of Augustine that He is *sacramentum et exemplum*, and he saw our sacramentum as a genuine humility towards God, our *accusatio sui* as the basis of receiving forgiveness.[26] Then in *Romans* he continued the image, and talked of Christ's utter abandonment to death of self as *sacramentum* which death is qualitatively more than that of the saints but theirs is to be a death of the same kind.[27] But is this for them a *sacramentum* or an *exemplum*? It is quite unclear.

But by 1519 all this is gone and was indeed clearly anticipated, as we have seen, in his *Two kinds of Righteousness*. In *On Christian Liberty*, 1520, he completely rejected any idea of good works as meritorious. Christian ethics were the ethics of gratitude and therefore of freedom and responsibility. From now on Christ alone is *sacramentum*[28] and by 1522 he abandoned the pair of terms *sacramentum et exemplum* and substituted in his *Christmas Postil* of 1522 *Donum* and *Exemplum*. Christ indeed is our example but only after we 'receive and recognise Him as gift'.[29] But more important for our study, he stated that only one thing was necessary for this 'Christian life, righteousness and freedom. That one thing is the most holy Word of God the gospel of Christ'. and he went on to define this one necessary Gospel virtually in terms of the *Apostles Creed*, quoting from Romans 1, 'What then is the Word of God? . . . The Word is the gospel of God concerning His Son, who was made flesh, suffered, rose from the dead and was glorified through the Spirit who sanctifies'. Here in this Trinitarian formula are combined the deity and humanity of Christ and his saving work.[30] Then when he discussed the power of faith he designated its 'third incomparable benefit' to unite 'the soul with Christ as a bride is united with her bridegroom'. By this means the great exchange takes place. Christ takes our 'sins, death and damnation' and gives the soul 'His grace life and salvation'. This is possible because 'Christ is God and man in one person'. By the wedding ring of faith He shares in the sins death and pains of hell which are His bride's. As a matter of fact, He makes them His own and acts as if they were His own and as if He Himself had sinned'.[31] This leads us to a profound and new emphasis upon the humanity of Christ which he developed so powerfully in his lectures on the Psalms and John of the fifteen twenties and thirties.

It is often affirmed that whereas the Antioch theologians emphasised the humanity of Christ and made it their starting point, and in the process tended towards Nestorianism, the Alexandrians started with the deity of Christ and tended to be

Apollinarian – that is, denied Christ's true humanity. As far as Athanasius and Cyril of Alexandria are concerned this is profoundly untrue. In his attack on Arius, Athanasius seized on all the passages Arius brought forward to show the frail humanity, (that is for Arius non-deity), of Christ, and insisted that this was the meaning of the incarnation—that God the Son really became this man and the weaknesses were not His by nature but by His choice and were for our sakes. And in the same way it is notable that Cyril attacked Apollinaris as sharply as he did Nestorius. Christ had to become like us, under the law that we might become like Him.[32] Because it is a unique event all analogies are misleading, and the 'how' of the incarnation must be unattainable, for efforts to describe it all fall short of the reality.[33] But the inadequacies of the description must not mislead us into equating these with the intention of the writer. There are remarkable similarities between Cyril and Luther, although I doubt whether Luther was deeply acquainted with Cyril, except probably in *catenae* of the Fathers.

In his quest for the meaning of salvation Luther at first had failed to see the importance of the humanity of Christ and what, after 1518, became for him the crucial issue of the unity of the two natures – that Christ was Son of God *and* Son of Mary in order that the great exchange could take place. In 1537 he wrote: '. . . Formerly I myself was a doctor who excluded Christ's humanity, supposing it was proper to separate his divinity and humanity. In the past the greatest theologians were wont to do this. They abandoned Christ's humanity and clung to his divinity on the assumption that it was unnecessary to recognise the former. But one must approach and hold to the divinity of Christ without overlooking his humanity or acknowledging only the divine nature. Otherwise in the name of all devils we tumble from the ladder that leads to Christ. Therefore beware of that! You must not know of any God or Son of God but Him who was born of the Virgin Mary and became incarnate . . . If you can humble yourself, adhere to the Word with your heart and hold to Christ's humanity – then indeed the divinity will become manifest. Then the Father, the Holy Spirit and the entire Godhead will draw you and hold you.'[34]

Luther's spiritual pilgrimage had drawn him to this position and this was reinforced once he realised that the righteousness of God was revealed completely in the coming of Christ. 'The incarnation of Christ', he wrote in his commentary of Isaiah of 1528, 'powerfully calls us away from speculations about the divinity. I learned from Staupitz that I had been carried away to the devil by my speculations for human weakness could not bear these if I did not gain access to God somewhere'.[35]

He had clearly begun to see some aspects of the importance of Christ's humanity by 1518 in the sermon on *Two Kinds of Righteousness* but the eucharistic controversy with the sectarians and Zwingli heightened his perception. Having resolved the problem of *sacramentum et exemplum* by seeing that Christ is first gift and then example, Luther naturally insisted when he came to discuss the question of sacrifice in eucharist, that it was never a meritorious act on our part and therefore it was all Christ's sacrifice though our response could be called a sacrifice of praise and thanksgiving. Against the sectarians and Zwingli, with his Platonising stance which denigrated the flesh and interpreted John 6 'The flesh profiteth nothing' in this fashion, Luther, realising that our salvation was wrought by the Son of God assuming our frail humanity, insisted therefore, that if the eucharist was to be a means of presenting us with the saving work of Christ, then the frail humanity of Christ must be present in it. 'Christ is our defence . . . The Sectarians will someday feel the sun without shade because they go to meet the naked majesty of God nakedly, casting aside the humanity and the flesh of Christ. This is possible only for a time. I have often advised younger theologians today that they must study the Holy Scriptures that they refrain from investigating the Divine Majesty and his terrible works . . . To keep us from striving to observe God in Himself in this matter, He came into the flesh presenting the flesh to us, in which we might observe God dwelling bodily as He answered Philip when the latter gazed at him, "He who has seen me has seen the Father". From this then you see the madness of those who say that the flesh avails them nothing, though on the contrary God is of no avail without the flesh. Indeed no God will avail for you except the God of Him who sucked the Virgin's breasts. On Him fix your eyes. For you cannot grasp God in Himself unless perchance you want a consuming fire.'[36]

Luther was not primarily concerned with the mode of Christ's presence in the Lord's Supper but with its purpose which was to sustain us by presenting us with the whole of Christ's saving work which now for Luther was always identical with his person. So against Zwingli who was putting forward the views of the Dutch theologian Hoen,[37] he insisted that this view denied Christ's true humanity, while against the commonly held view of trans-substantiation, although allowing it as a possible explanation,[38] much preferred the views of Scotus, d'Ailly and Occam of consubstantiation, though he never used the term himself. He supported this view by the Christological analogy of the Council of Chalcedon that the human and divine natures of Christ must not be confused and not separated,[39] so against trans-substantiation he would say one must not confuse the bread and the wine with the body and blood of Christ, and against Zwingli he would urge that one must not separate them. He came to see that Zwingli's position was essentially Nestorian and so like Cyril of Alexandria in opposition to Nestorius, insisted upon the unity of Christ's person, and strongly defended applying the term, *Theotokos*, the one who bore God, to Mary.[40] He had as a matter of fact usually spoken like this, but after the eucharistic controversy arose he eschewed any formulation that was remotely Nestorian in his work *On the Councils of the Church*, of 1539, where he uses technical Christological terms most frequently, after stating Nestorius' position within impartiality he continued, 'I too have been confronted be Nestorians who fought me very stubbornly saying that the divinity of Christ could not suffer. For example, Zwingli too wrote against me concerning the saying "The Word became Flesh". He simply would not have it that "became" should apply to the "Word". He wanted it to read "the flesh did not know at the itme that this resembled the notions of Nestorius, because I did not understand the Council either, but recognised it as an error on the basis of Holy Scripture, Augustine and the master of the *Sentences*.'[41]

'Through the manhood of Christ to the Father' could be said to be Luther's slogan. 'The Scriptures begin gently and lead us first to Christ as man, then as lord over all creatures, and then as God. Thus I come all the way to learning the knowledge of God',[42] through the manhood of Christ who showed the love of the

Father's will and heart.[43] He then developed his understanding of Christ's humanity essentially in the way in which he saw Christ's saving work. He insisted that though sinless He so identified Himself with mankind that He suffered all the consequences of sin. In the first place therefore Luther takes a very commonsense attitude to the ordinary aspects of Christ's humanity. 'What a strange game they played',[44] he remarked about the early heretics who denied Christ's true humanity. Christ let himself be seen, heard and touched. He ate, drank, slept, worked, suffered and died like any other human being.[45] He shared all our emotions – 'He was weak, tired, afraid, fled from danger, etc.'[46]

Luther scathingly attacked the legends about miracles that Christ performed in His childhood. 'He came and went and was brought up just like another child'.[47] As he grew up 'the humanity of Christ, like that of any holy and genuine man, did not always think, will, and notice everything, as some people make Him an omnipotent man' . . . but by so doing 'they blind themselves to the study of Scripture'.[48] In his comment on Luke 2:40 'Jesus increased in wisdom', he wrote, 'The Spirit descended more and more upon him and moved Him more as time went on . . . at one time it awoke Him to this, at another time to that'.[49]

From this basis Luther developed a most remarkable insight into the cost of our redemption. Mediaeval theologians like Anselm saw Christ in his humanity as the sinless one granting to his sinful brethren the merits of his obedience. But Luther, taking Gregory of Nazianzus' dictum 'the unassumed is the unredeemed' even more seriously, insisted that Christ so identified Himself with sinful humanity that He, though sinless, took on Himself the full consequences of sin and so He died in our place as if He were a sinner. There are a number of elements in this profound exposition.

First Luther especially stressed the fact that He shared in the agony of being rejected, opposed and misunderstood, partly perhaps because Luther himself had had similar experiences. Christ was filled with grief and anxiety at the approach of death, and felt wretched, lonely and forsaken when even his own friends left Him in His extremity.[50] Then in an exegesis of the genealogies of Christ, Luther on several occasions stressed the sinful nature of Christ's ancestors. In a sermon in 1522 he wrote 'The first thing to be noted in the lineage of Christ is the fact that the evangelist lists in it four women who were very notorious in Scripture – Thamar, Rahab, Ruth, Bathsheba. But nothing is said about the women of good repute – Sarah, Rebecca, Leah and Rachel . . . I hold that the first group was mentioned because these women were sinners and because Christ wanted to be born in that large family (Gechlecht) in which prostitutes and fornicators are found in order to indicate what a love He bore for sinners. This then is why Christ thrusts and sticks Himself into a family of sinners and lets them stand in the catalogue of his ancestry'.[51] And again, 'The highest patriarch Judah, a father of Christ, committed this unspeakable incest so that Christ might be born of flesh that was very sinful . . . to signify the unspeakable plan of God's mercy in that He assumed the flesh and human nature from flesh that was contaminated and horribly polluted'. As the genealogy also contained Canaanites, Luther commented, 'Christ wanted to be born from the Canaanites, a heathen nation and in this way to begin making peace between the Jews and Gentiles'.[52] Though 'He wanted to be born from the mass of the flesh and from that corrupted blood', yet, 'in the moment of the Virgin's conception the Holy Spirit purged and sanctified the sinful mass and wiped out the poison of the devil and death which is sin. Although death remained in that flesh on our account, the leven of sin was never-the-less purged out, and it became the purest flesh, purified by the Holy Spirit and united with the divine nature in the one Person'.[53]

This is Luther's attempt to show that Christ really took on Himself fallen human nature and yet was free from original sin. Several things should be noted. Christ's sinlessness, he insisted, was due entirely to the work of the Holy Spirit for Luther emphasised the sinfulness of the flesh He took from Mary, siding with the Augustinian view which denied her immaculate conception,[54] although he believed in her perpetual virginity.[55] He maintained that Christ's sinful ancestry was recorded in Genesis for 'His sake' because 'the Holy Spirit wanted Him to sink into sin as deeply as possible'[56] so that He could be identified with sinful mankind and take on the consequences of their sin including death, and, as we shall see, something more terrible.

Above all, Luther stressed, He was born a Jew under the law. 'And so the words "Christ was born under the law" are very meaningful and should be considered in this way: for they indicate that the son of God who was born under the law did not perform one or another of the works of the law or submit to it only in a political way, but that He suffered all the tyranny of the law. For the law exercised its full function over Christ; it frightened Him so horribly that he experienced greater anguish than any man has ever experienced. This is amply demonstrated by His bloody sweat, the comfort of the angel, His solemn prayer in the garden and finally by the cry of misery on the cross'.[57] This emphasis on Christ taking on the full consequences of our breaking of God's law to be in complete solidarity with mankind and to effect 'the blessed exchange' is at the very heart of Luther's thought and an essential place where he saw the complete unity of the person and work of Christ.

This is fully explored in his comment on Galatians 3:13 'Christ redeemed us from the curse of the law, having become a curse for us'. 'The whole emphasis', wrote Luther, 'is on the phrase "for us". Christ is innocent as far as His own person is concerned, therefore He should not have been hanged from the tree. But because, according to the law, every thief should have been hanged, therefore according to the law of Moses Christ Himself should have been hanged: for He bore the person of a sinner and a thief *Quia gessit personam peccatoris et latronis*[58] not of one but of all sinners and thieves. For we are sinners and thieves and therefore are worthy of death and eternal damnation. But Christ took all our sins upon Himself and for them he died on the cross'. 'He is not acting in His own person now' or as Luther expressed it a little later in his exegesis 'therefore we should not imagine Christ' [in this situation] 'as an innocent or private person' ('*innocentem et privatam personam*'[59] who is holy and righteous only for Himself' even although is the purest of persons.[60] 'Now', as the brother of sinful humanity, 'he is not the Son of God born of the Virgin, but He is a sinner . . . who has and bears the sins of all man in His body'.[61]

In this way in his comment on Psalm 22 of 1521 and Psalm 8 of 1537 he interprets Christ's cry of dereliction from the cross as His descent into Hell, as later did Calvin. On Psalm 8.5 'Thou wilt let Him be forsaken by God for a little while' he wrote 'In this verse David describes how miserably Christ will be forsaken . . . he is not speaking of the physical suffering of Christ which was also great and difficult, but of his sublime spiritual suffering which He felt in His soul, a suffering that far surpasses all physical suffering. He describes the highest degree of this suffering and says 'Thou wilt let Him be forsaken by God for a little while'. What this is, no man on earth understands and no man can reach or express it in words. For to be forsaken by God is far worse than death ... He struggles with death in the garden and cries out on the cross 'My God, My God, why hast Thou forsaken Me'. For that is His real sublime spiritual suffering which no man can imagine or understand ... And in fact He was forsaken by God. This does not mean that the deity was separated from the humanity – for in this person who is Christ, the Son of God and of Mary, deity and humanity are so united that they can never be separated or divided – but that the deity withdrew and hid so that it seemed and anyone who saw it might say, 'This is not God but a mere man and a troubled and desperate man at that' ... Thus the righteous and innocent Man must shiver and shake like a poor condemned sinner and feel God's wrath and judgement against sin in His tender innocent heart taste eternal death and damnation for us – in short He must suffer everything that a condemned sinner has deserved and must suffer eternally.[62]

Here Luther is straining the capability of language (and in this case the precision and concrete categories of Latin) in order to explore the ultimate mystery of our redemption, of God in whom there is only pure love, bearing the consequences of our sin, the most terrible of which is to separate us from God, to feel oneself 'forsaken and cast away from the presence of God'.[63] It was in this sense that Luther saw the cry of dereliction as God against God though of course this could never be the case. In us it would be blasphemy to say we are forsaken by God but 'in Him there was no sin as there is in us' ... for 'Christ loved the Father with all his strength, but those tortures which were beyond his strength forced his innocent and weak nature to groan, shout, shudder and flee just as if you load a beam beyond its strength, by necessity of nature through no fault of its own it creaks.'[64] It was not make-believe that cry 'My God, My God'! Luther concludes this section with the observation that 'when God was far at the same time He was near. He was far because Christ used the word forsaken. He was near because Christ said 'My God".'[65]

The problem with which Patristic theology wrestled was how could the infinite become finite. For Luther it was how could the perfectly obedient Son of the Father so identify Himself with sinful man that He underwent on their behalf the ultimate punishment of hell, namely separation from the Father. The reality of the two natures of Christ are essential for Luther's understanding and the way he stated the fact of the incarnation in 'Two Kinds of Righteousness' where in exegeting Philippians 2, 'He humbled Himself', he insisted that Christ always retained the 'essence of God'; that is if asked who He was the reply would have to be God who became this man Jesus Christ. But as man He did not act in the way His divine nature entitled him to.[66] But now Luther has gone deeper. As God He cannot sin: but as man he takes on the consequences of our sin, namely separation from God. Luther insisted, He stands as a sinner. Hence his phrase 'the deity withdrew and hid'. This 'withdrawing' and 'hiding' was in fact God's most costly and loving action for our sake and although the phrase can be criticised, any language to describe this unique mystery of the awful cost of our redemption will be ambiguous and inadequate. It is Luther's intention that must be kept uppermost and then one can see that the phrase points to something of this mystery.

Finally, Luther, following Paul saw the consequences of sin as death, and to be one with us, Christ had to be human in order to die.[67] It is clear that when Luther is talking of the humanity of Christ he is not speaking just of common anthropological or physical categories but basically theological. To be a man is to be confronted by the living God and in His presence to feel the accusation of the law. Thus Christ for Luther was truly man, like all of us except for sin but, voluntarily accepting the consequences of being as a sinner under the law – 'a true man on whom there came death, hell and sin with all their powers'.[68]

Cyril of Alexandria in his controversy with Nestorius saw the necessity of emphasising the unity of Christ's human and divine nature so that his most characteristic phrase is 'the One Lord Jesus Christ',[69] for otherwise Cyril realised our salvation was endangered. Because of this emphasis on the unity of Christ's person it is frequently averred that Cyril was not interested in

Christ's human nature and really held the view, later articulated by Eutyches, of divinising Christ's humanity. But this view fails completely to see that the genuine humanity of Christ was essential to Cyril's position.[70] In precisely the same way, it was essential for Luther's understanding of salvation that Christ's divine nature and human nature were united, and the most characteristic way he stated this was 'Jesus Christ Son of God *and* Mary's Son', which phrase or its equivalents can be found in innumerable passages, particularly in his sermons on St John. 'The statement "The Word became flesh" permeates John's entire Gospel. All he ever preaches is that Christ, the very and eternal Son of God is also true man, born of the Virgin Mary. And he unites wonderfully the two natures in the one person of Christ.'[71] It was the emphasis on the *and* in the formula which so characteristically expressed the thought of Luther. It prevented any trace of Nestorianism by showing the incarnation to be essentially the loving activity of God Himself in His standing beside sinful man *in* the vicarious humanity of Jesus Christ.

The controversy with Zwingli over the presence of Christ in the Lord's Supper forced him to develop this point with such emphasis that he accidentaly endangered the true humanity of Christ. The saving work of God and the man Jesus had to be identical in the person of the One Lord Jesus Christ and the incipient Nestorianism of Zwingli's position led him to search for a means to state this unambiguously. He took the traditional statement of the *communicatio idiomatum*, that one could predicate both divine or human attributes to Jesus Christ, but developed it in a way that made these predications quite indiscriminate[72] so that he could say *simpliciter* that Mary 'is the true natural mother of God and bearer of God ... that Mary suckled God, rocked God to sleep, prepared broth and soup for God, etc. For God and man are one person, one Christ, one Son, one Jesus, not two ...'[73] Conversely, one can say again, *simpliciter*, 'God was crucified by the Jews'.[74] Because the person of Christ carries the properties of both natures we must attribute to the entire person what pertains just to the one nature, though we must always distinguish the natures.[75]

Once the intention of Luther is perceived, one must not dismiss this as a form of Appollinarianism or Monophysitism any more than one should do so for Athanasius or Cyril who had similar difficulties in stating the truth of the unity of Christ's person.[76] Luther was primarily a biblical theologian and his great sensitivity in this area at times deserted him when he tried to put these insights into a dogmatic framework as, for example, his argument on *The Freedom of the Will* with Erasmus.[77] The strengths and weaknesses of Luther's statements are laid out with his usual brilliance by Karl Barth[78] where talking of the Reformed writers and particularly of Calvin he says 'They' (like Luther) 'had no desire to divide up Jesus Christ into the Son of God and Son of Man. They had no desire to seek or see or grasp the overcoming of the opposition between God and man, and therefore the reconciliation of the world with God elsewhere but in the humanity assumed by God, and therefore in the man Jesus of Nazareth'.[79] This comes out clearly in Calvin with his emphasis on the continuous obedience of Christ as man fulfilling the law of God; on Christ as man being the perfect high priest praying on behalf of his brethren, who now are united by the Holy Spirit through Word and Sacrament with him in his obedience and true worship.[80] It was no deeper interest in Christ's humanity than Luther's but it was developed more widely, though much of it is already in Luther in a less developed form.

Luther's whole position was based on the common bond of humanity between Christ and sinful men, so he concentrated his attention more on this in relation to the reconciling death of Christ. For example, he interpreted the verse in Hebrews (5:7) about Christ offering up 'prayers and supplications with loud cries and tears' exclusively to his passion.[81] But in his sermons on Matthew of 1523 his scope is much wider and he wrote of Christ fulfilling the law of God. 'He has fulfilled it all purely and perfectly and He gives Himself to us together with His fulfillment ... all must be accomplished and fulfilled even to the smallest dot, but only through this one Man'.[82] As man Christ rose from the dead and ascended into heaven and as man He rules in heaven as lord of all.[83] These themes are brought out with great power by Luther in his interpretation of the Second Psalm in 1532 'Having assumed our flesh, in our flesh He conquered Satan, killed death, laid waste and suffering humanity of Christ in the incarnation which displayed the love of God to which faith may hold with utter and destroyed hell. It proclaims that He alone is wise because He alone knows and does the will of God the Father'.[84] On verse eight he said, 'The psalm does not speak of the Son of God as He was from eternity, for in this capacity He is the Lord of all living creatures. It speaks rather of the King of Zion, that is of the incarnate Son of God, of the man born of the Virgin Mary, beginning His Kingdom on the physical Zion through the gospel. To this man, who is made humble below the angels, God gives authority over the nations ... He does not intrude, He does not seize it in His own accord. He remains in the humility of the cross'.[85] This is precisely the position of Athanasius that the incarnation is not only the love of God towards man but also the obedience of Christ as man on behalf of mankind towards God. 'True Christianity ... does not present God to us in His majesty, as Moses and other teachers do, but Christ born of the Virgin, as our Mediator and high priest'.[86]

Luther too combined Christ's work of salvation, the forgiveness of sin, the bestowing of His righteousness, with the gift of Himself. *Per Christum* and *in Christo* coalesce. Commenting on St Paul's phrase 'I live, yet not I, but Christ lives in me' (Galatians 2:20), he wrote, 'Christ is my *forma* which adorns my faith as colour or light adorns a wall. (This fact has to be expressed in this crude way, for there is no spiritual way for us to grasp the idea that Christ clings to and dwells in us as closely and intimately as light or whiteness clings to a wall.) "Christ", he says, "is fixed or cemented in me and abides in me. The life I now live He lives in me" '.[87] 'But faith must be taught correctly, for by it you are cemented to Christ, that by it you and He are one person which cannot be separated but remains attached to Him for ever, and declares "I am as Christ". And Christ in turn says, "I am as that sinner who is attached to me and I to him". For by faith we are joined together into one flesh and bone. Thus Ephesians 5:30 says, 'We are members of the body of Christ of His flesh and His bones'.[88]

These last two quotations come from his great commentary on Galatians of 1535 and illustrate the way in which Luther's Christology developed by integrating the great themes of faith and justification of his commentary on Romans, 1515–1516, with his more developed understanding of the significance of the vicarious confidence. This development can be gauged by comparing the exposition of this passage in 1535, with that of his earlier commentary on Galatians of 1516–17, in which one can see him groping his way towards a coherent understanding of what all the remarkable insights that he was discovering meant. But by the 1530s there is coherence. The saving work of Christ on the cross is the key which gives access to the meaning of who Christ was, while reflection on who Christ was, Son of God and Son of Mary, shows the cost of our salvation and that God 'abounds in unfathomable, ineffable love and grace'.[89]

An essential element of Christology has now been underlined – the cost of redemption – so that if one says *sola gratia* one points to the incarnation and if one says Jesus Christ, truly God and truly man, one can only say *sola gratia*. Adoration and theology are again knit together. 'Thus the devil has work to do and attacks Christ in three lines of battle. One will not let him be God, another will not let him be man, and the third will not let him do what he has done. Each of the three wants to reduce Christ to nothing. For what does it profit you to confess that he is God, if you do not also believe that he is man? Then you do not have the whole, real Christ with that, but only a phantom of the devil's. What does it profit you to confess that he is man, if you do not also believe that he is God? What does it profit you to confess that he is God and man, if you do not also believe that he has become everything and done everything for you?'[90] The grace of God, and the object of faith, Jesus Christ, are identical. Or as Luther summed up his discussion of Galatians 3:13 'Christ redeemed us from the curse of the law having become a curse for us'. 'For you do not yet have Christ even though you know Him as God and man. You truly have Him only when you believe this altogether pure and innocent person has been granted to you by the Father as your high priest and redeemer, yes as your slave. Putting off His innocence and holiness, He bore your sin, death and curse: He became a sacrifice and curse for you in order thus to set you free from the curse of the law'.[91] The grace of God and Jesus Christ the object of our love and faith are identical. Echoing Irenaeus, Luther said, 'He became incarnate for our sakes that we might enter into great glory'.[92]

NOTES

I am deeply indebted in this study to two excellent books in this area – Ian D. K. Siggins, *Martin Luther's Doctrine of Christ* (Yale, 1970) with its remarkable wealth of citations and general perceptions, and to Marc Lienhard, *Luther Temoin De Jesus-Christ*, (Paris, 1973), for its careful and balanced historical approach. I also owe a great debt to Professor David Cairns of Aberdeen for many stimulating and clarifying conversations on this issue and for much assistance in translation, and to Father Daniel Olivier, Professor of Lutheran studies at the Institut Superior d'Etudes Oecumeniques at Paris for many insights.

1. *W*, 45:548; *LW*, 24:97.
2. *W*, 46:43; *LW*, 24:346.
3. ibid. *LW*, 24:347.
4. *LW*, 22:25.
5. *W*, 45:589; *LW*, 24:141 and *W* 33:94; *LW*, 23:63–64. See I. D. K. Siggins, *Martin Luther's Doctrine of Christ*, Yale, 1970, 88 ff., for many other references.
6. M. Lienhard, *Luther Temon De Jesus-Christ*, (Paris, 1973), 145.
7. *W*, 45:589; *LW*, 24:140–1.
8. *W*, 40; *LW*, 12:20.
9. *W*, 46:627; *LW*, 22:105.
10. *W*, 8:111–39 ff. *LW*, 32:235–6.
11. *W*, 56:275. *LW*, 25:263. See also W. von Loewenich, *Luther's Theology of the Cross* (trans. Minneapolis, 1976), 52 ff.
12. S. Ozment, *The Age of Reform* (Yale, 1980), 239.
13. ibid.
14. *W*, 3:291., *LW*, 10:240, quoted Ozment, ibid.
15. For Luther's view of sin in *Romans* see my previous essay above, pp. 9–10.
16. When I first embarked on this essay it never occurred to me that it would throw light on the dating of Luther's 'Tower Experience'. But going through Luther's Christological statements chronologically made the change of emphasis and language abundantly clear and showed why Luther now saw the crucial importance of the humanity of Christ and why the sacraments loomed large in his subsequent theology, and why the language of mysticism is now totally excluded in favour of biblical and creedal language.
17. *W*, 2:145–52. *LW*, 31:297–306. For a discussion of its dating see 'Les deux sermons sur la double et triple Justice' by Daniel Olivier in *Oecumenica*, 1968, 39–69.
18. ibid., *LW*, 31:297.
19. ibid., 298. Notice how this is spelling out his comment in 1516 on Romans 1:17 (*LW*, 26:151) with considerably more theological precision and in specifically Christological terms.
20. *LW*, 31:299–300.
21. Athanasius, *Contra Arianos*, 3:30.
22. *LW*, 31:301.
23. For a penetrating analysis of Athanasius and Cyril see T. F. Torrance, *Theology in Reconciliation*, chapters 4 and 5, particularly pp. 224–31.
24. M. Lienhard, op. cit. 147. 'On the Councils of the Church' *LW*, 41:105.
25. *W*, 10/1/1:238; *LW*, 52:82.
26. N. Nagel 'Sacramentum et Exemplum in Luther's understanding of Christ', in C. S. Meyer, *Luther for an Ecumenical Age*.
27. ibid., 177 and *LW*, 27:382.

28. *W*, 6:86; *LW*, 36:93, 4.
29. *W*, 10/1, 10, 20. See Nagel 187–9 for penetrating discussion and full documentation.
30. *W*, 7:51, *LW*, 31:345–6.
31. *LW*, 31:351–2.
32. T. F. Torrance, *Theology in Reconciliation*, 277–31; 161–7.
33. Karl Barth, *Church Dogmatics*, 2:2, 51 ff. where in a brilliant extended footnote he shows the inadequacies of all analogies to the incarnation and also quotes Gregory of Nyssa's insistence that the 'how' of the incarnation is impossible for us to know, just as we cannot know how God creates *ex nihilo*.
34. *W*, 33:154; *LW*, 23:102.
35. *W*, 31/2:38; *LW*, 16:55.
36. ibid.
37. H. Sasse, *This is My Body* (revised edition, Adelaide 1977), 97 ff.
38. *The Babylonish Captivity of the Church*, *LW*, 36:30–1. Transubstantiation was the most widely held view of the time, but it was not made binding on the Church until after the Council of Trent.
39. ibid., 35. Calvin also based his understanding of the way of stating Christ's real presence on Chalcedon 'A Short treatise on the Lord's Supper', *LCC* 22, 147.
40. *W*, 47:51; *LW*, 22:323 – 24. For Cyril see note 54 below.
41. *On the Councils of the Church*, *LW*, 41:105.
42. *W*, 10/1/2:297. Quoted Siggins, 181.
43. See Siggins 181.
44. *The Three Symbols*, *W* 50, 268:4; *LW*, 34:208 (Siggins translations, 201).
45. *W*, 46:69; *LW*, 24:375. See also on John 1.14: *LW*, 22:110.
46. *W*, 46:102; *LW*, 24:413. See Siggins 198–201.
47. *W*, 10/1/1:444–5.
48. Lienhard, 170, 174. *W*, 10/1/1:445.
49. *W*, 10/1/1:446. See P. Althaus, *The Theology of Martin Luther*, 196–7. But Luther failed to develop this view of Christ as man being dependent on the Spirit so deeply, as did Athanasius or Calvin, largely because of the eucharistic controversy which made him avoid any possible Nestorian formulation. Both Athanasius and Calvin emphasised Christ's anointing by the Spirit so that as man He lived by full obedience to the Spirit. Athanasius saw Christ as Son of God by nature, Son of man by nature, and as man Son of God by grace – that is through the aid of the Spirit rendering to God the true worship and obedience of man – a theme taken up by Calvin.
50. *W*, 46:103; *LW*, 24:413.
51. *W*, 10/111:136, in *Luther Speaks*, 1:150.
52. *W*, 44:311, 313; *LW*, 7:12, 15.
53. *W*, 44:311; *LW*, 7:13.
54. *W*, 46:136 in *Luther Speaks*, 1:152. Despite the insight of Athanasius for the absolute necessity for the true humanity of Christ, (see T. F. Torrance *Theology in Reconciliation* chapters 4, 5), and of the basic statement of the Cappadocians 'What He did not take up He did not redeem', as Joseph Jungman, S.J., has shown (*The Place of Christ in Liturgical Worship*), the Church tended to underplay the rôle of the humanity of Christ in the work of salvation, and as a consequence this rôle was taken over by the priest or by the saints or by Mary. Marian devotion developed in the Church without sufficient control by the doctrine of the incarnation. The whole Church became increasingly interested in the holiness of Mary and in the Western Church this interest became absorbed into the question of her immaculate conception. This was because St Augustine, in his controversy

with Pelagius, had emphasised the ravages wrought on mankind by original sin which he insisted infected every member of Adam's race, including Mary, and which he postulated was transmitted in the act of sexual intercourse.

Almost all the great Western theologians until the later Middle Ages followed Augustine. An essential element of Anselm's argument in *Cur Deus Homo* depends on the fact that all Adam's descendants are infected by sin (*Cur Deus Homo*, 2:8). Aquinas in all five works in which he discussed the issue, insisted that Mary was not completely preserved from original sin. The same position was maintained by St Bernard and that great anti-Pelagian, Gregory of Rimini. (*A Catholic Dictionary of Theology*, 1962, *sub* 'conception, immaculate' and H. Oberman, *The Harvest of Mediaeval Theology*, 289 ff.).

But in the later Middle Ages Duns Scotus and William of Occam, strongly supported by the Franciscan order, put forward the view that Mary was freed from the taint of original sin from conception. Those who held this position were in constant danger of undermining the crucial issue of the true humanity of Christ as did Gabriel Biel who in strongly upholding the immaculist position said 'Christ is not fully man but the God-man'. Mary, he said, was more allied to the created order than Christ and therefore had a greater sympathy for human weakness than he. She represented love and pity in contrast to the severity of Christ as judge. (Oberman op. cit., 319).

It is in this theological climate that Luther discussed this question. As we have shown, the full humanity of Christ was essential for his whole understanding of the Gospel. Conversely, he saw faith – that is, total response to the grace of God – as the highest form of Christian commitment. Hence Mary's 'Lord be it unto me according to Thy will' was a paradigm for Christian faith. From this stance this would be the highest honour one could pay her – the true representative of faithful Israel.

The belief in the immaculate conception was not made a dogmatic statement until 1854, and it is notable that Vatican Council II insisted that the Marian dogmata should not be given a place of their own but must be understood in the context of the Christological and ecclesiological dogmata, much more in line with Luther and much less in line with Biel. (E. L. Mascall, 'Mary the blessed Virgin', in *A Dictionary of Christian Theology*, ed Alan Richardson). For the importance of this issue on Christology see T. F. Torrance *The Mediation of Christ*, (Paternoster Press, Exeter, 1983), 48–50.

55. *LW*, 22:23 and note 2, p. 215.
56. *W*, 44:311; *LW*, 7:13.
57. *W*, 40/1:567; *LW*, 26:372.
58. *W*, 40/1: 433/20; *LW*, 26; 277
59. *W*, 40/1: 448/17. *LW*, 26:287.
60. *LW*, 26:287.
61. *LW*, 26:277.
62. *LW*, 12:126–7.
63. *W*, 5:603 – 16. Luther's Commentary on Ps.22, 1522, trans. Henry Cole, *Select Works of Martin Luther*, (1826), Vol.4:362 – 67.
64. *W*, 5:605–25.
65. *W*, 5:606.
66. See above p. 6.
67. *W*, 46:759; 47:52 and 71, *LW*, 22:324 and 341.
68. *W*, 10/111/74.
69. For example, Cyril 'Second Letter to Nestorius' in *Creeds, Councils and Controversies*, ed. J. Stevenson, 277, 78.

70. Cyril of Alexandria, *Scholia on the Incarnation* (Library of te Fathers) s12. See also T. F. Torrance, *Theology in Reconciliation*, 156 ff. and especially 161–2.
71. *LW*, 22:346. See Siggins 207 ff. for many other examples.
72. For a full discussion see Siggins 221–39; Lienhard 345 ff.; Karl Barth *Church Dogmatics*, 4:2, 62, 69.
73. *On The Councils of the Church*, 1539, *LW*, 41:100.
74. ibid., 101.
75. *W*, 45:556–8; *LW*, 24:105–7.
76. For Cyril see G. L. Prestige *Fathers and Heretics*, 160; for Athanasius ibid., 179 for a translation from Athanasius' Fourth Letter to *Serapion* (not in the Robertson edition of Athanasius) for a striking similarity to Luther's statements. But notice Cyril's subtle statement of the problem in his *Second Letter to Nestorius*, s 24a, in Stevenson, op. cit. 277.
77. See also Siggins, 233–4.
78. Barth *Church Dogmatics* 4:1–63.
79. ibid., 4:2–68. See also 71–2.
80. This emphasis of Calvin on the rôle of the humanity of Christ is not often seen but it is quite clear from the structure of the *Institutes*, Books 2 and 3. See especially 2:16–19; 3:1–1; 3:20–19; 3:24–5. See also J. B. Torrance 'Vicarious humanity and the priesthood of Christ in the theology of John Calvin' in *Calvinus Ecclesiae Doctor*, ed W. H. Neuser, Kampen, 1980 and T. F. Torrance *The Mediation of Christ*, Paternoster Press, Exeter, 1983, chapter 4.
81. *W*, 57/111/173; *LW*, 29:174.
82. Com. on Matthew 5.19: *LW*, 21:72–3.
83. Siggins, 203, *LW*, 36:342 and *LW*, 13:236.
84. Psalm 2:3; *LW*, 12:20.
85. Psalm 2:8; *LW*, 12:55.
86. *W*, 40/1.77; *LW*, 26:28.
87. *W*, 40/1.282; *LW*, 26:167.
88. *W*, 40/1.285; *LW*, 26:168.
89. *W*, 33:149; *LW*, 23:98.
90. 'The Three Symbols or Creeds of Christendom", *LW*, 34:210. See also *LW*, 52:82.
91. *W*, 40/1.448; *LW*, 26:288.
92. *W*, 46:631; *LW*, 22:110.
93. This theme has recently been developed by T. F. Torrance, 'Karl Barth and the Latin Heresy,' *Scottish Journal of Theology*, Vol.39 No 4, 1986.

HOC EST CORPUS MEUM:
THE CENTRALITY OF THE REAL PRESENCE FOR LUTHER

Basil Hall

Martin Luther celebrated his first mass at Erfurt on May 2, 1507, and, as he remembered later more than once, it was an occasion which included fear and trembling. Three times he referred to his anxiety at that mass in the *Table Talk*, and once more fully in his *Lectures on Genesis*. Since that occasion left so deep an impression on him it is worth examining his account of it. In the *Table Talk*, the essential point he made was on such fear at being in the presence of the awe-inspiring majesty of God whom he was about to address in the *Commemoratio* the second prayer of the canon, 'Offerimus ... aeterno, vivo, vero Deo ...' that he felt like running from the altar. He elaborated this later by saying that it was having to speak to God without a mediator that increased his anxiety: 'Who can bear the majesty of God without Christ as mediator?'[1] In the *Lectures on Genesis* he added a further point about his feeling, namely, that he was stunned by his own impudence in addressing the majesty of God, but 'faith which relies on the mercy and word of God overcomes and prevails over that fear.'[2] This reference to faith occurs because Luther is writing in the context of Genesis 25:21 about the faith of Isaac in praying to God that his barren wife Rebecca might have a child. Luther wrote of Isaac's courage in lifting up his eyes and hands to the divine majesty and commented on our weakness and unworthiness which too often leads us to say: 'Who am I that I should have the courage to lift up my eyes and to raise my hands ... shall I wretched little man say to him "This is what I want" ... I who am ashes, dust and full of sins am addressing "the living eternal and true God".' It is immediately after this emphasis on the need for humility, faith in effective prayer and after these last words 'living and true God' from the canon of the mass, that Luther turns to the description of his fear and trembling at his first mass.

It is interesting that Luther is emphasizing throughout these accounts that it is only at that point in the mass at which the priest begins the words of offering not long before the consecration and immediately after the words, 'Whose faith is known unto thee', that the crisis occurred. In the earliest parts of this first mass Luther had already addressed God, 'the God of joy and gladness', he had already pronounced forgiveness of sins, he had already come before God in the solemnity and humility of the secret prayers, he had already 'washed his hands in innocence', and he had again addressed the 'almighty and everlasting God' in the Preface and sung the Sanctus, why is it that only at those particular words of the Canon, on faith, that Luther fell into fear and trembling and wished to flee from the altar?[3] Since he himself does not say precisely why his crisis occurred at that stage of the mass it is dangerous to be positive about his reasons. In any event some may wish to point out that Luther is making these statements many years after the event, therefore it could be argued that his later development of the concepts of justification by faith, and the centrality of Christ's saving work, were colouring his account. This, however, would not do justice to Luther's vivid memory of the crisis and his insistence on why it was so great a shock. We should remember also that his crisis occurred at that point of the mass where he was coming to the central action, the words of consecration would soon be said, then he would be holding in his hands the central mystery of his religion, the elements of bread and wine which were the body and blood of Christ – moreover it was precisely at this point that he had said, 'Whose faith is known only to thee'. Again, he made the astonishing statement in his *Table Talk* cited above that he had to approach the prayer of consecration without a mediator, 'Who can bear the majesty of God without Christ as mediator'. But what had he been doing so far but pray throughout the mass in the name of Christ? What he was offering was through Christ. Had not the mediation of Christ for our sins been sung in the Gloria and in the Creed? It would be merely pedantic to note that the words, 'Through the mediation of Jesus Christ our Lord' had probably not been actually used. Luther's shock and hesitation during the prayer of consecration, this disabling sense of his own unworthiness and of the awe-inspiring otherness of God in May 1507 at the altar in Erfurt, shows Luther being jolted by what was to become increasingly a trouble to him, the need to know forgiveness of sins and how this was to become fully effective. Without the confident assurance of forgiveness how could one approach the majesty of God; without a living and vital faith how could one validly stand at the altar and pray; and without the crucial acceptance of Christ incarnate, crucified and risen as our mediator how can we present ourselves before God at the altar?

Prior to the development of intensive Luther studies which has come to be known as the *Lutherforschung*, traditionalist Catholic apologists on the basis of this Erfurt experience of Luther described him as neurotic and unstable and saw the event as foreshadowing his future break with the church since he was showing himself thus early to be unsuited to the life of a regular priest – at best this event pointed to a dangerous subjectivism in Luther.[4] However, many a priest before and since could recall the sense of awe and personal unworthiness when celebrating his first mass: such humility is in fact much to be desired. But one point that those Catholics wished to make was that Luther exaggerated, for he failed to understand the gifts of grace, including forgiveness of venial sins, flowing from these words and acts at the altar, and he underestimated the mercy of Christ in emphasizing the majesty of God. With some reservations this view could be accepted; but it is too simple an answer. Luther was beginning to ask himself questions which would reflect what was to be the chief preoccupation of his life before 1521: 'How can we understand God and what he requires of us' (how should I address him?); and 'How can we find effectual knowledge of forgiveness of our sins and be at peace with God' (I . . . full of sin)? In sum, how are we to be justified in his presence? From the stance of technical thoroughness in scholastic theology from Duns Scotus to Thomas Aquinas all questions on what, how, why, and by whom, concerning the mass had been answered, yet these questions were still not essentially those which Luther was asking.[5] From his first mass onward Luther had been thrust beyond the satisfactions of technical theology into the challenge of the living God. This challenge with its implications on sin and forgiveness and on justification 'coram deo' was the beginning of a labour of self-examination, stimulated by his vocation as a friar, and undertaken alongside of that study of Scripture which was to become officially his life's work from 1512 when he was made *Doctor in Biblia* at the university of Wittenberg. The consequence of this intensive effort was Luther's challenge to contemporary Catholicism on the doctrine of grace and the repudiation of the validity of obtaining justification through merit-earning works which has been so thoroughly analysed during the *Lutherforschung*. Amid this considerable literature the studies in English *Let God be God* and the 'coram deo' section of *The Righteousness of God* suffice to show by their titles alone – as well as by their weight of learning – the revolutionary force of Luther's developing thought.[6] Yet in works by these and other non-Lutheran English-speaking writers not much attention has been given to Luther's teaching on the sacrament of the Eucharist. There has been a marked tendency to do no more than state his views briefly and not to see them as integral to his doctrinal work – this sacrament is discussed almost as an appendix to his work or as a peripheral and controversial subject. However, when Luther through the repristination of the theme of the dynamic word of God in Scripture which came from his intensive biblical studies, and through the reassertion of the centrality of the incarnation in his Christology as central to our relations with God in grace, came to his fulfilled doctrine of justification by faith he associated it most closely with his doctrine of the sacraments. He shows the eucharist to be the objective declaration and assurance of forgiveness of sins and the place where the incarnate Christ is known and received uniquely in his very flesh and blood for our salvation and eternal life. So strong was Luther's insistence on the centrality for the Christian life of the sacrament of the eucharist seen as only effective by the real presence, that he divided the Reformation movement rather than compromise this conviction. This has caused considerable embarrassment to non-Lutheran Protestants who hold to Zwinglianism, Anabaptism or some variation of these, as well as to some later Lutherans. This embarrassment has led to the well-intentioned tendency to regard Luther's doctrine on this sacrament as a consequence of his Catholic upbringing and as something which may be disregarded while holding in honour the great contribution of Luther in other doctrines to the life of the church. It has been the custom in the writing of theological textbooks and histories of doctrine to consider Luther's view of this sacrament as emerging somewhat perfunctorily in 1519, then developing to his attack on transubstantiation and other aspects of catholic teaching on this sacrament in 1520 and 1521, and thereafter exploding into his attacks on Zwinglian views in and after 1528.[7] This is to assume that Luther had little interest in the sacrament before 1519, or if he showed any interest it was expressed only in the usual traditional Catholic terms and that he did not begin to write thoroughly and effectively on it until 1524 and later. It is one purpose of this essay to challenge this assumption.

Luther's studies received new depth upon his appointment as a 'doctor in a general free university, a doctor of holy Scripture, I began at the command of pope and emperor to do what such a doctor is sworn to do expounding the scriptures for all the world and teaching everybody'.[8] Part of the fruit of this duty was the *Dictata super Psalterium* his lectures at Wittenberg on the Psalms.[9] That there are problems concerning the manuscripts which lead to caution in the use of them will be acknowledged and set aside, because there are characteristic notes in them of Luther's theological and exegetical development which are sufficiently clear to be cited with confidence. One leading theme concerns the justice of God, that *justitia dei* which has been so prominent in discussion of Luther's theology and its origins for the mid fifty years of this century, and the thrust of his solution lay in his presentation of Christ. He sees it as essential to hold together Christ's person and work as showing forth God and his purposes. For Luther Christ is always seen as he who is human and divine, as the incarnate redeemer. Luther provided the energizing concept that it was in Christ's humanity that our sins are forgiven, and it is in bread and wine that the body and blood of Christ are set forth.[10] Alongside of this theme goes the theme of the word of God which he showed as the energizing concept of the word of God as God speaking through Scripture in an arresting and vital way since God speaks not just *formaliter* but *effective*: in this Luther was making fresh discoveries in exegetical method.[11] It is this freshness in exegesis, this sense of the dynamism of the word of God, taken together with his increasing and positive christological emphasis which provide the insights which Luther was now bringing to his view of the mass. This did not take the form of a discussion for its own sake of the doctrine of the mass and of the doctrine of the sacraments: Luther is writing exegesis not prologomena to systematic theology. He used the ideas associated with sacraments, not least the mass, illustratively in his work of exegesis on the Psalms. Here are foreshadowed sacramental ideas which he will develop later after 1521.

From the traditional position of seeing Christ in the mass as an example to which we should conform our lives, Luther can be seen as beginning to emphasize Christ as the gift of God to men, an unmerited and undeserved gift. In this view of Christ as gift he stresses the incarnation, for the human as well as the divine nature of Christ are important together and the way they are conceived together is central for man's salvation. God's saving will is only understood when seen in Christ through whom is the only way to come to God – he is God's gift in his being incarnate, crucified, raised from the dead, and coming in judgment. This theological development in Luther's *Dictata* can be seen to occur through his exegetical work on scripture. His increased understanding of the person and work of Christ is seen in his finding the living Christ in the Psalms themselves, as the traditional exegetical method emphasized by Augustine had done rather than by following the more recent historical method of Nicholas of Lyra. Both from Augustine and from the piety of the usage and contemplation of the Psalms as the centre of monastic worship in the choir offices and the breviary, Luther saw Christ as interpreting the mind and work of God. Eventually Luther will be able to say: 'In the whole Scripture there is nothing else but Christ either in plain words or involved words.'[12] In association with this view of the centrality of Christ for grasping the meaning of Scripture is the view of it as the word of God that is the speech of God; God creates by his word and brings through it his redeeming love. For the word of God is also Christ himself the word made flesh. In him God speaks and God acts and the Scripture records this. Luther rediscovered the force of the Hebrew for word which meant not only a word spoken but deed, when God spoke something happened.[13] For Luther Scripture related to Christ and Christ is he who redeems and is present as redeemer – his chief acts are set forth in the sacraments. Only through hearing God speak, that is, by attending carefully to what is said in Scripture the external word can we understand that

117

Christ is the full work of God. Through careful listening to the word we can find the grace of humility, and after being humbled at finding ourselves without righteousness can we come to righteousness through faith – this justification is in Christ. It is through the word of Scripture that Christ and truth are brought to our hearts, for when God speaks he gives what he says. Luther can even illustratively give force to this by using the symbolism of eating and drinking concerning the truth of Scripture: Christ devours us and transforms us into himself and we are his food; we are drink to Christ and we drink Christ and we are incorporated in one another.[14]

It is this nexus of Scripture as showing forth Christ as gift and of the word of God as God's speech and act, and of sacraments as external signs whereby we may certainly believe that God is favourable and merciful, which form central themes for Luther's theological development from 1513 to 1519 – indeed they remained so all his life. While it is obviously true that Luther still uses traditional piety as well as the terminology of technical theology in referring to the mass and in his illustrative use of it, yet the central themes of the nexus of Christ and his sacrifice as God's gift, of the vivifying word of God, of sacraments as giving God's favour, point forward, just as his exegetical work in the *Dictata* on the meaning of justice and justifying faith points forward, to the future Luther. This nexus is given greater impact by Luther's giving the traditional usage of *sacramentum* and *exemplum* in the *Dictata* a new emphasis. Luther pushes the concept of Christ as *exemplum* beyond the customary *imitatio Christi*, for that *imitatio* could rest content with the works of penance and the works of love. Luther instead insists that these works done in following the example of Christ are a false beginning, for we should begin rather with *sacramentum*. Christ went the way of suffering and death and draws men to these and makes these effective in men – this is *sacramentum*. It is Christ's humanity which is our protection and our salvation from eternal judgment. The purpose of the incarnation was for Christ to suffer and as a pattern, so to speak, provide *sacramentum* and *exemplum* for our being made whole and enabled to pass from this world to future glory. For Luther *sacramentum* speaks directly of Christ and not of the mass, not that Luther at this stage is seeking to undercut the mass for as a regular priest he was celebrating it daily; rather he was bringing a new depth of understanding of Christ as *sacramentum* to the mass which was eventually, when the other theological work of Luther was achieved, to show a great change from its traditional form.[15]

When we turn to the *Theses* of 1517 and the *Heidelberg Disputation* of 1518, that emphasis on humility shown in his *Lectures on Hebrews*, and which was associated with his development of the *theologia crucis*, is strongly present: this is an idiom which does not give much scope for the discussion of Luther's major theme of justification by faith nor of his insights on the nexus of Christ for us, the dynamic word of God and *sacramentum* as the gift of mercy.[16] Nevertheless, apart from this *theologia crucis*, Luther affirms that the sacraments are effectively means of grace not just because they are performed but because they evoke faith, because they are believed. We are present at the sacraments because we need them out of our unworthiness – we do not come presenting our worthy state of mind or the quality of our works. We come drawn by faith: the instituting words in the sacrament draw out effective faith from us. Luther is increasingly demonstrating that man achieves nothing towards his own salvation, Christ is the sole means. What he will understand more fully later concerning gospel and sacrament has not yet been achieved but he is insisting that the words, for example, from the gospel when cited in the sacraments, bring grace therewith. The word of promise is given in the sacraments: faith answers the word and receives the promise.[17]

The Lectures on Hebrews of 1517/18 show Luther emphasizing that man is delivered from the anxiety of sin not by following the example of Christ but by Christ's blood alone. Faith sees this and knows that sins are washed away by it: faith accepts the words of God which declare that the blood of Christ was shed for the remission of sins.[18] He even rebukes Chrysostom's discussion on testament for leaving aside the greatest of blessings through Christ's giving as a will or testament the forgiveness of sins and eternal life. For these are bequeathed to us in the testament, the words of Christ at the last supper.[19] We must not go to the sacrament relying on our confession, freedom from mortal sin and so on: the right preparation lies in faith alone, for no one receives grace automatically, 'It is not the sacrament but faith in the sacrament which justifies.' The sacrifice we offer is the remembrance of Christ's sacrifice.

By this stage the threshold has been reached of the customary interpretation of Luther's doctrine of the eucharist. The *Dogmengeschichte* and the monographs begin with the sermon of 1519, *A Sermon concerning the Blessed Sacrament of the Holy and True Body of Christ and Concerning the Brotherhoods* where the meaning of the sacrament is said to be *communio*, that is, fellowship with Christ and with each other realized in eating the bread and drinking the wine, and affirms that the bread is changed into Christ's true natural body and the wine into his natural and true blood – how and when this occurs we commit to Christ.[20] To start with this bluntly as Seeberg does is to fail to have before us the context of all that Luther had already been writing of Christ, of the word, of faith, of the objective givenness of the sacraments. It is also to neglect the context of the other sacramental sermons which Luther preached at this same period, not to mention the treatise *Asterici*.[21] Further, it would leave the unwary reader with the impression that by 1519 Luther has achieved nothing more significant to say on this sacrament than traditional ideas from Augustine for the notion of the mass as *communio* and Aquinas for the real presence, though ignoring the language of *substantia* supporting that presence. Again, Sasse wishes to show that this sermon of 1519 demonstrates Luther's first doubt on the official language of transubstantiation citing the passage where philosophical subtleties are dismissed by him: 'It is enough that it is a divine sign in which Christ's flesh and blood are truly present – how and where we leave to him'. Sasse deduces from this that it is the first step in Luther's rejection of philosophical support for the doctrine of the real presence, whether transubstantiation or otherwise.[22] But Luther's view of the real presence was already coloured by his biblical work wherein he saw the whole Christ as present in the bread and the wine, that this is God's gift, and that the words of the institution are dynamic in the concept of the presence. His own biblical thoroughness had provided Luther with what he needed at this stage without recourse to philosophical support for the presence. As Thimme said Luther's 'thought is existential and not substantial' – and this goes back before 1519. He had not formally rejected transubstantiation hitherto because he had not discussed the mass as a *locus* before this, he had only been concerned illustratively with its purpose and effects; also he was to reject it on scriptural rather than on christological grounds.

As was mentioned above other sermons were preached in 1519 and 1520 about the sacraments which should be noted as the context for this sermon.[23] In writing of the sacrament of penance Luther affirms that it is the words of Christ ('What you loose . . .') pronounced by the priest which give certainty, they are the first essential part of the sacrament, and the second part is the grace and peace of forgiveness; the third part is faith.[24] In a sermon on baptism of the same period occurs again this threefold emphasis on sign and the words of Christ spoken; grace and forgiveness are given in Christ and in the life of faith the grace of baptism is renewed.[25] In a sermon on preparation for death he affirms among other statements which are based on traditional piety (for example, the dominant theme of Christ in us and for us because of the *corpus mysticum* his body the Church) that the sacrament of the body of Christ promises and ensures that we may rely on all saints for love and support, and the ground for this is God's word and Christ – this is because we believe his word and cling to his sacrament.[26] In another sermon on the worthy preparation of the heart for receiving the sacrament *communio* or fellowship in the saints is emphasized, but also we are warned against the great error of relying on our confession and prayers or anything that is ours for our assurance is only in Christ and his word who gives us peace.[27] This last point is shown in the *Lectures on Hebrews* as the essence of the sacrament. With these contemporary utterances in mind and looking again at the Sermon of 1519 Luther is seen to stress the sacrament as the *communio* of saints in which we have all things in common with Christ and in addition there is the need to *communicare* that is to receive the sacrament. It is not enough to speak of the *opus operatum* (that is, a work of itself pleasing to God) for this brings harm to the sacrament: there must be *opus operantis* (that is, something done in faith) through which our faith is active. But this is the only challenge to customary ideas.[28] If this sermon of 1519 were undated it could be taken as belonging to an earlier period, but taken with the contemporary writings it can be seen as making a point which while customary in its

Augustinianism (the *communio* theme) is a further step in the road to Luther's developed conception of the sacrament. In any case there is no ground for the assertion sometimes made that Luther ignored here the doctrine of the real presence, or was to introduce it arbitrarily later as though he had not arrived there yet, for this doctrine had never been formally questioned by him nor was it to be. When Luther came to the achievement of seeing that Christ's whole work is unique as completed gift, to which we add nothing, then that together with his conception of justification by faith, with the forgiveness of sins, completes his essential Reformation theology – and it is through his sacramental theology that this achievement is effected.

Luther was different from most if not all other protestants in not desiring a breach with Rome as his starting point: his Reformation like his Protestantism was thrust upon him by the institutional aspects of Rome and those who defended them. Conscience and his vocation as a Doctor he said, compelled him to make his challenge. In an earlier day certain Czechs had protested against communion in one kind and Wyclif in England had opposed transubstantiation; both protests were bitter and divisive, but neither topic seemed important enough to Luther to attack until nearly three years after his first challenge in the Theses of 1517. [29] As he pointed out frequently, abuses in the Church or problems created by immortality in the clergy, factors so stimulating to a Protestant schism in others, were not matters he thought requiring to be attacked. It was the doctrine of justification by faith, and that which was so conjoined with it, the doctrine of Christ our incarnate saviour who took our flesh and died for our sins, and gives us forgiveness through the word of the gospel and the sacraments – these, he said, we believe and receive but can do nothing through our works and merit to earn – it was these doctrines which, when they were rejected by controversialists led Luther to his breach with Rome. After the disputation with John Eck at Leipzig in July, 1519, who had avoided discussion of the central issues, had insisted on requiring Luther's obedience to the pope and general councils, Luther grasped what institutionalized Roman Catholicism could do to overwhelm the teaching which he saw as scriptural truth and realized a breach was before him. Thereafter he attacked what he called the Babylonian Captivity of the Church but before the treatise of that title appeared he had written another against reliance on good works, a subject increasingly disturbing to the laity, showing his opposition to justification by these works which he said were only good when they flow from faith. While discussing the third commandment Luther wrote: 'Oh how many masses there are in the world at present! but how few who hear them with faith and benefit . . . Our masses at present are merely celebrated without our knowing why or wherefore and consequently we neither give thanks nor love nor praise, remain parched and hard, and have enough with our little prayer. Of this more another time.'[30] Two months later appeared a sermon on the new testament, that is the holy mass in which he set aside for the first time clearly the Roman teaching on the mass as a bloodless repetition of the sacrifice of Christ on Calvary. Luther states that this view is untenable since the mass is not a sacrifice but a testament and sacrament in which God provides us with Christ crucified and risen as a gift: we cannot give or offer, we can only receive. It is true that sentences on sacrifice have been added in the rite but these are due to the Holy fathers. We can bring sacrifices of ourselves our praise and thanksgiving, but we cannot offer Christ for that would be to go against Christ's own words and against God's gift; it is Christ who offers us not we Christ.[31] This theme was to be given greater weight in his treatise on *The Misuse of the Mass* in November the following year, but his concern in the months May 1520 to November 1521 is shown by his writing eight treatises on the mass itself or containing sections on it.[32]

Luther is now disentangling himself from Roman teaching which he considered to be confusing or denying those truths which he sees as the essentials of the sacrament of the Eucharist. Forcefully and with increasing weight of analysis he gives to the words of institution the greatest emphasis as the *testamentum* of God's gift to us in Christ, for it is here that there is certainty of the forgiveness of sins and the giving of faith through the gospel: 'What is the whole Gospel but an explanation of the testament (This is my body, this is my blood)?' Christ has comprehended the whole gospel in a short summary with the words of this testament or sacrament. 'For the whole gospel is nothing but a proclamation of God's grace and of the forgiveness of all sins granted us through

123

the sufferings of Christ, as St Paul proves in Romans 10 and Christ in Luke this same thing the words of this testament contain . . .' – the force of the words of institution is evident.[33] The primary importance of Christ is now not in his mystical body (as Luther had once written in the earlier stages of the *Dictata* and the *theologia crucis*) but in his body given and blood shed 'for you' for the remission of sins. The vital quality of the real presence lies, for example, in the sentence: 'In the mass there are to be found Christ's words and the confirming signs of his body and blood'. As he said elsewhere of this sacrament it is, *'ein felz in Christum gegrundet'*.[34] By now it is plain that the fulness of the answers to the questions which lay behind his spiritual crisis at his first mass had been found. From about 1513 the threads were being woven which were eventually to attain this completed pattern. He had now found when he stood at the altar the confident assurance of forgiveness which could enable him to stand before God, he had found a new meaning for faith, he had found the meaning of Christ as God's gift incarnate crucified and risen mediator.[35]

In October 1520 appeared not a sermon for edification but a vigorous polemic weapon of attack in *The Babylonian Captivity of the Church*. Here the mass is shown as in bondage through the withholding of the cup from the laity, through the imposing of transubstantiation teaching, and finally through the most dangerous abuse in its being made into a sacrifice and a good work done by men.[36] This sums up Luther's challenge to Rome and its institutions which overturn or obscure the Gospel even as this treatise marks his final break with the papacy. Here he expands what he has said already about the impossibility of the testament of Christ being a work or a sacrifice but in the discussion of transubstantiation he now becomes positive and full in his rejection of it as an irrelevance derived from Aristotle and his, 'it is the essence of an accident to be in something'.[37] It is unnecessary to introduce this 'pseudo-philosophy' of accidents and substance and he will not allow the words of institution to endure any petty arguments to override them or wrest them to meanings foreign to them for the 'honour of the holy words of God'. Yet even so Luther agrees 'I permit other men to follow other opinions' and he was to write in *Adoration of the Sacrament of the Blessed Body in 1523*: 'No great importance attaches to this error, if only the body and blood of Christ are left together with the word'.[38] That it was the 'holy words of God' that held him and strengthened his grasp of the doctrine of the real presence there can be no doubt, especially since he was able to pass through the period of turmoil, when so many doctrines were being put to the test by him after the break with Rome, through the hold these 'holy words' had on him on the presence when it was rejected by Karlstadt and others. This crisis of questioning can be seen in 1524 in his address to the Christians of Strasbourg who had consulted him on Karlstadt's views:

> This I admit; if Dr. Karlstadt or someone else had told me five years ago that in the sacrament there is nothing but mere bread and wine, he would have rendered me a great service. I passed through great inner struggles in that respect and had to fight hard to overcome the temptation. For I was well aware that by these means I could strike the hardest blow against the papacy. Besides, there were two men who wrote to me about this in a far more able way than Dr. Karlstadt without torturing the words according to their own ideas as he does. But I am captured by the word of God and cannot find a way out. The words are there and they are too strong for me. Human words cannot take them out of my soul. Yea, even if it should happen today that someone should prove with strong reasons that only bread and wine are there it would not be necessary to attack me so furiously. For, according to my old Adam, I am unfortunately, very much inclined to that view. However, the way Dr. Karlstadt talks wantonly about it does not tempt me at all. On the contrary, it only confirms me in my opinion.[39]

Perhaps it is as well to recall as Sasse reminds us that 'there is no utterance of Luther's in which he expresses any doubt concerning the belief that the body and blood of Christ are truly present in the Lord's Supper and distributed to the communicants'.[40]

After the rejection of **Rome Luther faced next** another form of bringing men's **own** effort into the work of salvation when, as he saw it, Karlstadt and the Swiss from different starting points sought to do this. Karlstadt introduced a form of **mysticism which** relied on men's experience and Zwingli introduced human reason to provide differing though converging roads to God and salvation.[41] For Luther the doctrine of the real presence could save us from the recurring errors of men, which were seen first in seeking through their reason the way to interpret God's will; next, through their legalism by which God's will could be found by setting themselves rules, obedience to which could bring them on the way of salvation, and finally through the belief that their spiritual insights, based on the religious experience of individual believers, opened the way to understanding God's will. It will be the second purpose of this essay to bring out the force of Luther's challenge to all three positions. He had already dealt with the legalism of Rome supported by canon law and its reliance on the merit of works, and proclaimed the liberty of a Christian man. He was to find it to be ironical that those even more opposed to everything Rome stood for than himself would again be turning to some form of reliance on human effort or feeling, and restoring legalism.

When Karlstadt said, 'participation in the suffering of Christ and participation in Christ's body and blood are the same thing' Luther saw here the overtones of the *Theologia Germanica*, the mystical way to salvation and forgiveness.[42] But this was not new to him if it was to Karlstadt; Luther had already tried the mystical way of contemplation in the quest for evangelical perfection in his earlier years in the monastery. Luther saw in Karlstadt's iconoclastic alterations to worship and Christian life at Wittenberg a falling back on works again and therefore legalism, since this meant drawing up rules based upon a radical simplification which meant for Luther an alteration of the gospel. Karlstadt had commanded, during Luther's absence the removal of elevation, of the word mass, of vestments, singing, images, all titles of clergy and of honour in the congregation, and insisted on a specific way of breaking bread and on the need for sabbath observance and rules of mortification. For Luther this was like going back to where he had started and he had already found it useless for salvation; he refused to be 'swallowed up in works again' with Christ made not a gift but a lawgiver because of Karlstadt. Those familiar with Luther's theological method in establishing his liberating doctrine of justification by faith know his emphasis on law and gospel in which law comes first and shows us our sin then comes the gospel in which the gift of Christ frees us from sin.[43] Karlstadt was seeking to repristinate the tradition of mortifying our sinful flesh and thereby increase in holiness: in so doing he was putting law after gospel and turning Christ into a second Moses. It is mere speculation to say as did Karlstadt that Christ pointed to himself when he said 'this is my body', though when he said that the presence of Christ is a remembrance of that last supper and within our minds only and not through eating and drinking, he was sharing a view which was becoming widely held.[44] Of this Luther wrote: 'I could go on thinking about it until I died, acknowledge it with all desire and have a great passion ... and remembrance of the treasure until I became ill over it. But of what help would all that be if this same treasure were not opened to me, given, brought and put into my keeping'.[45] Karlstadt also said that Christ is in heaven and therefore he cannot be in the bread of the sacrament for us who are earthbound. Luther immediately suspected that this meant a denial of Christ being incarnate in our humanity, and that Christ is being confined to a specific place, whereas Christ is everywhere and fills all things and comes to us 'for us' in bread and wine as he promised. It seemed to him that Karlstadt was in effect spiritualizing away not only the sacrament but Christ himself.

Cornelius Hoen (Honius) from Holland had written a letter, perhaps to Erasmus, copies of which were circulated and one was sent to Luther in 1521 (Zwingli also was to receive a copy of this letter and in 1524 take up its ideas enthusiastically) in which Honius suggested that 'est' in the words of institution should be rendered as 'significat' since 'est' is often so used in scripture.[46] After this time Luther strengthened his insistence on his exegesis of the words of institution as meaning and conveying exactly what they say and also his insistence that the body and blood of Christ are in with and under the elements of bread and wine. The body is not just a means of knowing the gift of Christ in the sacrament but as being the gift itself. The words of institution are not a matter of hearsay or something remembered from the past they are 'living things', *res viventes* which give life to those who hear them here and now.[47] In setting aside Honius Luther was not opposing one man or a minor and small group since Honius reflected spiritualistic tendencies in intellectual circles which were influenced by the Brethren of the Common Life, most notably Erasmus himself – Luther's comment was, 'Erasmus, Oecolampadius, Zwingli, Karlstadt, omnia sua sapientia metiri volunt et ita confunduntur.'[48] Luther turned to the Swiss views of the sacrament through his controversy with Karlstadt and he later judged them all as *Schwärmgeister*: 'enthusiastic' or fanatical, they were all rationalizing. In the Swiss as well as Karlstadt he saw a revival of an ancient dualism that of contrasting spirit and body to the discredit of the latter when they should have realized that scripture was to be followed and not antiquity and its speculations, for in scripture 'flesh' meant not body but sinfulness. This position was to lead to the confrontation between Zwingli's view of the relation of flesh and spirit in John 6:63 as the superiority of spirit over flesh and Luther's view that flesh meant sin in opposition to spirit, moreover Luther said the passage was irrelevant.[49] Luther felt that exegesis was not being effectively undertaken by the Swiss and their supporters. To him it seemed that they were using exegesis to defend the prior conclusions arrived at by rationalist processes. For Luther exegesis was impossible if a text of scripture was not accepted as it was written, unless very positive reasons required it to be read otherwise. If a text was considered to be unclear then it could be clarified by referring to other texts which were clear. The words 'This is my body' are direct and clear and mean what they say. Zwingli's use of the rhetorical term alloiosis to interpret the two natures of Christ whereby we can use the terms appropriate to one nature to refer to the other, enabled him to write that scripture can be said to use figurative language and 'my body' could mean 'a sign of my body'.[50] For Luther this was to be handing over scripture to the manipulations of human reason which would then become the master of scripture; not only this but the figurative interpretation divided Christ and in the end left us with no more than a human Christ. It was Zwingli, in spite of his later denials, who initiated the controversy which, however regrettable it was to become, required Luther to give a more thorough account of his exegesis of the scriptural passages in debate.[51] In doing so he was answering positions set forward by Zwingli and in terms and methods he had not hitherto used and was not to emphasize again after the Marburg Colloquy.

Zwingli had arrived at his view of this sacrament by 1524 a thankful memorial of Christ on Calvary and a means of mutu witness to the faith of members of a congregation. In November of that year he wrote to the Lutheran Alber expounding this view forcefully stating that there is only a spiritual eating which is no more than the remembering Christ's death, to think of it as essential to eat Christ bodily is utterly false.[52] This letter was widely circulated. Oecolampadius, a faithful follower of Erasmus at Basel published a treatise in which he sought to demonstrate that the patristic writers not only did not hold transubstantiation but did not hold Luther's position either, and that they affirmed that *soma* was a 'sign of the body'.[53] By now both he and Zwingli were associating Luther's interpretation with that of Rome, whereas Luther was coming to the conclusion, through the correspondence of his outraged supporters, that Oecolampadius and Zwingli were identifiable with Karlstadt, but he still did not publish anything against them. However, pressure from friends led to the publication of a treatise edited by them from three sermons by Luther, entitled *A Sermon on the Sacrament of the Body and Blood of Christ against the Fanatics* since they feared that his silence was being interpreted as capitulation to the views of the Swiss.[54] Here the Swiss conception is attacked of remembering and announcing the death of Christ as the forefront of the sacrament, whereby the body and blood are set aside and it is implied that the sacrament is something we perform to witness to our faith. 'They set up these dreams of theirs without any scriptural basis . . . some of them are crude, grammatical fanatics, the others are subtle philosophical fanatics.'[55] He is not making a sustained argument but homiletic declarations; for example, the body and blood of Christ have won forgiveness and impart it, we receive them corporally in confirmation of this and this is our great treasure.[56] In two treatises, Luther made his fullest and deepest statement on the real presence: *That These Words of Christ 'This is my Body' still stand firm against the Fanatics*, 1527; and *Confession concerning Christ's Supper*, 1528.[57] Here are brought together those themes of the real presence, the word of God and the person of Christ which had already been used by him since 1513, but now they are given their clearest expression. He succinctly shows what he will attack: 'On the sacred text "this is my body" Doctor Karlstadt tortures the word "this", Zwingli tortures the word "is", and Oecolampadius tortures the word "body" '. His first target is what he sees as Swiss attempts to define and limit the extent of God's purposes and powers with measuring rods.

After some sarcastic mockery of his opponents by showing how he could play at *Schwärmarei* himself he takes up what he rightly sees as a fundamental point, the meaning of the phrase 'the right hand of God'.[58] The Swiss say, following the creed, that Christ is ascended and therefore since he is at God's right hand he cannot be on earth in bread and wine. Luther asserts that this is a childish notion for it is to bind God himself to one place in heaven, but where is the scripture which thus limits the right hand of God? For Luther Christ must be with us and not remote from us: it is consistent with both scripture and the creed for Christ's body to be at the same time in heaven and in the sacrament. We cannot confine Christ to a specific local 'right hand' in heaven like 'a bird in its nest' for that would be to make him a prisoner in something created, but God is free from all patterns of man's making as to place, for his 'right hand' means not a place but his power.[59] God is there for you when he puts himself there and binds himself to that place saying 'here you are to find me', and he does this by placing the 'right hand' in the humanity of Christ and dwelling there. In any event what an enormous consolation it is not to have God as sheer spirit, but incarnate and wrapped in baptism and the eucharist.[60]

It is sometimes assumed that Luther was unfair to Zwingli in identifying his theological views with those of the Anabaptists, and later with Karlstadt and Schwenkfeld, since it is obvious that Zwingli opposed the Anabaptists vigorously and could not be said to follow the spiritualistic patterns of Karlstadt and Schwenkfeld in his theology. Nevertheless Luther drew all these people together into one net labelled *Schwärmarei* on the matter of the real presence in the sacrament. Since Zwingli and others had ceased to regard the sacrament as a means of grace, and reduced it to a sign of divine grace which could well be received otherwise than through this sacrament, Luther is justified in his attitude. Pelikan in his useful account of Luther's doctrine of the real presence as a case study in exegesis wrote: 'Luther countered the Swiss accusation "that he was in effect supporting Roman Catholicism" by his view of the sacrament "with a weird rumour that their theories were being well received by some papal circles as support for the sacrificial interpretation of the mass".[61] But this is not so 'weird' if we remember that Zwingli had written that the sacrament is essentially man's commemorative act and a sacrifice by believers to God – for Luther this seemed to be the rejected ground of Romanism that the mass is a sacrifice and a meritorious work so that the sacrament no longer represents what God's grace does in the soul but what man does.[62] Since Zwingli regarded the Lord's Supper as a *sacramentum* in the old meaning of the word as a soldier's oath of allegiance, and therefore our witness of allegiance to God and a declaration of faith and no more, Luther could see further evidence of this sacrament being essentially for Zwingli man's action towards God and not God's gift and grace coming to us.[63] Indeed Zwingli's symbolic understanding of the sacrament was linked to activism: the eucharist is never more than the act of giving thanks, it is not the body and the blood of Christ.

Luther himself, in replying to Zwingli's insistence that the idea of the real presence was impossible on philosophical grounds, resorted to philosophical analysis to show that there are more modes of a presence than that called 'local' according to the schoolmen. Out of this arose that defence by Luther of his doctrine of the omnipresence of Christ's body which was to be called by later writers the doctrine of ubiquity. It should be realized that this interpretation of omnipresence by Luther originated in the controversy with Zwingli and was not essential to Luther's teaching on the real presence, it arose in response to Zwingli's declaration that the real presence was contradicted by philosophy so Luther with the help of Occamist definitions demonstrated in his *Confession concerning the Lord's Supper* that there was a distinction by the sophists between *praesentia localis sive circumscriptiva*, a *praesentia definitiva* and a *praesentia repletive*.[64] He shows that this means being present locally if the space and object exactly correspond (wine in a cask); present definitively where an object can occupy either more room or less (an angel in a chest); or present repletively where the presence is supernatural (Christ after the resurrection passing through a closed door) and is then present in all places whole or entire. Of this last mode of presence Luther said it is altogether incomprehensible and can be maintained only through faith in the word of scripture.[65]

Luther had found part of his answer to Zwingli's challenge that the real presence was impossible through his use of scholastic terms, another part of his answer lay in the use of the patristic christological theme of the *communicatio idiomatum* which had been used by the Cappacodians, and Cyril of Alexandria, as well as later by Aquinas and Bonaventura. Expressed most simply this theme asserts that the divine nature conveys its attributes to the human nature and the human nature conveys its attributes to the divine nature. Luther from this showed that God dwells in Christ bodily so that the person of Christ is God and man in such a way that the two natures of Christ human and divine are one person in inseparable union. 'Whatsoever I behold in Christ is at the same time both human and divine.' He had always held this christology and he saw Zwingli's alloiosis as the 'devil's mask' through which Zwingli was separating the two natures.

For him the poles of the discussion, in spite of this philosophical excursus, in spite of alloiosis, synechdoche, or any other grammatical or rhetorical trope, are still christology and scripture. His main grounds of the defence of the real presence were still as he wrote in words to be copied later into the *Formula of Concord*: 'Jesus Christ is essential natural true complete God and man in one person undivided and inseparable; the right hand of God is everywhere; the word of God is not false nor deceitful; God has and knows of various ways to be present at a certain place not only the single one of which the fanatics prattle which philosophers call "local".'[66] Luther insisted that this omnipresence of God, otherwise terrifying if left as a concept in itself, is in Christ: it is effective for us only in Christ, giving us through his body and blood forgiveness life and salvation. Luther is saved from the rationalism of philosophical defence and from the pantheism of declaring *simpliciter* God's omnipresence, through his body and blood forgiveness, life and salvation. Luther exposition of scripture is always more important than theological system-making and he did not deduce the real presence from speculative theory or philosophical definitions but from the words of scripture itself. Christ's omnipresence which gives body and blood through bread and wine is received not by acceptance of a philosophical demonstration but by faith, not faith in the omnipresence but faith in God's promises – and yet the real presence is not dependent on our faith.[67] One of Luther's constant themes is that Christ is not present in saving grace except it is 'for you': those who come without faith in God's promises eat of the body and blood but it is not effective for them. It should be understood that no one sees, eats or chews the body of Christ as we see clearly and chew other flesh.[68] There is nevertheless a genuine unification of the body of Christ with us and not only a spiritual one through the mind and will. But this oral eating is spiritual, for the heart must believe the presence of Christ in the bread which the word announces. This oral eating with its consequence that unbelievers eat the body but to their own hurt was to be the focus of trouble later.[69] A curious variant on this was his suggestion later that the fanatics who do not at all believe in the words of institution (in the sense of finding through the *verba* the real presence) receive nothing but bread and wine.

Apart from the discussion on the omnipresence of Christ another special focus of attention for the Swiss and their supporters was chapter 6 of John. For them this was the essential biblical basis for their rejection of the real presence especially verse 63 ('the flesh is of no avail') which Zwingli called 'his diamond'. For him this chapter concerns that spiritual eating and drinking which is faith: it showed explicitly that Christ taught a spiritual eating and clearly set aside those views of a bodily eating affirmed by Rome and by Luther. Luther replied that John 6 did not deal directly with the eucharist but was about faith; and particularly verse 63 had nothing to do with the sacrament. For Luther the words 'flesh' and 'spirit' are contrasted with each other in scripture where flesh is used not to describe the body of Christ but first the flesh born of the flesh which means 'the world', that is, what is opposed to God, and secondly our flesh our humanity. Both senses are used he said in John 6 and Zwingli was obtuse in not seeing the change of meaning. Further, Luther held that whenever Christ speaks of his flesh he calls it 'my flesh': in John 6:63 if Christ were speaking of his body he would have used 'my' and not the definite article 'the' – but he was in fact speaking of 'the world'. Luther considered he had won the argument when

Zwingli did not cite this verse in his last book. In any case Luther was not himself making John 6 central to the discussion, it was Zwingli who did so, since Luther saw the words of institution as the central scriptural passage in the discussion.[70] Luther was accused of being indifferent to spiritual insights but he insisted that communion was a spiritual act not by spiritualizing the 'body' into something non-material, but by receiving the real body through the Holy Spirit. The words of Christ, the *verba* of the institution, assure us of Christ's body being present – if, says Luther, the body is so useful on the cross why not in the bread? It is for man's sake that the words are linked to Christ and his body, and the words must not be divided from Christ's body in the eucharist. For if a separation is attempted between words and body this would separate Christ from the communion, leaving us on earth and Christ in heaven, a gap which could only be bridged by some effort of man's will or mind – but God is merciful and comes to use through these words and this body. The words are indeed external but they are made vital by the creative power of the Holy Spirit. This further means that we are always dealing with Christ present in the saving power of his incarnation, cross and resurrection, and not someone in the past or remembered only. We have through the words, energized by the Spirit, the present and living Christ and not a historical Christ only. It is worth noting that Luther's insistence on the body and the blood in the bread and the wine gives a more secure link with the historical Christ than remembering him. What we present makes no difference, it is not our worthiness as priests nor our faith as recipients that count, Christ has given everything to his word and not to man's holiness, so that we may be certain of the word and the sacrament.[71] The gospel sets forth, in preaching and hearing, Christ's death which brings forgiveness of sins; and also the gospel in the words of institution communicates forgiveness of sins through the eating and drinking of Christ's body and blood. Luther sees a peculiar advantage of the sacrament over the spoken word since the preached word reaches out to all in general, but the sacrament brings the content of the word to each individual person, 'for you': preaching in public cannot speak so directly to the individual, nor so intimately.[72] A collateral development of his insistence on eating the flesh of Christ was Luther's adoption of the view of Irenaeus, and of other Greek patristic writers, that the body and blood of Christ are the medicine or food of immortality. We are given a pledge here that our bodies too shall be immortal, though changed, for they partake here on earth of this everlasting food; though with the reservation that the gift is only made to faith. This is a departure, according to Althaus and Sommerlath, from Luther's insistence on the relation between word and sacrament, and, Althaus added, Luther refers to this topic most frequently in the controversial treatises, and significantly it is not mentioned in the Catechisms.[73] But more probably it is a further example of Luther taking an old and mismanaged tradition and giving it new depth and force through his scriptural insights. The 'magical' overtones are set aside by Luther's discovery of the scriptural meaning of body as the sphere of God's creative action, and not merely to be dismissed as the regrettable accompaniment hindering our spiritual nature. Luther could use this idea of the body in describing Christian marriage (an inheritance from Luther to be found in the English *Book of Common Prayer* in the marriage service), since our bodies are part of our life in God on earth and they too therefore can be benefited in the sacrament. 'For (the body of Christ) must be beneficial and cannot be present without a purpose, therefore, it must give life and blessedness to our body.'[74]

Luther regarded his *Confession Regarding Christ's Supper* as definitive for it is a thorough, cogent and full account of the whole doctrine of this sacrament, and he wrote no more at any length on it until 1544 in his *Brief Confession Concerning the Holy Sacrament* apart from his attack on private masses, and his *Admonition Concerning the Sacrament* which dealt with its place in the life of the Christian community.[75] In the *Brief Confession* he roused himself in the year before his death to attack the 'fanatics' for the last time, his target being Schwenkfeld who 'disregarded' said Luther 'the words "this is my body" since they hinder the spiritual understanding.' 'If you want to become a theologian' he adds ironically, 'you must carefully observe this rule, namely, where the clear word of God contradicts your understanding look for some other word which pleases you and say that it is [found] through the Holy Spirit. After that you may arrange and interpret the words as it seems good to you.'[76] Luther drew attention to the fact that apart from Schwenkfeld and the other Sacramentarians there was a further view increasingly prominent which said with cool indifference that no article of faith was at issue in the matter of the real presence, therefore, there should be no occasion to quarrel about it, and in this matter 'everyone can believe what he likes' – however dead may seem the views of some of Luther's opponents this one is widely prevalent today, acceptable no doubt because it represents the spiritualizing away of the sacrament into nothing much at all that Luther had feared.[77] To the criticism from Protestant opponents, which in their eyes was a serious indictment, that he was a Papist he equably replied that what he taught was taught under the papacy and that it was also taught in the true ancient christian church of 1500 years ago, since the Pope did not institute it or invent the sacrament as the 'fanatics' themselves also must admit although they want to make this belief papistical. Luther had expressed this more fully elsewhere: 'The witness of the entire holy christian church (even if we had nothing else) should be enough for us to maintain this doctrine and neither to listen to nor tolerate any sectarian objections. For it is dangerous and terrible to hear or believe anything contrary to the common witness, faith and doctrine which the entire holy christian church has maintained from the beginning until now for more than 1500 years.'[78] One might add to this the evidence of Luther's liturgical writings for his concern to preserve as much as possible from the traditional worship of the church. Those writings also show the depth of spiritual power which Luther's doctrine of the real presence could give to worship: but this material is an investigation in itself and beyond the range of this essay.

It is significant that in his last writing on the sacrament Luther states that he left the Marburg Colloquy with real hope that in time the Swiss would come to share his point of view since they 'agreed to all the christian articles of faith and on this point gave up their previous error that it was merely bread.' But the Marburg Colloquy was essentially an unreal affair, unreal because it did not go to the depth of the argument and was political and not theological in origin. That Luther felt the insincerity of the Swiss in signing articles for political ends is shown in his adding that he was badly betrayed at Marburg since Zwingli in his last book rejected the intention of many of the articles of agreement and according to Luther dealt deceptively at the Colloquy. Certainly the Colloquy was not initiated by Luther but came about largely because of the fears of the Protestant leaders, especially the princes, about the theological division. From 1525 at different times Oecolampadius, then Zwingli and Capito, proposed a colloquy, and Bucer wrote to Wittenberg urging a settlement of the sacramental controversy by a meeting of Zwinglians and Lutherans. The Landgrave Philip of Hesse wanted a political alliance among Protestants as protection against Catholic attack by imperial forces which was regarded as increasingly probable after the rift at the Diet of Speyer, 1529.[80] When Luther was approached by him for a Colloquy to heal the division Luther refused on the ground that there were no new arguments available to discuss and the old ones had been thoroughly debated in print. However, the elector of Saxony agreed with the Landgrave and the Colloquy was called at Marburg later that year. It would not be useful to give extended attention to what was said there since the reports of the private sessions were fragmented, sketchily written down as the discussion progressed or from memory later, and since the proceedings were soon over.[81] Luther was proved right that nothing new of any substance would emerge. It can be seen from the reconstruction of the discussion that Zwingli and Luther and their associates were debating formulations which had been derived from and hardened in the printed controversy: neither side provided the range and depth which had been shown before. The attempt by Bucer, supported by Oecolampadius, to focus the debate on the 'spiritual presence' brought about by the Holy Spirit, was ignored by Luther who feared that a compromise would be taken by Zwingli to his own advantage. He went to Marburg convinced that Zwingli celebrated a commemoration of a past event with an absent Christ instead of the essential principle that we are shown a divine initiative there and then with the bread and the wine. A reconstruction of the end of the second session bears this out:

> Luther lifts the tablecloth and reads the passage which he had written with chalk on the table. '*Hoc est corpus meum.* This is our scripture passage. You have not yet taken it from

us, as you promised to do. "This is my body." I cannot pass over the text of my Lord Jesus Christ, but I must confess and believe that the body of Christ is there.'

Zwingli, jumping to his feet, 'Thus you also Doctor, assume that the body is in the Supper locally. For you say "The body of Christ must be there". There! There! This is certainly an adverb of space!'

Luther: 'I have simply quoted the words of Christ, and I was not prepared for such a conclusion. If we want to deal cunningly with one another, then I testify that I have nothing whatever to do with mathematical reasons, and that I exclude and reject completely from the Lord's Supper the adverb of space. The words are: "this is my body", not "There is my body". Whether it is there locally or not locally, I do not want to know. For God has not yet revealed anything with reference to that, and no mortal man can prove it one way or the other.'

Zwingli: 'Should then everything go according to your will?'[82]

It is curious that Zwingli did not show at Marburg that for him the Supper was an act of divine good will towards us – *gnädiger Handel Gottes mit uns* – but then he in his turn may have been afraid of giving away a debating point.[83] The result of Marburg was an agreed statement of faith drawn up by Luther, the Marburg Articles, the first fourteen of which, to Luther's surprise were signed without controversy by the Swiss but the fifteenth was the result of much diplomatic activity by the Landgrave to bring both sides to agree on a formula on the Supper.[84] This article had six points of which five were agreed but the last showed the unhealed division, 'Although at this time we have not reached an agreement as to whether the true body and blood of Christ are bodily present in the bread and wine nevertheless each side should show brotherly love to the other side insofar as conscience will permit.' However, soon after Zwingli showed his differences from the Articles by publishing appended notes. Each side had signed with a different intention; Luther signed what was essentially a statement of faith, Zwingli gave his signature to no more than a demonstration of a common front against Rome in which individual choice of interpretation of the Articles was of no consequence.[85]

This division between the Lutherans and the Reformed has remained and increased since, in spite of occasional attempts to heal it from Bucer's Wittenberg Concord (which the Swiss refused to accept) to those ecumenical activities of the last two decades which have proved to be more sympathetic if not wholly successful. In spite of the sacramental realism of Calvin, whose theme was the *sursum corda* so that our souls are fed with the body and blood of Christ through the power of the Holy Spirit when we eat the bread and wine, the Reformed Churches in their varieties, like other forms of Protestantism (whatever the degree of official recognition of Calvin's legacy), are in practice Zwinglian at the Communion. The tendency to Nestorianism at least latent in Reformed theology has played its part here. Also, remembrance has been given the further dimension of sealing and fulfilling the new covenant to which promises for obedience are attached. In the seventeenth century and later this covenant or federal theology brought back again what Luther had sought to abolish, the trust in works righteousness which led to emphasizing that moralism which reduces the sacrament to being an appendix to or recognition of moral virtues attained. All the varieties of federal theology are destructive of sacramental theology. Whatever modifications to Reformed theology were brought about through Anglican evangelicalism, through the Methodist movement, or through the post-Ritschlian theology, the Zwinglian remembering and not sacramental realism has essentially triumphed for the majority of non-Lutheran Protestant laity. That Lutheranism could fall into the narrowness of excess of dogmatizing and other defects including some loss of Luther's original freshness of approach will be plain to non-Lutherans at least, but it is still possible to find behind the denominationalism the quickening theology of Luther himself which could change for the better the sacramental aridity just mentioned. In the running tide of change in Christian faith, morals and religious practice which is so evident today would it not be fruitful in this time of testing of all traditions to seek what Luther was attempting to achieve by his scriptural, christological and soteriological concern for the doctrine of the real presence in the sacrament of the eucharist?

For Roman Catholics interest in Luther's holding to the real presence has been manifest again in these last decades as, for example, Killian McDonnell shows in his comments on some passages in Luther and on Calvin, and in the last chapter of his book which concerns the mass and ecumenical outreach today.[96]

In this ecumenical outreach many will require a reconsideration of the theme of sacrifice in the eucharist. Luther believed the view of his Catholic contemporaries that the sacrifice of the mass was a work performed by us to be unscriptural and repudiated it. Many now will think that he rejected the subject of sacrifice too brusquely and that it must in some sense be part of ecumenical discussion on the eucharist in the future.

To Luther let us give the last word: 'May God grant to all devout Christians such hearts that when they hear the word "sacrament" or "Lord's Supper" they might dance for pure joy, indeed, in accordance with genuine spiritual joy cry sweetly. For I am very fond of the precious blessed Supper of my Lord Jesus Christ in which he gives me his body and blood to eat and to drink even bodily with my own mouth along with these exceedingly sweet and kind words "Given for you, shed for you ..." '.

NOTES

1. *D. Martin Luthers Werke* (Weimar, 1883 ff.) *Tischreden* (1912–21) V, No. 5357. Also American Edition of *Luther's Works* (Philadelphia and St. Louis, 1955 ff.) *Tabletalk*, 54 No. 1558, 3556a. Hereafter these editions will be cited as *WA* and *LW*.
2. *LW*, Genesis 4:341.
3. Whatever variations from the standard form of the mass may have occurred in the Missal of the Augustinian Eremites at Erfurt it is unlikely that the main sections of the mass referred to here would be absent.
4. Luther has been regarded, conveniently for critics, as a man driven by psychological pressures to exaggerated statements and excesses of egotism and subjectivism cf. e.g. J. Lortz, *Die Reformation in Deutschland* (Freiburg, 1950), I, 402 ff. E. Erikson provided a psycho-analyst's variation of this theme in *Young Man Luther* (New York, 1958).
5. From Aristotle who had provided a distinction between substance and accidents writers as early as the twelfth century drew the doctrine of transubstantiation, which Aquinas elaborated, adding the notion of concomitance, to describe the miracle of the transformation of the elements into the real presence, (*Summa*, Q 76, Art. 5). Scotus and Occam provided further discussion: but the work of Biel on the canon of the mass would be of greater interest to Luther.

6. P. S. Watson, *Let God be God* (London, 1949), E. G. Rupp, *The Righteousness of God* (London, 1953) both point to the emphasis of Luther on the initiative of God in grace.

7. Reinhold Seeberg, *Lehrbuch der Dogmengeschichte* (4th ed. Basel, 1953), IV, 1. H. Cunliffe-Jones, *A History of Christian Doctrine* (Edinburgh, 1978), 348.

8. *LW*, 13:66.

9. For what follows on the writings of Luther from 1513 to 1519 the Dissertation for the degree of Ph.D. in the University of Cambridge, 1961, by Dr N. E. Nagel, *Luther's Understanding of Christ in Relation to his doctrine of the Lord's Supper*, has been useful. Grateful thanks are due to Dr Nagel for his permission to quote from his work which should be more widely known for its thorough investigation which provides a mine of materials as well as a close analysis of Luther's christological insights.

10. Nagel, op. cit., 23.

11. For a full discussion of Luther on the Bible as the Word of God cf. Jaroslav Pelikan, *Luther the Expositor: Introduction to the Exegetical Writings*, *LW*, Companion Volume, 48 ff.

12. *WA* 11, 223:f. 1.

13. Pelikan, op. cit., 54.

14. Nagel, op. cit., 77 ff.

15. Nagel, op. cit., Ch. 2.

16. Walther von Loewenich, *Luther's Theology of the Cross* (E.T.) Belfast, 1976.

17. The Faith/Promise theme goes back to Augustine: Luther was to elaborate it on various occasions e.g. *WA*, 8:440.

18. *WA*, 57, 3:208, 23.

19. *WA*, 57, 3:610, 17.

20. *WA*, 2:743 ff.

21. *Eyn Sermon von der Sacrament der Puss*, *WA*, 2:714: *Eyn Sermon von den Heyligen Hochwirdigen Sacrament der Tauffe*, *WA*, 1:727: *Eyn Sermon von Hochwirdigen Sacrament des Heyligen Waren Leychnams Christi und von den Bruderschaften*, *WA*, 2:742: *Sermo de digna preparatione cordis pro suscipiendo Sacramento Eucharistie*, *WA*, 1:329: *Eyn Sermon von der Bereytung zum Sterben*, *WA*, 2:685. *Asterisci*, *WA*, 1:286 'sed requiritur fides ante omne sacramentum fides autem est gratia. Ideo gratia semper praecedit sacramentum.'

22. Hermann Sasse, *This is my Body*, rev. ed., Adelaide, 1977, 80.

23. Nagel, op. cit., 175.

24. *WA* 2, 716:35.

25. *WA* 2, 727:23, 30.

26. *WA* 2, 695:16.

27. *WA* 1, 331:30.

28. *WA* 2, 751:29.

29. E. Peschke, *Die Theologie den Böhmischen Brüder in ihrer Früzheit*, 2 volumes. Stuttgart, 1940. H. B. Workman, *John Wyclif*, 2 volumes. London, 1926.

30. *WA*, 6, 224.

31. *WA* 6, 369:3.

32. *De feste Corporis Christi sermo*, 1519–20, *WA*, 4:700. *Antwort auff die Tzedel szo unter des Officials tzu stolpen sigel ist aus gangen*, 1520 *WA*, 6:137. *Vorclerung Doctoris Martini Luther etlicher Artickell yn seynen Sermon von dem Heyligen Sacrament*, 1520, *WA*, 6:78. *Sermon von der wurdigen Eruffahung des heiligen wahren Leichnams Christi gethan um Gründonnerstag*, 1521, *WA*, 7:692. *Von den guten werckenn*, 1520, 6:353. *Eyn Sermon von dem newen Testament das ist vom der heyligen Messe*, 1520, *WA*, 6:353. *De Captivitate Babylonica ecclesiae praeludium*,

1520. *WA*, 6:497. *De Abroganda messa privata Martini Lutheri sententia*, 1521, 8:440. *Von Miszbrauch der Messe*, 1521, 8:482.
33. *WA*, 6:360.
34. *WA*, 4:658. '... quia Christus in verbo est annexus, esz musz nicht Pampeln sacramentum est ein pelsz in Christum gegrundet'.
35. cf. 3 above.
36. *LW* 36, 47:48.
37. *WA*, 6:508.
38. *WA* 2, 441:18.
39. Sasse, op. cit., 64, *WA*, 15:394.
40. Sasse, op. cit., 65.
41. E. G. Rupp, *Andrew Karlstadt and Reformation Puritanism*, J.T.S., Oxford, 1959, vol. 10, 308–26: E. Seeberg, *Der Gegensitz zwischen Zwingli, Schwenkfeld und Luther, Reinhold Seeberg Festschrift*, ed. W. Koepp, Leipzig, 1929, vol. 1, 43–80.
42. *WA* 23, 732:8, 'Ich bin auff der selben treppen gewest ich hab aber ein bein druber zubrochen.' Cited from Nagel, 308.
43. *WA* 18, 117:20. In this *Wider die himmlischen Propheten*, Luther expresses the distinction between law and gospel and rejects the Puritan reliance on works which Karlstadt showed in his changes in worship and the practice of the christian life at Wittenberg.
44. *WA* 18, 149:26.
45. *WA* 18, 203:5.
46. W. Koehler, *Huldrych Zwingli*, 1943, 175. To whom the 'letter' was addressed is not known, Koehler suggested plausibly that it was Erasmus. The 'letter' was widely circulated, and published by Zwingli in 1525. Sasse gives an account of Honius suggesting that he took the interpretation from Wessel Gansfort also a follower of the *devotio moderna*, 97, 98.
47. *Von Ordenung Gottes Diensts ym der Gemeyne*, *WA*, 12:37.
48. *WA* TR 5, No. 5760 and 3, No. 3442.
49. Sasse, op. cit., 143, 144. Pelikan, op. cit., 145, f. 28, points out that Luther had already criticized the eucharistic interpretation of John 6:55 ff. in a sermon of June 4, 1523, *WA* 12, 580:584.
50. *Zwingli's Werke*, Schuler and Schulthess, 3:525, 'Est ergo alloiosis ... permutatio, qua de altera in eo natura loquentes alterius vocibus utimur.' So for him too the *communicatio idiomatum* was no more than a figure whereas for Luther there was a real exchange of properties – Zwingli's view for Luther meant rationalism. '... the old witch Lady Reason, the grandmother of alloeosis.' *LW* 37, 206:f. 63, 210.
51. 'Zwingli vielmehr hat die Trennung in der Abendmahlsfrage zuerst vollzogen'. W. Koehler, *Zwingli und Luther. Ihr Streit über das Abendmahl nach seinen politischen und religiösen Beziehungen* (2 volumes Gutersloh, 1924–53), I, 73.
52. Zwingli could go as far as writing: 'Nor do I believe that there ever was a person who believed that he ate Christ bodily and essentially in the sacrament.' Huldreich Zwingli's *Sämtliche Werke*, (vols. 88 ff. of the *Corpus Reformatorum*, ed. by Egli, Finsler et al., Leipzig, 1905), 90, 335.
53. *De genuina verborum Christi ... expositione*, Basel, 1525.
54. There are long insertions in this treatise which do not fit appropriately the argument surrounding them. This suggests that Luther himself did not prepare it for the press: the original sermons were popular accounts for laymen and the addition of attacks on the 'fanatics' was irrelevant to these sermons. (*LW*, 36:333.) However, he did not complain when opponents attacked it as his own work. It was the first of his treatises in the controversy on the eucharist with the Swiss and their supporters.

55. *LW*, 36:346.
56. *LW*, 36:366 ff.
57. Both treatises are translated in *LW* 37. '*This is my Body*' is *WA*, 23:64 ff. *Confession concerning Christ's Supper* is *WA*, 26:261 ff.
58. *LW*, 37:41.
59. *LW*, 37:63 ff.
60. *WA* 25, 128:38.
61. Pelikan, op. cit., 119.
62. *The Latin Works of Zwingli*, ed. S. M. Jackson, 3 volumes, New York and Philadelphia, 1912–29, vol. III, 234.
63. Sasse, op. cit., 103.
64. *LW*, 37:214 ff.; *WA* 26, 326:12 ff.
65. *LW*, 37:223. But it should be noted that while Luther uses this scholastic terminology it is not essential to his position since he finds what the terms intend are already available in Scripture. Nagel, 389: '. . . the ubiquity of Christ the man is not a ubiquity of spatial extension but simply and soteriologically where God is there He must be also otherwise our faith is false.' The repletive presence is not, moreover, the sacramental presence for Luther, the 'in, with and under' are of the definitive presence. Nagel, 390, fn 1. For Luther these scholastic explanations are possibilities only, they propose means to an end which can be reached by other means.
66. *Formula of Concord: Solid Declaration*, VII, 98 ff.
67. A frequent 'reformist' tendency was to deny the validity of consecration by a bad priest, or to say that faith like morals conditions the validity of a sacrament. One of the achievements of Luther was to challenge these man-made restrictions on the grace of God.
68. *LW*, 37:238.
69. *WA*, 29:346; 30:132. The *manducatio oralis* and the *manducatio impiorum* were to be a serious ground of criticism of the consequences of Luther's doctrine of the real presence among those of the Reformed, who sought reconciliation with Luther, on the ground that the glorified Christ could not be reduced to the blasphemous indignity of being consumed by the wicked and unfaithful. The modification was made to *manducatio indignorum* to accommodate this concern.
70. For the background to Zwingli's view of John 6:55 ff. Cf. Sasse, op. cit., 97 ff., and Pelikan, op. cit., 122 ff.
71. *LW*, 37:367.
72. Pelikan is useful on Luther not equating the Word of God and the Bible, but less useful in suggesting that Luther makes the proclamation of the Word a Sacrament alongside the other sacraments – the notion of sacramentalized preaching would be all too heady a theme for too many clerics. There is no clear support in Luther for this notion.
73. Paul Althaus, *The Theology of Martin Luther*, (E.T.), Philadelphia, 1966, 402. E. Sommerlath, *Der Sinn des Abendmahls nach Luthers Gedanken uber das Abendmahl*, 1527–29, Leipzig, 1930, 81–90.
74. *LW*, 37:134. Luther uses this theme of the 'bodily' saving work of Christ in his sermon April 17, 1538, *WA*, 66:256–65. Note cited from Pelikan, 176.
75. *Von der Winckelmesse und Pfaffen Weighe*, 1533. *WA*, 38:195–256. (E.T., *LW*, 38:147 ff.) *Vermanung zum Sacrament des leibs und bluts unsers Herrn*, 1530, *WA* 30, 2:595–626, (E.T., *LW*, 38:97 ff.) Luther had written more than once against private masses before this date: as early as August 1, 1521 he wrote to Melanchthon: 'I will no more celebrate a private mass for ever.' *WA*, BR, 2:372.

76. *Kurtz Bekentniss D. Martin Luthers vom heiligen Sacrament*, 1544, *WA*, 54:141–67, (E.T., *LW*, 38:286 ff.), *LW*, 38:297.
77. *LW*, 38:298.
78. *LW*, 38:292 and *WA* 30, 3:552. Althaus, op. cit., 334.
79. *LW*, 38:289 and 291.
80. *Weltgeschichte: Geschichte der Neuzeit das religiöse Zeitalter* 1500–1650. ed. J. von Pfluge-Hartung, Berlin, 1907, 337 ff. Also *LW*, 38:7.
81. Note-taking during the Colloquy was forbidden. 'A reconstruction of the Colloquy on the basis of reports which were afterwards made either from notes taken during the sessions or entirely from memory must consequently remain fragmentary.' *LW*, 38:10. However, there are interesting reconstructions in W. Koehler, *Das Marburg Religions Gesprach: Versuch einer Rekonstruktion*, Leipsig, 1929, and Sasse, op. cit., 215–68.
82. Sasse, op. cit., 207.
83. Cf. R. Ley, *Kirchenzucht bei Zwingli*, Zurich, 1948, 70 and Zwingli, C. R. ed. vol. 89, 138.
84. Sasse, op. cit., 216. The articles are a monument to the Landgrave's diplomatic skill. Further, W. Koehler, *Huldrych Zwingli*, 212.
85. Sasse, op. cit., 225.
86. Kilian McDonnell O.S.B., *John Calvin, the Church and the Eucharist*, Princeton, New Jersey, 1967. 'Open Questions', 294–361.
87. *Ein Brief D, Martin Luther von seinem Buch der Winckelmessen, WA* 38, 267:13. *LW* 38:227.

THE ESCHATOLOGY OF FAITH: MARTIN LUTHER

T. F. Torrance

In turning from the literature of medieval theology to the works of Martin Luther one is arrested immediately by an expression such as *'Regnum fidei'*, and the contrast it presents to the whole of mediaeval thought. For almost a millennium the eschatology of the Scriptures and the Early Fathers had been adapted to the prevailing cosmology. The language of primitive cosmology had certainly been used in the Scriptures in the communication of the eschatological message of the Bible, but not in such a way that eschatology was redacted to a particular cosmology or determined in its main features by it, for the very nature of Biblical eschatology made that impossible. But in the mediaeval world it was quite a different story; eschatology was almost wholly determined by a pre-Copernican geography of heaven and hell, with its dominating conception of purgatory. The whole of that way of looking at things was torpedoed by Luther's doctrine of the *Regnum fidei*, and Purgatory was regarded as *'ein lauter Teufelsgespenst'*, for the perverse eschatology it enshrined turned the Mass into sheer *Abgötterei*.[1]

Typical of this position was Luther's interpretation of the parable of Dives and Lazarus.[2] 'Abraham's bosom' was not to be understood in any corporal sense, but solely in terms of the Word of God, and as nothing else than God's Word in Genesis 22:18, in which Christ was promised to Abraham: 'Through thy seed shall all the nations of the earth be blessed.' All the fathers who believed this Word of God were blessed, that is, were redeemed from sin and death and hell. They belonged therefore to 'Abraham's bosom', and having died in faith they remain there until the day of judgment. Similarly, when we die, we must die believing in the Word of Christ: 'He who believes in me shall never die' (John

145

11:26), for then we are embraced in the 'bosom of Christ' and are kept in Him until the day of judgment. That is the same Word of God that was spoken to Abraham, so that the *sinus Abrahae* is fulfilled in the *sinus Christi*.³ On the other hand, 'just as Abraham's bosom is God's Word, within which believers through faith rest and sleep, and are kept until the last day, so hell must be understood on its part as where God's Word is not, where the unbelieving through unbelief are expelled until the last day. That can be nothing else than an empty, unbelieving, sinful, evil conscience.'⁴ By that Luther means, as he goes on to explain in the same sermon, that when a man dies his conscience is opened up so that even in his unbelief he sees 'Abraham's bosom' and those in it, that is, the Word of God, in which he ought to have believed and has not and from which he suffers the greatest pain and anguish without any help or comfort. That does not mean that Luther simply interprets hell in subjective terms, but that he refuses to understand it in the terms which 'carnal reason' had so long supplied.

The difficult thing to grasp in Luther's thought here is that he should think of the 'bosom of Abraham' or the 'bosom of Christ' in terms of the generations of history of those who have believed the Word of God, and in terms of the ultimate refuge of the believing beyond history – and yet it is just this very fact that injects into Luther's theology the utmost eschatological concentration and urgency. In answer to the question whether Dives continued daily to suffer such torments, Luther declared that here we have to put out of our minds all notions of time, for in that world '*nicht Zeit noch Stund sind, sondern alles ein ewiger Augenblick*'.⁵ In another sermon on the same passage preached during the following year, 1523, Luther speaks of the fact that *coram Deo* a thousand years are not even a day, so that when a man rises from the dead Adam and the fathers will rise with him just as if they had been living but half an hour before. '*Dort is kein Zeit ... Es ist vor Gott alles auf einmal geschehen. Est ist nicht weder vor noch hinter, jene werden nit eh kommen an den jüngsten Tag denn wir.*'⁶ The impact of that eternal moment (in which all action is concentrated) upon the life of the believer in time gives it intense eschatological potency, for it is life in the 'hour' when the mighty last things knock at the door. That is what Luther characteristically called the *Stündlein*.[7] Nowhere is the eschatological perspective which this brings better expressed than in his Commentary on Peter and Jude.[8] 'There are two ways of viewing things – one for God, the other for the world. So also this present life and that to come are twofold. This life cannot be that, since none can reach that but by death – that is by ceasing from this life. This life is just to eat, drink, sleep, endure, bring up children, etc., in which all moves on successively, hours, day, year, one after another: if you wish now to apprehend that life, you must banish out of your mind the course of this present life; you must not think that you can so apprehend it, where it will all be one day, one hour, one moment. Since then in God's sight there is no reckoning of time, a thousand years must be before Him, as it were, a day. Therefore the first man, Adam, is just as near to him as he who shall be the last born before the last day. For God sees not time lengthwise but obliquely, just as when you look at right-angles to a long tree which lies before you, you can fix in your view both place and parts at once – a thing you cannot do if you only look at it lengthwise. We can, by our reason, look at time only according to its duration; we must begin to count from Adam, one year after another, even to the last day. But before God it is all in one heap; what is long with us is short with Him – and again, here there is neither measure nor number.'[9]

To refer back again to the exposition of the parable of Dives and Lazarus, the ultimate division which the *Stündlein* reveals between the 'bosom of Abraham' and 'hell', so sharp that an impassable gulf is seen to exist between them, is read back into our life before the day of judgment, so that Lazarus and Dives represent the Kingdom of faith with its poor despised Church on the one hand, and the kingdom of this world with its external wealth and splendour on the other. It was in those terms that he expounded the Book of Genesis, his longest and most sustained exposition, for throughout it the whole of history, life and theology is interpreted in the light of ultimate judgments and distinctions. That, then, is the idea that dominates Luther's thought and makes it eschatological through and through – the dialectic between heaven and earth, grace and nature, gospel and law, the true Church and the false.

JUSTUS ET PECCATOR

All this, however, is also rooted in Luther's own spiritual pilgrimage, which made him react against a superficial conjunction of heaven and earth and against the easy relation of grace and nature[10] or the easy transfiguration of nature which he found in mediaeval theology, both in its Dominican and in its Nominalist form. His Augustinian training, his searching experience in the monastery, and his lectures on Scripture all combined to convince him that grace and nature as we know it in this world today are in the sharpest tension, a tension which goes down into the depths of man's being[11] – so he interpreted Romans 7[12] and Galatians 5.[13] Furthermore, Luther's conflict with a Papacy hostile to the proclamation of the Biblical Gospel of grace shocked him into the conviction that the same tension ran clean through the official Church from top to bottom.[14] The inner conflict of his soul had a counterpart within the Church on earth.[15]

Luther's own inner conflict found its answer in the doctrine of justification by faith through which the believer, though *semper peccator*, knew himself in Christ to be *semper justus*.[16] The outstanding characteristic of this teaching is that justification was understood as the eschatological act of pure grace which anticipated Christ's ultimate vindication of the sinner at the final judgment. And so with reference to the words from John's First Epistle, 'If our hearts condemn us God is greater than our hearts', Luther wrote: 'Greater, infinitely greater, is the counsel for the defence than the counsel for the prosecution. God is the Defender, the heart is the accuser. What, is that the proportion? Thus, thus, even thus, it is. "Who shall lay anything to the charge of God's elect? Nobody. Why? It is Jesus Christ (who is very God) who died, nay, rather, who is risen again. If God be for us, then, who can be against us?" '[17] No wonder Luther came to long for the day of judgment as '*lieben jüngsten Tag*'.[18]

As early as his lectures on Romans Luther had come to use the terms '*reputatio*' and '*imputatio*' to describe that act of pure grace.[19] 'The saints are inwardly always sinners and thus outwardly they are always justified. The hypocrites inwardly are always just, and thus outwardly they are always sinners. By inwardly, I mean, as we are in ourselves, in our own eyes, in our own estimation. But outwardly what we are in God's sight, in His *reputation*. Therefore we are outwardly just when we are just, not of ourselves or of our own works, but only by the reputation of God.'[20] 'Since therefore the saints always have their sin in view and implore righteousness from God according to His mercy, by this fact they are always *reckoned* just by God on account of this confession of sin. For they really are sinners, but they are just by the merciful *reputation* of God. Ignorantly they are just, they know themselves as unjust: sinners indeed they are none the less just in hope.'[21] 'For righteousness and unrighteousness are taken in Scripture very differently from the way in which the philosophers and lawyers interpret them. For they assert it to be a quality of the soul, but in the Scriptures righteousness consists rather in the *imputation* of God than the essence of the thing itself. He is a possessor of righteousness, not only who has a certain quality, nay rather, he is altogether a sinner and unjust, but whom God on account of the confession of his unrighteousness and his imploring mercifully *reputes* the righteousness of God and wills to regard as just in His presence. Thus we are all born and die in iniquity, i.e. in unrighteousness. We are just by the sole *reputation* of the merciful God by faith.'[22]

It was in the great *Commentary on Galatians* that that teaching was fully developed and the eschatological character of *imputation* was powerfully brought out. In the *Lectures on Romans* Luther had been concerned to emphasise the fact that justification is on the ground of Christ's substitutionary and atoning exchange, thus involving the believer in objective righteousness, the righteousness of God, so that it is God's righteousness which is the real heart and substance of man's righteousness, but in the *Commentary on Galatians* Luther is also concerned to emphasise the fact that we can only understand justification in terms of a duality which reaches out to the advent of Christ, when our perfect righteousness in Christ will be revealed. 'Christian righteousness consists in two things, faith in the heart and God's imputation.'[23] Faith is a formal righteousness (*formalis iustitia*), and yet this righteousness is not enough, for after faith, there still remain remnants of sin in our flesh. This sacrifice of faith began in Abraham (Romans 4:20–22), but at the last it was finished in his death. Wherefore the other part of righteousness must be added

149

also, *to finish the same in us*, that is to say, God's imputation. We have received the first fruits of the Spirit, but not yet the tenths . . . We conclude, therefore, that righteousness indeed begins through faith, and by the same we have the first fruits of the Spirit; but because faith is weak, it is not made perfect without God's imputation. Wherefore faith begins righteousness, but imputation makes it perfect unto the day of Christ.'[24] Or again: 'Hereby we may see how faith justifies without works, and yet how imputation of righteousness is also necessary. Sins do remain in us, which God utterly hates. Therefore it is necessary that we should have imputation of righteousness which we obtain through Christ, and for Christ's sake, who is given unto us and received of us by faith. In the meanwhile as long as we live here, we are carried and nourished in the bosom of the mercy and longsuffering of God until the body of sin is abolished and we are raised up as new creatures in that great day. Then there shall be new heavens and a new earth in which righteousness shall dwell.'[25]

Here it is clear that *imputation* is essentially an eschatological concept. Certainly it indicated that justification is forensic in the sense that it is grounded on the judgment of Christ on the Cross, for He the Just dies for the unjust that we may be made the righteousness of God in Him, but it also indicated that what happened in the judgment and death of Christ for us is yet to be fully disclosed at the advent of Christ. *Imputatio* is the concept which holds together those two moments, the forensic and the eschatological, in one.[26] That the believer is imputed righteous means that he possesses a righteousness which is *real* (*justus*), though not yet fully *realised* (*justificandus*),[27], as real as Christ who dwells in his heart by faith, but who as yet is discerned only by faith and not by sight.[28] *Imputatio* describes the *hic et tunc* of our salvation in Christ,[29] and tells us not to judge our actual righteousness by the appearance of the flesh, for it is concealed under hope until Christ comes. 'We through the Spirit wait for the hope of righteousness by faith' (Galatians 5:5). Every word here is pithy and full of power . . . Hope after the manner of the Scriptures is taken two ways: namely, for the thing that is hoped for, and for the affection of him that hopes. For the thing that is hoped for, it is taken in the first chapter to the Colossians: 'For the hope that is laid up for you in heaven' (v. 5), that is, the thing we hope for. For the affection of him who hopes it is taken in the eighth chapter of Romans (v. 24): 'For we are saved by hope.' So also in this place hope may be taken in two ways: first, 'we wait in Spirit, through faith, for the hope of righteousness', that is, the righteousness hoped for, which shall be revealed when the Lord will; the second, we wait in Spirit by faith for righteousness, with hope and desire. That is to say, we are righteous, although our righteousness is not yet revealed, but hangs yet in hope. For so long as we live here, sin remains in our flesh; and there is also a law in our flesh, and members rebelling against the law of our mind, and leading us captives unto the service of sin (Romans 7:23). Now, when these affections of the flesh rage and reign, and we on the other side wrestle against them, then there is room for hope. Indeed, we have begun to be justified through faith, whereby we have also received the first-fruits of the Spirit, and the mortification of the flesh is also begun in us, but we are not perfectly righteous. It remains, then, that we be perfectly conformed, and this is what we hope for, so our righteousness is not yet in actual possession but lies under hope (*nondum est in re, sed adhuc in spe*).[30] Or, as Luther puts it a little later in the same *Commentary*: 'We possess Christ by faith and in the midst of our afflictions through hope we wait for that righteousness which we possess already by faith.'[31]

That is the relation between *having* and *not-having* which lies at the heart of Luther's eschatology.[32] It is thus neither a realised eschatology, for the *having* here and now is offset by a *not-having*, nor is it a futurist eschatology, for the *not-having* is a *not-yet-having* which is offset by a present *having*. It is the eschatological dialectic of *justus et peccator*.[33]

It is with the same doctrine that Luther faced the conflict with the official Church. At first he believed that the hostility of the Papacy to his doctrine of grace must be due to a misunderstanding, that it was only temporary, and that he would be vindicated in his difference at a General Council of the Church, because the Church itself was sound. But then when he saw that the tension between grace and nature ran right through the fabric of the institutional Church, he knew that the only General Council which would vindicate him would be the final judgment of Christ at His advent.[34] As he recovered from his shock of horror at the conflict of the Church with the Church, Luther could only interpret the conflict as an adumbration of the final judgment when the children of light would be divided from the children of darkness.[35] To Luther the Reformation was a divine act[36] which startled him into the realisation that he was living in the last times, so close to the impending judgment that already he could see the Church of Jesus Christ being unmasked of its anti-Christian secularisation. 'If the Last Day were not so close at hand it would be small wonder if heaven and earth were to fall at such blasphemy. The fact that God can tolerate such things as this is a sign that the Great Day is not far off. And yet they laugh at that, unmindful that they have made God out to be blind, crazy, mad, and foolish, and they think that their doings are wise and manly. I, too, would be as carefree as they are, if I regarded only their raging; but the wrath of God, which is shown upon them, terrifies me sorely, and it is high time that we all wept and prayed earnestly, as Christ did over Jerusalem, when he bade the women weep not for Him, but for themselves and their children. For they do not believe that the time of their visitation is near, and they will not believe it, even though they see it, hear it, smell it, taste it, touch it, and feel it.'[37]

THE TWO KINGDOMS

The characteristic way in which Luther stated his whole position was his doctrine of the two kingdoms, the '*geistliches Regiment*' and the '*weltliches Regiment*'.[38] That was his way of expressing the Biblical doctrine of the two ages, the αἰὼν οὗτος and the αἰὼν μέλλων. The Christian who is *simul justus et peccator* lives, as Luther puts it, in two kingdoms, two ages, or 'two worlds, the one heavenly, the other earthly'.[39] But there are differences between Luther's understanding of the two ages or worlds and that of the primitive Church. The New Testament writers and the early Fathers thought of the two aeons in terms of a *Heilsgeschichte*, in terms of a divine action within, as well as transcending, the course of history. In that historical perspective the age of the Kingdom of God is partially telescoped into this present age, so that there is an area in which they overlap each other. The Church on earth has her existence in that overlap of the two ages, living at once in the time of this present age and in the time of the Kingdom of God.

In contrast to that historical perspective, Luther's doctrine of the two ages or regiments is primarily dialectical.[40] The historical element, however, is by no means wanting in Luther's thought. It is apparent, for example, in the temporal order in which he expounded the relation of Law and Gospel, although these two times, of Law and Gospel, are also thought of as persisting side by side in the present, cleaving the Christian himself in two, as it were. 'A Christian is divided into two times. In that he is flesh, he is under the law; in that he is spirit, he is under grace. But these days must be shortened, or else no flesh should be saved. The time of the law is not perpetual, but has an end, which is Jesus Christ. But the time of grace is eternal.'[41] The same historical perspective is to be found in Luther's notion of the *novum regnum* which Christ came to set up in distinction to the old kingdom[42] which has persisted ever since God said to Adam: 'Be fruitful, and multiply, and replenish the earth and subdue it and have dominion over the fish of the sea, and over the fowls of the air and over every living thing that moves upon the earth' (Genesis 1:28). That 'old kingdom' founded in Adam concerns our temporal life and relates to *die weltliche Oberkeit*. But afterwards God has established another *Regiment* which is *zweierley*. On the one hand, it is the regiment of the law which was founded through Moses to reveal sin but it has little to do with grace. On the other hand, however, there is '*alterum regnum, das resurrectio Domini hat gestifftet, wil ein new Reich, wesen einsetzen*'. This is the Kingdom of Christ, who is enthroned as King to have dominion over life and death and to reign over sin and death, which we have inherited from Adam, but in distinction to the temporal nature of the old kingdom this is the '*regnum coelorum, non terrestre*'.[43] It is the '*regnum remissionis peccatorum*' through which heaven is opened and hell is closed.[44]

Luther has another way of speaking of the historical perspective of the two kingdoms, the *duplex ecclesia* which dates from the beginning of history.[45] We shall examine that later, but here it must be noted that the *geistliches Regiment* as even *novum regnum* is not thought of in positive relation to the temporal kingdom of this world but is sharply distinguished from it like the *sinus Abrahae*. That kingdom has no need of the Gospel,[46] no need of the Word of God, for it has its own *ratio*.[47] And yet there is no doubt that Luther does think of this temporal kingdom as taking on through sin the form of the law[48] upon which, therefore, the *geistliches Regiment* supervenes as a *novum regnum* in a mighty operation of the Word of God. The *novum regnum* is involved in history, therefore, so that Luther sometimes interpreted it in terms of the prophecies of Ezekiel and Daniel,[49] but his attempt to relate eschatology to the actual course of history was strangely confused. Nowhere is that more apparent than in his second preface to the book of Revelation written in 1545, in which he sought to give it a detailed historical interpretation.[50] The fact is that on the one hand Luther was powerfully influenced by the popular apocalyptic literature in which the later Middle Ages abounded, literature from Wyclifite England, from Taborite Bohemia, and above all from the many successors of Joachim of Fiore and the Fraticelli,[51] and yet, on the other hand, his training in scholastic philosophy and theology had so indoctrinated him with a conception of eternity as '*totum simul, alles auf einmal*',[52] or 'all in one heap', as he put it in the Commentary on Peter and Jude,[53] that he found it extremely difficult to think of duration or time in the Kingdom of God, and had to think in terms of mathematical points and lines.[54] Consequently, apocalyptic for Luther pointed not so much to the engagement of the Kingdom of God with history, as to its abrupt termination, '*consummans et abbrevians*' (Romans 9:28), for the nearer the day of judgment comes the fewer will be the faithful, as in the days of Noah.[55] That is to say, Luther's was an apocalyptic view in the Donatist or sectarian rather than in the Biblical sense, for to him 'the whole world is evil and among thousands there is scarcely one true Christian'.[56] As early as 1530 Luther was so convinced that the end was about to break in with catastrophic swiftness that he resolved to publish his translation of the book of Daniel right away in order that it might do its work before the mighty and terrible day of the Lord, so full of fear for the godless, and so full of consolation for the believing.[57] 'Therefore we commend all earnest Christians to read the book of Daniel, to whom it will be a consolation and a great profit in these wretched last times: but to the godless he is of no profit, as he himself says, in the end, "The godless remain godless and do not heed" (Daniel 12:10) . . . As Christ in Luke 21 encouraged His own with terrible news, and says. "When ye shall see all these things, then look up and lift up your heads, for your redemption is near" (21:28), so here too we see that Daniel always ends all his visions and dreams, however terrible, with joy; namely, with Christ's Kingdom and Advent, and it is on account of this Advent, as the most important and final thing in them, that these visions and dreams were given, interpreted and written.'[58]

Throughout the year 1530 Luther was working and writing in '*Johannine haste*' (*in festinantia Ioniana*).[59] He was afraid that the advent would take place before he had finished translating the Scriptures. 'The world runs and hastens so diligently to its end that it often occurs to me forcibly that the last day will break before we can completely turn the Holy Scriptures into German.[60] For it is certain from the Holy Scriptures that we have no more temporal things to expect. All is done and fulfilled: the Roman Empire is at an end; the Turk has reached his highest point; the pomp of Papacy is falling away and the world is cracking on all sides almost as if it would break and fall apart entirely. It is true that this same Roman Empire now under our Emperor Charles is coming up a bit and is becoming mightier than it has been for a long time, but I think that that shows it is the last phase, and that before God it is just as when a light or wisp of straw is burnt up and about to go out, then it gives forth a flame as if it was going to burn brightly and even at the same moment goes out: even so Christendom now does with the light of the Gospel. Moreover all prophets in and out of the Bible write that after this time, namely, after the present year of 1530, things will go well again. That which they so rightly point to and prophesy will be, I hope, the last day, which will free us from all evil and help us to everlasting joy. So I reckon this epoch of the Gospel light as none other than the time in which God shortens and restrains tribulation by means of the Gospel, as Christ says in Matthew 24: "If the Lord shortened not these days, no man would be saved." For if the world had to stand longer as it has hitherto stood, the whole world would become Mohammedan or sceptical, and no Christian would be left, as Christ says (Luke 18:8): "When the Son of Man comes, shall He find faith on the earth?" And, in fact, there was no more right understanding nor doctrine in the Christian faith present, but mere error, darkness and superstition with the innumerable multitude.'[61]

That fervid eschatological expectation kept up its force until Luther's death, but it became more and more calculating. In 1541 he published a book called *Supputatio annorum mundi*, which he reissued in an enlarged edition in 1545.[62] In it he calculated in old Patristic style, finding that the year A.D. 1540 corresponded to the year 5500 after creation. There were still five hundred years to go before the eternal Sabbath, but the Lord had promised to shorten the time for the sake of His elect, and as the Lord Himself did not stay the full three days and nights in the grave, the day of the Church's resurrection would be hurried on. There might be no more than a hundred years to go![63] It was during the Easter season that Pharaoh was overthrown in the Red Sea and Israel was redeemed out of Egypt. It was during the same season that the world was created, and that Christ rose again from the dead. Perhaps it will be at Easter too, thought Luther, that the Last Day will arrive, when God's gracious *imputation* will be fulfilled crowned with glory.[64]

There can be no doubt that Luther's realistic eschatology revived a Biblical emphasis which he preached with great power and comfort to the flock of Christ hungering for the righteousness of the Kingdom of Heaven. There were also these other aspects of his eschatology which were rather unfortunate and came to have too great an influence, particularly in England, but after all they are but a minor aspect of his theology. More important than any correlation between prophecies and contemporary events was his apocalyptic cast of thought which allowed him to see movement and divine intervention in history, for the Word of God preached throws the world into tumult. 'The world and its god cannot and will not bear the Word of God; and the true God cannot and will not keep silence. While, therefore, these two gods are at war with each other, what else can there be in the world but tumult? Therefore to wish to silence these tumults is nothing else than to wish to hinder the Word of God, and to take it out of the way. For the Word of God, wherever it comes, comes to change and renew the world.'[65] And that is the '*Verbum Dei* by which we receive testimony of future and invisible things'.[66] Indeed, it is just because the Word of God is the sceptre of His Kingdom that by bringing the future things into the present it creates *commotiones.*[67] '*Verbum non est opus nostrum, sed est regnum Dei efficax et potens in cordibus nostris.*[68] *Regnum habet fundamentum, columnam in verbo Dei.*'[69] That, however, is the very fact that determines the dialectical character of eschatology for Luther. 'Here thou hearest that His Kingdom is on earth, and that it is not visible but is in Word.'[70] Just because the Word of God is His sovereign and mighty action, His Kingdom operates wherever the Word is heard – that is the '*Regnum fidei*',[71] as he is so fond of calling it. But, as a *hearing Kingdom*, it is not a *seeing Kingdom*.

THE KINGDOM OF GOD

At this very point, however, Luther sometimes speaks of '*duplicia regimina dei*'.[73] One is the *Regnum dei invisibile*, the invisible Kingdom of the invisible God. Because it concerns the hidden will and council of God it is utterly incomprehensible to us, for His eternal decisions and judgments are far beyond our knowledge and he who would pry into that Kingdom will only 'break his neck'.[74] The other Kingdom is the Kingdom of the Incarnate Son, 'the visible God', '*Gottes Regiment auff Erden, das sichtbar Regiment Gottes, welches uns Christen angehet und heisset das Reich Christi*'. This is the revealed Kingdom in which Christ as King and Lord rules through the Word of the Gospel, through the Spirit and the Sacraments; it is the Kingdom of the Incarnation and the mighty deeds of Christ for our salvation.[75] Jesus Christ is God, Creator and Lord over all, and He participates in God's invisible Kingdom as well as rules over the visible Kingdom of God on earth. *Secundum Deitatem* Christ rules in the invisible Kingdom along with the Father, for He is equal to the Father, but *secundum humanitatem* He reigns in the *Kirche* and *Christenheit* on earth, although He is also Head of the whole worldly regiment on earth because of His Deity.[76] In so far as Christ's Kingdom is involved '*in den heimlichen, verborgenen Rath und in das unsichtbar, unbegreiflich und unerforschlich Regiment Gottes,*' it is beyond us, but what concerns us is the visible Kingdom of God on earth, where we have to do with the Humanity of Christ.[77] That is the Kingdom which is the object of our faith and which therefore

Luther calls '*Regnum fidei*'. This is the revealed Kingdom visible to faith, but in contrast to the worldly regiment it is invisible because it is not discerned through our senses or by our natural reason. The visible Kingdom on earth is invisible because it concerns hearing rather than seeing, faith rather than works, Gospel rather than Law. That takes us back in our discussion to Luther's primary emphasis upon the eschatological tension between *believing* and *seeing*, between *having* and *not-having*, which assumes its large and masterful aspect in the dialectical relation between the two Kingdoms, *geistliches Regiment und weltliches Regiment*.[78]

Luther employs a wealth of expression to distinguish the two kingdoms, such as '*regimen spirituale/regimen corporale*',[79] '*regnum gratiae/regnum rationis*',[80] '*regnum fidei/regnum operum*',[81] '*regnum Christi/regnum Caesaris*',[82] '*regnum aeternum/regnum seculare*',[83] '*Reich des Glaubens/Reich der Tat*',[84] '*Hörreich/Sehreich*',[85] '*regnum coelorum/regnum mundanum*',[86] '*regnum dei/regnum humanum*',[87] etc. It is clear that Luther does not think of these two regiments as two magnitudes excluding each other or competing with each other for rule, but as two overlapping aspects of the one *Regnum Dei invisibile*.[88] The Kingdom of God in the supreme sense, '*das hoch Regnum der Göttlichen Majestet*',[89] assumes a dual aspect within this world, and each aspect is unthinkable without, and inseparable from, the other.[90] 'There are two kinds of regiment in the world (*zweyerley regiment auff der wellt*), as there are also two kinds of people (*wie auch zweyerley leut sind*), the believing and the unbelieving. Christians yield themselves to the control of God's Word; they have no heed of civil government for their own sake. But the unchristian portion require another government, even the civil sword, since they will not be controlled by the Word of God. Yet if all were Christians and followed the Gospel, there would be no more necessity or use for the civil sword and the exercising of authority; for if there were no evil doers there certainly would be no punishment. But since it is not to be expected that all of us should be righteous, Christ has ordained magistracy for the wicked, that they may rule as they must be ruled. But the righteous He keeps for Himself, and rules them by His Word.'[91]

Both these Kingdoms are involved in our relation to God the

Creator and Redeemer. In the spiritual realm the relation to God is direct, in the secular realm it is indirect, but even the *regnum seculare* or '*weltliches Regiment* is spoken of as *Gottes Reich*, for God wills it to remain and wishes us to be obedient within it. It is the Kingdom of God's left hand', says Luther, 'where God rules through father, mother, Kaiser, king, judge, and even hangman, but His proper Kingdom, the Kingdom of His right hand, is where God rules Himself, where He is immediately present and His Gospel is preached'.[92] 'As Christians we must not place the *Datum* of our life here on earth, but know that He will come from heaven, and so we are to be ready to expect His coming every hour. Therefore we are only half and with the left hand, within the life of this world, for with their right hand and their whole heart they live in expectation of the hour of His Coming.'[93] When, therefore, Luther speaks of one Kingdom as 'spiritual' in contrast to the other, which is 'corporal', it does not mean that one has to do with pure spirit and has nothing to do with our physical life on earth. 'Spiritual' distinguishes this Kingdom of Christ or of faith in two main respects: (*a*) It is spiritual in that its *end* is different, for its end reaches beyond the earthly life as we know it into a new existence beyond death and sin and all corruption. The spiritual Kingdom is thus essentially an eschatological expression for the fact that in God's redeeming purpose this present evil world is to be renewed through the Spirit – it is with that *causa finalis* that the spiritual Kingdom is supremely concerned.[94] In contrast the worldly or secular kingdom is concerned with earthly matters only and with earthly peace. (*b*) It is spiritual in that a different means is employed for its operation in the world: the Word and Spirit of God or the sword of the Spirit, as against the sword of steel which is employed by the *Obrigkeit*.[95] This division is also an essentially eschatological expression, for it means that in His mercy God wills that His power shall operate through preaching of the Gospel, and that the Omnipotent Judgment of God is suspended until the Last Day.[96]

THE KINGDOM OF CHRIST

To these two differences in end and method between the *geistliches Regiment* and the *weltliches Regiment* there correspond two other

159

distinctions which Luther constantly makes: (*a*) The spiritual Kingdom is distinguished as the *new Kingdom*, as we have already seen. That is well expressed in the Preface to the Book of Ezekiel. 'The old, worldly, temporal regiment remains in all the world, and does not at all prevent the establishment of the new, spiritual, everlasting rule and Kingdom of Christ under it and within it, though this Kingdom has its own peculiar nature. Especially is this the case where there are righteous kings and princes, who tolerate this new, everlasting Kingdom of Christ under their old government, or accept it themselves, promote it, and desire, as Christians, to be in it. Otherwise the greater part of the kings, princes and lords hate the new covenant and kingdom of Christ as poisonously and bitterly as the Jews at Jerusalem, and persecute it and would wipe it out, and like the Jews, they go to destruction because of it. That is what happened to Rome, and will happen to others also, for it is promised that Christ's new Kingdom shall be an everlasting Kingdom, and the old Kingdom must perish in the end. It is well to remember, too, that since God Himself calls this Kingdom a new Kingdom, it must be a far more glorious Kingdom than the old Kingdom was or is, and that it was God's will to make it a far better Kingdom than the old one; and even though it had no other glory, this alone would be enough to make it glorious beyond measure – that is to be an everlasting Kingdom that will not come to an end like the human kingdom.'[97]

(*b*) This very Kingdom of Christ, however, just because it has moved into history, and operates under and in this old world reaching out in its *causa finalis* beyond, must itself be considered as two-fold. '*Regnum Christi est duplex*. On the one hand, it is the Kingdom which Christ has from eternity with the Father and the Holy Spirit which He will never lay down. On the other hand, it is the Kingdom which He now has, which is the Kingdom of remitting sins and governing His Church. This Kingdom Christ will lay down at the Last Judgment, for no more will there be sin or death or any calamity or misery.'[98] Another way Luther had of speaking of that was to distinguish between the *Regnum gratiae* (or *Regnum fidei*) and the *Regnum gloriae*. 'The *Regnum gratiae* is the *Regnum fidei* in which Christ reigns as Man, set over all things by God the Father. The *Regnum gloriae* is the Kingdom in which God Himself through Himself (*Deus ipse per se*) will reign no longer through humanity in faith. *Non quod aliud et alius sit Regnum, sed aliter et aliter. Nunc in fide et aenigmate per humanitatem Christi, tunc in specie et revelatione divinae naturae.*'[99] This was a theme on which Luther was fond of preaching in connexion with 1 Corinthians 15:24. Thus in 1532 he declared: 'All Scripture shows that this worldly life will cease, the nasty devil with his regiment, and all worldly regiment and all spiritual *Aemter*, for that life is ordered very differently from this. "He will hand over the Kingdom to God the Father" refers then to the Kingdom of faith. Christ now rules through the Word, in faith. Christ and God are already reigning, for there is only one Kingdom of Christ and God. The difference is this, that now it is a Kingdom that is made secret and invisible (*heimlich und nicht sichtbar*), hidden, covered, veiled and grasped in faith and Word. That is how Christ rules now.'[100] Luther goes on to say that because the Kingdom now operates in this way through the Word, 'we see nothing but the Gospel, the Sacrament, Baptism, and that we ought to honour our parents',[101] but when we see God in His majesty without Word and Faith, that will mean that 'the eternal Kingdom of Light will bring the Kingdom of faith to an end. *Das Weltreich will er zerstören, und das Reich Christi wird aufhören.*'[102] In the following year Luther preached again from the same text. 1 Corinthians 15:24 'speaks of the Kingdom of Christ now upon earth which is a Kingdom of Faith, wherein He rules through the Word, not in a visible, public character (*Wesen*), but like the Sun which we see through a cloud, for then we see the light but the sun itself we do not see. But when the cloud is removed we see both light and sun together, *in einerlei Wesen*. And so Jesus Christ now rules along with the Father, and there is *einerlei Reich*. The only difference is that it is now dark and hidden, or veiled and covered, grasped in Faith and in the Word so that we do not see any more of it than Baptism and the Sacrament, or hear any more than the external Word: *das ist alle seine Kraft und Macht, dadurch er regieret und Alles ausrichtet ... bis so lange das Stündlein kommt*, when Christ will make an end and openly manifest Himself in His Majesty and Power ... Then it will be called the Kingdom of God.'[103]

Sometimes it looks as if Luther held that with the coming of that absolute Kingdom of God the *regnum corporale* will be completely set aside for some empyrean heaven, but that is not the case. In the sermon just cited, for example, he explains the words 'and then God will be all in all' to mean that each one will then himself have in God everything he now has, for when God manifests Himself, '*werden wir alle genug haben an Seele und Leib, und nicht mehr so mancherlei bedürfen, wie wir jetzt auf Erden müssen haben*'.[104] Both the Kingdom of Christ which is described as 'spiritual' and the Kingdom of God in glory have to do with the *whole man, body and soul,*[105] and indeed with the whole of creation.[106] Like the other Reformers Luther held that the whole of nature would be recreated in the Kingdom of God, but so long as this fallen world remains in its present state, the one invisible Kingdom of God at work in it *necessarily* wears a dual aspect in which the direct action of God's grace appears under the contrary aspect of sight and might. If we live in sin and the midst of death and hell, then it is into sin and death and hell that the Word made flesh has come, made like us in our condition that we through grace may be made like Him in glory. That is the *wonderful exchange* that lies at the heart of Luther's theology, the *theologia crucis*.[107]

The Kingdom of grace means that God's Kingdom has penetrated into the midst of our life and taken on the aspect of our life, so that its very hiddenness in the darkness of our sin is the token of its real presence and activity on earth. 'If we follow the judgment of reason, God sets forth absurd and impossible things, when He sets before us the articles of the Christian faith. Indeed it seems to reason an absurd and foolish thing that in the Lord's Supper is offered to us the Body and Blood of Christ, that Baptism is the laver of the new birth,[108] and of the renewing of the Holy Spirit, that the dead shall rise at the Last Day, that Christ the Son of God was conceived and carried in the womb of the Virgin Mary, that He was born, that He suffered the most reproachful death of the Cross, that He was raised up again, that He now sits at the right hand of the Father, and that He has power both in heaven and in earth. For this cause Paul calls the Gospel of Christ crucified the word of the Cross and the foolishness of preaching which to the Jews was offensive, and to the Gentiles foolish doctrine. Wherefore when God speaks reason judges His Word to be heresy and the word of the devil, for it seems unto it absurd and foolish.'[109] That is the way in which Luther understands the *Regnum fidei*, understands Christ as the object of faith. 'Christ is the object of faith, nay, He is not the object of faith but, as it were, in the faith itself Christ is present (*imo non objectum, sed, ut ita dicam, in ipsa fide Christus adest*). Faith therefore is a certain obscure knowledge or rather darkness which sees nothing, and yet Christ apprehended by faith sits in this darkness: as God in Sinai and in the Temple sits in the midst of darkness (Exodus 19:9; 20:21; 1 Kings 8:10, 12).'[110] '*Ut ergo fidei locus sit, opus est, ut omnia quae creduntur abscondantur. Non autem remotius abscondantur, quam sub contrario objectu, sensu, experientia.*'[111] 'For our good is hidden, and that so deeply that it is hidden under its contrary. Thus our life is hidden under death, our joy under our hatred, glory under shame, salvation under perdition, the Kingdom under exile, heaven under hell, wisdom under foolishness, righteousness under sin, strength under infirmity.'[112]

THE ESCHATOLOGICAL PERSPECTIVE

Since this is so, that the Kingdom of Christ has come to us in the midst of our wretchedness and sin and weakness, then the very measure of its hiddenness is the measure of its penetration and actual presence. But that makes it imperative that we learn how to distinguish between the Kingdom of Christ and the aspect which it wears in our corporal and earthly existence, for unless we distinguish them, we lose the Kingdom of Grace by losing its identity in our sin and shame under law and the worldly kingdom. 'In this life God does not deal with us face to face, but veiled and shadowed from us. That is, as Paul said in another place: "We see Him now through a glass darkly" (1 Corinthians 13:12). Therefore we cannot be without veils in this present life. But here wisdom is required which can distinguish the veil from God himself, and that is the wisdom the world does not have.'[113] Though the creation which has been deformed and demonised by sin comes under judgment, it belongs nonetheless to God's Kingdom, and there are not two Kingdoms of God but one. The fact, however, that God has reserved to the last day the renewal of all creation and 'has reserved the displaying of His greatness and majesty, His glory and His effulgence', so that we have but a 'narrow view' of Him,[114] means that we have to exercise faith within that action of divine *reserve*. We must not therefore confound the two realms which God deliberately keeps apart in His eschatological purpose. To confuse the two kingdoms, to join together in the present hearing and seeing, heaven and earth, word and power, *religio* and *politia, fides* and *mores, gratia* and *opera, iustitia Christiana* and *iustitia civilis*, etc., is to usurp the Kingdom of God or to force God's hand – and that is the very mark of Antichrist.[115] '*Das ist invadere regnum et majestatem Dei.*'[116] The two realms or kingdoms may be confounded either by the subordination of the spiritual kingdom to the worldly kingdom as among the Turks, or by the subordination of the worldly kingdom to the spiritual, as in the Papacy, but whether the movement comes from the one side or the other it is really the same act of the devil, for what he seeks to do in each instance is to gain the mastery by anticipating the final judgment and usurping the prerogative of God. Precisely the same attempt to force the Kingdom of God Luther saw in the *Schwärmer*. 'There are two kingdoms, one the Kingdom of God, the other the kingdom of the world. I have written this so often that I am surprised that there is anyone who does not know it or note it ... God's Kingdom is a kingdom of grace and mercy, not of wrath and punishment. In it there is only forgiveness, consideration for one another, love, service, doing of good, peace, joy, etc. But the kingdom of the world is a kingdom of wrath and severity. In it there is only punishment, repression, judgment and condemnation, for the suppressing of the wicked and the protection of the good. For this reason it has the sword, and a prince or lord is called in Scripture God's wrath, or God's rod (Isaiah 14) ... Now he who would confuse the two kingdoms – as our false fanatics would do – would put wrath into God's Kingdom and mercy into the devil's kingdom; and that is the same as putting the devil in heaven and God in hell.'[117]

On the other hand, it is the part of faith to maintain the eschatological perspective by distinguishing sharply between the two kingdoms, the *Reich der Gnade* and the *Reich der Tat*, the Kingdom of God and the kingdom of this world. In this way the Church of Christ waits in faith for God's final action and does not attempt to usurp His power by execution or to force His hand by a preliminary decision.[118] To distinguish the two kingdoms is an act of humility before the impending judgment, and that carries with it the recognition that the final judgment sets limits and boundaries to our obedience in time in respect both of the Church and of the State, the representatives of the two kingdoms on earth. Neither the Church nor the State can assume absolute power. Both are under the judgment, both will pass away in their present forms, and that final judgment relativises and restricts the authority of each.[119] Rebellion against that limitation is apparent in the welding of spiritual and worldly authority into one, the *potestas tyrannica* which Luther discerned in the action of the Papacy on the one hand and the action of the *Schwärmer* on the other.[120]

At the same time, this does not mean that the two realms are to be separated from each other, for the visible and outward realm is also under Christ and belongs to the Kingdom of God, and therefore must listen to the Word of God's Kingdom as proclaimed in the Gospel.[121] But just because Christ's Kingdom is inward (*internum Regnum*[122]) and spiritual it has no right to rule over the corporal realm or to exercise authority over it as though it were itself an external kingdom.[123] That would be to act against its own essential law and to confound the kingdoms again.[124] Though distinct the two realms are involved in each other and must not be separated; they are differentiated and yet unified under the overarching *Regnum Dei*.[125]

CHRISTIAN ORDER?

That brings us to ask an important question, and for Luther's eschatology it is perhaps the most significant. Apart from the ultimate unity between the two kingdoms which will be revealed only in the advent of Christ in glory and power and the over-all rule of the Word of God, is there no positive connection between the two kingdoms in history, no *tertium comparationis* which faith at least may discern here and now in this world?[126] In answer to that question we may turn to Luther's conception of *Christenheit* which stretches over the whole mass of the people in the world who are baptised and are Christian in name.[127] This does not mean that Luther held that there could be any Christian regiment in or over the world or over any country.[128] So that even with *Christenheit* Luther has to draw a distinction between the true believers and those who are nominally Christian,[129] and the true *Christenheit* which is free of all external things,[130] and nominal believers who must come under the external jurisdiction of the sword.[131] Far from providing any real *tertium comparationis*, the notion of *Christenheit* tends to move in the direction of an *ecclesiola*, that is, of an inner community of believers within the larger mass which Luther always thought of as unchristian.[132] The notion of *Christenheit* does carry with it, however, the idea that the Kingdom of God is actually present within this world, within history, as well as future. '*Idem Christi regnum hic et in futuro: hic per fidem incoatum, in futuro consummandum per gloriam.*'[133]

To answer the question as to a *tertium comparationis* we have to inquire whether the *geistliches Regiment* ever assumes order and concrete form within the world of here and now. It is not often that Luther uses the term '*ordo*'.[134] No doubt the two regiments do acquire some kind of *ordo* in history, and so far as they do, that is in the nature of the case only observable empirically, but an empirical *ordo* cannot be the object of faith, cannot in the nature of the case belong to the *Regnum fidei*, so that such *ordo* as is acquired in history comes under the judgment of the last day. The real nature of the two regiments, however, Luther preferred to understand in terms of a divine *ordinatio*,[135] that is, in terms of the Word of God,[136] the Word which created heaven and earth, the Word which has broken into our estranged world in Jesus Christ and clothed itself once and for all with His humanity. While therefore Luther makes a sharp distinction between the two regiments, he thinks of the mighty, active, living divine-human Word as operating behind both and it is through that Word that God's will is performed. It is the Word of God which is the third dimension between heaven and earth, between spiritual regiment and earthly regiment, and it is through that Word of God that the heavenly realm is made relevant to the earthly, and the last things are made relevant to the present, and the present things of the earth are taken in control and ordered in accordance with God's final purpose for the renewal of heaven and earth.

THE ORDERS OF CREATION

To see how Luther works out that idea we must examine his difficult doctrine of the '*larva dei*', a term which he apparently took over from mediaeval theology.[137] '*Larva*' means at once a mask or a veil and a ghostly presence. In the world which God has created all creatures and all ordinances are designed to be veils or masks of God's presence,[138] but in this life or in this world that mask or veil can never be removed so that we may see God face to face.[139] The Creator is concealed behind the creature as his *larva* or his *persona*.[140] '*Universa creatura eius larva.*'[141] But this world is estranged from God and the powers of evil have entered to extend their kingdom in it, so that while the whole realm of creation (*universa creatura* or *tota creatura*)[142] is to be regarded as *larva*, and to be nothing in itself but only what it is with respect to the Word of God,[143] yet it may be turned into its opposite by corruption and may even be spoken of as devilish. In this way Luther can speak of *weltliches Regiment* and even of the Law as devilish.[144] As a matter of fact sin has entered creation and therefore all the *larvae* are involved in this demonic perversion and cannot be used directly without correction and judgment, i.e. without the realisation that at the final judgment as they are now, perverted and twisted masks, they will be done away with. Meanwhile, however, the *larva dei* veils the presence of God, not just because it is creaturely but because it is impregnated with evil. Estrangement and perversion therefore turn the *larva dei* into a ghostly presence,[145] so that now *larva* becomes, so to speak, a haunted mask, and it is only an angry God who can be known behind it and only God's strange work which can be encountered through it apart from the Gospel.[146]

This concept Luther also applies to official persons ('for *persona* is properly speaking only "face" or "countenance" or "*larva*", and is that quality or quantity by which a man may be considered from without'),[147] offices and authorities, capacities and institutions, for God uses them as His 'instruments' of action and communication – though there is a difference here between the way He uses them in religion and in the worldly realm.[148] 'So the prince, the magistrate, the teacher, the schoolmaster, the scholar, the father, the mother, the children, the master, the servant, the maid, are *personae, larvae* which *religiose* God will have us to acknowledge, love, reverence as His creatures.[149] We must have them in this life, but He does not wish divinity to be ascribed to them.' We must not so reverence them that we forget Him. In order that we may not magnify the *personae*, or put any trust in them, God leaves in them offences and sins, yes, great foul sins, to teach us what a difference there is between the *persona* and God Himself.[150] Everything depends then on the way these *larvae* and *personae* are used. '*Personae, larvae debent esse, Deus dedit eas, sed non debeo accipere, respicere. Es ligt in usu rerum.*'[151] It belongs therefore to theology to draw the proper distinction between the *larva* or *persona* as a God-given *creatura*, and then to pass behind it to God Himself. Thus when we hear the word in St Paul we adore it as Christ Himself speaking; it is not that we adore St Paul. But this is only possible through the Spirit. It does not belong to political man, naturally grounded. 'Only a spiritual person distinguishes acutely the appearance from the Word, the divine *larva* from God Himself and God's work. Hence our science, to distinguish divinity from *larva. Hoc non facit mundus.*'[152] This is of prime significance for the whole realm of the Church and the two kingdoms on earth, for it means that we must not be 'respecters of persons' – that is, must not render to the *persona* an importance in himself which he does not have but exercises only as a servant of God, to whom it is his duty to point.[153] That is particularly the case in religion and with respect to the Word of God. 'But out of religion, and in matters of *politia*, we must have regard to the *persona*: for otherwise there will necessarily be confusion and an end of all respect and order. In this world God will have order, a reverence and a difference of *personae*. For else the child, the scholar, the servant, the subject would say: I am a Christian as well as my father, my schoolmaster, my master, my prince. Why then should I reverence him? Before God, then, there is no respect of persons, neither Greek nor Jew, but all are one in Christ – although not so before the world.'[154]

Luther attacks both the Papacy and the *Schwärmer* on the ground that they fail to make the proper theological distinction between the *larva* or *persona* and *divinitas*. 'Scripture is full of examples to warn us not to put our trust in the person and not to think that when we have the person we have all things, as it is in the

Papacy where they judge all things according to the outward *larva*, and therefore the whole Papacy is nothing else but a mere respecting of persons. God has given us His creatures for our use and to do us service, and not as idols that we should do service to them. Let us then use bread, wine, apparel, possessions, gold, silver, and all other creatures. But let us not trust or glory in them; for we must trust and glory in God alone. He only is to be loved. He only is to be feared and honoured.'[155] 'We could be content to suffer the dominion of the Pope, but because he abuses the same so tyrannously against us, and would compel us to deny and blaspheme God, acknowledging the Pope only as our lord and master, clogging our consciences and spoiling us of fear and trust which we should have in God, therefore we are compelled by the commandment of God to resist the Pope: for it is written: "We must rather obey God than men" (Acts 5:29). Therefore without offence of conscience, which is our singular comfort, we contemn the authority of the Pope. Müntzer and other mad heads desired the destruction of the Pope, but they sought to accomplish this with arms, not with the Word; and so they withstood him for the sake of his person, and not for God's sake. We for our part would gladly show favour to Behemoth and his scales, with all the persons and dignities which they have, if they would but leave us Christ. But because we cannot obtain this of them, we contemn their persons and say boldly with Paul: "God respects no man's person." '[156]

THE CHRISTIAN PERSONA

These passages, mostly from the great *Commentary on Galatians*, show us how extremely important this idea was for Luther, for it is nothing else than the fundamental distinction between the two kingdoms and indicates clearly why that distinction is to be made. But Luther was not content to leave the distinction in this dialectical contrariety, and it is at this point that we see how deep is the significance of the conception of *larva vel persona*. And here once again he has in mind the significance both of *larva* and of *persona* on the stage, where an actor assumes a rôle and a public face which he does not have privately, so that he can be spoken of

169

as having '*two persons*'.[157] That is particularly true of the Christian who has become a new man in Christ. Thus, for example, he is at once a member of the *geistliches Regiment* and yet also participates in the *weltliches Regiment*.[158] In the *geistliches Regiment* he may also be a preacher[159]; and even as an individual Christian is 'a person for himself who believes for himself and for no one else',[160] and yet we must speak of him 'not as one Christian but *in relatione* as bound in this life to another person'.[161] The fundamental distinction here is between the person which a man is *coram Deo* and the person he necessarily is *coram mundo*, for he lives in the world and uses the Kaiser's world and goods as well as any heathen.[162]

The supremely important fact here, however, is Christological, for the Eternal Son of God, the second Person of the Trinity, came down and wore our humanity and suffered under Pontius Pilate. He did that 'not for His own *Person* but for our person'.[163] 'Thus making a happy exchange with us, He took upon Him our sinful *person*, and gave unto us His innocent and victorious *person*, with which we are now clothed and are freed from the curse of the law. For Christ was willingly made a curse for us, saying: As touching my own *person* both as human and divine (*pro mea persona humanitatis et divinitatis*) I am blessed and need nothing. But I will humble myself (*exinanibo*) and put upon me your *larva*,[164] that is to say, your human nature, and I will walk in it among you, and will suffer death and deliver you from death. Thus when bearing the sin of the whole world in our *larva* He was taken, suffered, was crucified and put to death, and became a curse for us. But because He was a divine Person and eternal, it was impossible that death should hold Him. Wherefore He rose again the third day from death, and now lives for evermore. And there is neither sin nor death in Him any more (*nec amplius invenitur peccatum, mors et larva nostra*) but mere righteousness, life and everlasting blessedness.'[165] Through faith, that is, reason enlightened by faith (*ratione illuminata fide*), we lay hold of this victory of Christ and enjoy it.[166] 'If you believe sin and death to be abolished they are abolished. For Christ has overcome and taken away these in Himself, and will have us to believe that as in His own person there is now no *larva peccatoris, nullum vestigium mortis*, so there is none with us since He has accomplished and performed all things for us

... Therefore the victory of Christ is most certain, and there is no
defect in the thing but in our incredulity: for to reason it is a hard
matter to believe these inestimable good things.'[167] 'If we look
upon our own person or the person of our brother, we see that it is
not holy, but Christ has sanctified and cleansed His Church.'[168] 'If
therefore in the matter of justification you separate the Person of
Christ from your person, then you are in the law, you remain in it,
and live in it yourself and not in Christ, and so you are condemned
by the law and are dead before God.'[169] 'By faith, however, you are
so entirely and closely joined to Christ that He and you are made,
as it were, one person.'[170] 'By the inseparable union and
conjunction Christ and I are made as it were one body in Spirit.'[171]

The Christian then is two persons because of union with Christ.
'He uses the world and all creatures so that outwardly there is no
difference between him and the infidel. "In outward appearance
they are like", as Paul says also of Christ: "In outward appearance
he was found as a man" (Philemon 2:7). Yet, notwithstanding
there is a great difference.'[172] In so far as the Christian is one
person with Christ he is hid with Christ in God and his union with
Christ is '*in medio tenebrarum*',[173] but in so far as he still lives *in
mundo* he presents to the eyes of the world a person that is to all
appearances sinful. But faith discerns that that person is *larva*, and
behind it faith discerns the new man in Christ. At the very heart of
this teaching is the fact that the eternal Son or Word of God was
found as a man wearing our *persona* and *larva* in order that we
might be translated into the Kingdom of Christ. It is an operation
of the *Verbum Dei*.[174]

VERBUM DEI

Fundamentally the Word of God is Christ Himself,[175] but Christ's
Word, Christ Himself, comes to us through the Holy Scriptures as
the Word of God. Here our human words are used as *instrumenta*
or *larvae* by means of which the mighty living Word of God
communicates Himself to us and acts upon us.[176] In the passages
from the *Commentary on Galatians* cited above we say that Luther
regarded the Apostles, Paul for example, as *larva* or *persona*
through which *Christus loquens* comes to us speaking through the

mouth of the Apostle.[177] A proper theology distinguishes between the person of the Apostle and Christ Himself. So in the Scriptures the *Verbum Dei* comes to us using creatures as His *larvae*, but here we must think of *larva* in a different sense from the general sense in which all creation is *larva* haunted by the presence of a strange God, or in which we have to deal very indirectly with a distant God. 'God is indeed to be left to remain in His own nature and majesty, for in this respect we have nothing to do with Him, nor does He wish us to have, in this respect, anything to do with Him: but we have to do with Him as far as He is clothed in and delivered to us by His Word, for in that He presents Himself to us.'[178] Here the *larva* is filled with the gracious presence of God, and so Luther speaks of it as *iucunda larva* through which God reveals Himself directly. That is His 'proper Kingdom where He rules Himself, where He is Himself, for there the Gospel is preached to the poor.'[179] And yet, because this Word is none other than Christ Himself who was crucified and resurrected for us, this is the Word which slays and makes alive, and operates law and Gospel, by crucifixion and resurrection.[180] It is through that operation of the Word that the Christian is united to Christ according to Galatians 2:20.

But that mighty Word of God, that slays and makes alive, comes not simply to the individual believer, but is injected into the whole situation, where every creature is *larva dei*, and where all the *ordinationes* are *larvae dei*.[181] When that Word comes to us in this creaturely context we can discern the presence and glory of God in nature and behind it, and so the *larvae* become not veils that conceal a terrifying ghostly presence but such veils that, while they cover the majesty of God, they serve as a means to unveil to us His will and His purpose of love in our human life. But in order to do that the Word of God must intervene as it did in Jesus Christ in mercy and judgment, in death and resurrection.[182] Under this activity of the Word Luther can speak of Preachers of the Word and Sacraments, and of the Church itself, as well as of Apostles and Holy Scriptures, as *larvae Dei*, for through their instrumentality Jesus Christ is preached and delivered over to men and His Kingdom is established.[183]

Luther was particularly concerned to apply this teaching to the whole secular life and regiment of man. He gives a sustained discussion of this in his exposition of the 82nd Psalm: 'God stands among the congregation and is judge among the gods', etc.[184] In accordance with his teaching elsewhere,[185] he speaks of 'the whole temporal estate as an ordinance of God which everyone ought to obey and honour'.[186] Within this temporal estate the ruler is God's minister, for God as Creator, preserving His own creatures, works and ordinances, has instituted and preserved rulership. But God Himself stands in the congregation and is the ruler of rulers and the judge of these 'gods' whom He has set over the temporal estate. That temporal estate and its whole ordinance rest ultimately upon God's creation but special communities were formed in the fallen world by a 'special Word of God'[187] – the communities of the people of Israel. But the temporal estate is 'established anew through Christ by a special Word'. For Christ says: 'Give unto Caesar what is Caesar's' (Matthew 22:21); 'Be subject to every ordinance of man' (I Peter 2:13); and 'Let every man be subject to his rulers' (Romans 13:1).[188] Luther then reminds us that the 82nd Psalm says nothing good about the rulers or gods and their virtues. God stands in their midst and judges them. He rebukes them. It is His will that they should be subject to His Word and either listen to it or suffer all misfortune. It is enough that they have to rule over all else, but over God's Word they have no control. For God's Word appoints them and makes them gods and subjects everything to them. 'Therefore they are not to despise it, for it is their instituter and appointer; but they are to be subject to it, and allow themselves to be judged, rebuked, made, and mastered by it.'[189] How does that take place? Through the preaching of the Gospel in the midst of the congregation, for it is there that God stands: in the midst of the congregation, and He judges through the preaching of His Word. God stands behind the congregation over against the rulers, for the congregation is His ordinance; but God stands behind the rulers over against the congregation, for they are His ordinance as well. And in the midst of both is the mighty Word of God. 'He who does not heed and keep the Word of God, sets God Himself at naught. He who would honour and have God, must have Him in and through His Word,otherwise it is impossible to get Him, have Him or know Him.'

On the other hand, 'the Word of God hallows and makes divine everything to which it is applied. Therefore those estates that are appointed by God's Word are all holy, divine estates, even though the persons in them are not. Thus father, mother, son, daughter, master, mistress, servant, maid, preacher, pastor, etc., all these are holy and divine positions in life even though the persons in these positions may be knaves and rascals. So, because He here founds and orders the office of rulership, the rulers are called "gods" and "children of God", for the sake of the divine office and the divine Word and yet they are wicked knaves, as He here calls them.'[190]

Because they are wicked 'God will depose them and take away their godhead so that they die and go to destruction not as "gods" or "children of God" but as men, so that both in life and death they may be like men who are without God's Word, and are lost. For God's Word makes a distinction among the children of Adam. Those who have God's Word are not merely men, but holy men, God's children, Christians, etc.; but those who are without God's Word are merely men, that is, in sin and eternally imprisoned in death, under the power of the devil and are altogether without God . . . A Prince who is without God and His Word is also assuredly lost, and when he falls and passes away, he loses his godhead, that is God's appointment, and passes away as tyrants are wont to pass.'[191]

'The Psalmist therefore prays for another government and kingdom in which things will be better, where God's name will be honoured, His Word kept, and He Himself will be served: that is the Kingdom of Christ. Therefore he says: "O God, come and be the Judge upon earth. Be Thyself King and Lord. The gods have a lost cause. For to thee belongs the kingdom among all the heathen in the whole world, as is promised in the Scriptures." This is the Kingdom of Christ: this is the true God who has come and is judging: that is to say, He is Lord in all the world, for no empire has spread so far among the heathen as has the Kingdom of Christ . . . Arise O God and judge the earth . . . For the righteousness of this world has an end, but the righteousness of Christ and those who are within His Kingdom abide for ever.'[192]

Such preaching of the Word of God was certainly mighty. Whenever that Word is injected into the Church and State, the representatives of the *geistliches Regiment* and of the *weltliches Regiment*, there is inevitably tumult and upheaval, for, as we have seen, the Word challenges their disobedience to the divine *ordinatio* and calls in question their compromised and hardened institutional patterns. The Word of God does not destroy the *ordinationes* but it comes to reshape them in obedience to the Word and Will of God.[193] This is the point where we can see most clearly both the greatness and the weakness of Luther. In contrast to Erasmus, who was afraid of tumult, Luther insisted that the Kingdom of God is only taken by violence and determined action, and yet when Ulrich von Hutten wanted to unsheath the sword for the sake of the Reformation, Luther wrote powerfully against it.[194] 'By the Word the world was conquered, by the Word the Church has been preserved, and by the Word also she shall be restored. Antichrist, as he began with violence, will be crushed without violence, by the Word.'[195] But if the Word inevitably creates tumult, even when it comes not to destroy the ordinances of the world but to restore them, how can you avoid violence? That was the problem which Luther never succeeded in facing properly; in the last resort he appears to have been afraid of the consequences of the mighty Word of God.

Perhaps the most significant of his smaller writings in this respect is the *Second Wittenberg Sermon*, in which he says: 'We should give free course to the Word and not add our works to it. We have the *jus verbi*, but not the *executio*. We should preach the Word, but the consequences must be left to God's own good pleasure.'[196] In the actual situation foretold by the Zwickau prophets to which this particular Word was preached Luther achieved a remarkable result, and yet the failure to go beyond the Word had a great deal to do with more extreme action by the *Schwärmer* later. What is at stake here? Luther sees quite clearly that the Word exercises in our human situation a critical, eschatological action in anticipation of the final judgment, for the final judgment of the Word of God is suspended until the last day. It is the duty of the Church therefore simply 'to let the Word work alone, without our work',[197] to work in its own time, but for Luther that actually means that before the last judgment the Word uses the *weltliches Regiment*, which is entrusted by God with the power of the sword to enact a temporary judgment, but only such a temporary judgment as to preserve the *status quo* and make room for the free course of the Word of God. In this way, as we have seen from Luther's *Exposition of the 82nd Psalm*, the Word addresses itself critically to all the *larvae Dei*, to every ordinance and aspect of human life in this world, calling them in question and refashioning them in accordance with their own true end and authority, and it is through them alone and their co-operation with the Word that the Word becomes action in the world. In the last resort Luther appears to resign the *executio verbi* to the secular power, for in so far as anything is *larva* it belongs to the *weltliches Regiment* and comes under its authority. And yet the difficulty Luther found here, as expressed in the *Exposition of the 82nd Psalm*, is that 'the princes and lords, who ought to be advancing God's Word, do the most to suppress, forbid and persecute it'.[198] Quite clearly Luther did not give sufficient attention to the corporeal embodiment of the Word here and now within the world, an embodiment which already spans the distinction between the two kingdoms as a *tertium datur*.

THE KINGDOM OF FAITH

Corresponding to that view of the Word is Luther's view of faith. Faith is the dimension of Christian existence over against the Word, an existence on the frontiers of the two kingdoms where the Word bears down upon this world and calls man into such obedience to it that he finds the real substance of his life in the Word, not in himself but in the Kingdom of God. 'Therefore faith in Christ is the most arduous of all things, for it is a *translatio et raptus* from all things of sense, within and without, into those things beyond sense within and without, into the invisible, the most high and incomprehensible God.'[199] The believer therefore lives and moves between two realms. He is involved by the Word in a world which is hid with Christ in God[200] and yet he is involved in this visible and tangible fallen world where God has placed and called him. The Christian, in fact, as we have seen, is divided between two times, and the two times are spoken of as the time of heaven and the time of earth, or the time of grace which is eternal and the time of the law which is not perpetual but which has an end.[201] Faith is an existence therefore in which man hangs between heaven and earth, without any earthly security, but in sheer trust in God alone.[202] Because Christian existence is found at a point where two times meet or two worlds meet, Luther can even speak of faith as a *punctus mathematicus*,[203] on the analogy, however, of the relation of God and Man in Christ.[204] Faith is always encounter, always the tangential point where the divine bears upon the human, grace upon nature. Faith is the point where the invisible and the visible meet, where the invisible reality is given to us '*sub contrario objectu sensu, experientia*', as he says in the *De Servo Arbitrio*.[205]

There is no doubt that the tendency of Luther is to think of the encounter of faith as a timeless event within time, like the notion of continuous crisis and critical decision with which we are familiar in modern theology, but in spite of that the Christological analogy is all-important in Luther's thought. It is Christ Himself, the Word made flesh, who bears upon us and encounters us in this way, so that the 'mathematical point' is really Christ Himself, into union with whom believers enter by faith and sacramental incorporation. That does not only mean that in and through faith the Christian is formed anew in Christ and refashioned according to His image so that his true form is the form of Christ,[206] but, as we have seen, that Christ Himself sits in faith, so that faith encompasses Christ.[207] 'Christ is formed in us for the life of the Christian is not of himself but of Christ living in him – although that does not mean that Christ is formed in any one *personaliter*.'[208]

The Christological analogy means that faith has two aspects to it. On the one side it is union with Christ, the invisible Head of the Church, so that faith is a translation into the invisible realm of the risen and ascended Christ. But on the other hand, just as Christ was found as a man and came down to our earthly life, so faith is involved in a physical context. As there is no disembodied Word, so there is no disembodied faith. To have faith, then, means on the one side to be involved in the spiritual Kingdom of Christ which cannot be felt or grasped by the finger, any more than the forgiveness of sins can be grasped in my fingers – it has to be believed.[209] But nevertheless this takes place only in a bodily context – that is the sphere of the external Word and Sacraments. Even here it is a spiritual event, but it is not apart from seeing, hearing, speaking, grasping, eating, drinking, etc.[210]

177

In the *Commentary on Galatians* Luther works out this Christological analogy very fully in the relation between faith and works, in terms of a *'tertium datur'*, a *'fides operans'* which is a new *thing*, a *new doing*, unknown to the philosophers or to reason.[211] It must be understood therefore in quite a different way: on the analogy of the Incarnation of the Word.[212] Luther makes a distinction then between a *'fides abstracta vel fides absoluta'*, on the one hand, and a *'fides concreta, composita seu incarnata'*, on the other.[213] When the Scriptures speak of justification or imputation they are speaking of faith as abstract or absolute, but when they speak of rewards or works they speak of faith as composed, concrete and incarnate. In the same way the Scriptures speak of Christ. When they speak of His whole Person as God and Man they speak of Christ *compound and incarnate* (*composita et incarnata*, that is, of the divine nature united in one person to the human nature). When they speak of the two natures apart they speak *absolutely*. On this analogy then, in terms of this *new theological grammar*,[214] we must speak of faith first as naked, simple and abstract like the divinity spread throughout the humanity of Christ. Like His divinity, faith is the *'divinitas operum'*, the divinity which is diffused throughout the works, and so faith is the supreme agent (*est Fac totum, ut ita loquar*).[215] 'Faith is universally the divinity in work, person, members, as the one and only cause of justification, which nevertheless is attributed to the matter because of the form, that is to the work because of the faith.[216] Eternal and infinite power is given unto the man, Christ, not because of His humanity, but because of His divinity. For the divinity alone created all things, without any help of His humanity; nor did the humanity conquer sin and death, but the hook under the worm, whereon the devil did fasten, conquered and devoured the devil, which sought to devour the worm. Therefore the humanity alone would have effected nothing, but the divinity, joined with the humanity because of the divinity. So here faith alone justifies and does all things: and yet notwithstanding the same is attributed to works but because of faith.'[217]

On this ground we may speak of faith in its other aspect as concrete, composed, and incarnate, as 'faith that incorporates the doing and gives it its form (*ut fides incorporet et informet "facere"*)

... First ought reason to be enlightened by faith before it works, but when a true opinion and knowledge of God is held as right reason, then the work is incarnated and incorporated into it, so that whatsoever is attributed to faith is afterwards attributed to works also, but on the ground of faith alone.'[218]

THE NEW MAN

This is a highly significant account of faith, for it shows that Christologically Luther passes beyond a merely dialectical relation and thinks of faith as involving a *new operation*; but just because it is new, it is not discerned by the natural reason, so the dialectical relation between believing and seeing remains.[219] Behind this lies also Luther's doctrine of the *new man* in Christ, that is, of regeneration, spiritual resurrection, or the new creation. In his *Third Disputation against the Antinomians* of 1538 Luther spoke of it in this way. 'In Christ who is arisen there is certainly no sin, no death, no law, to which He was subjected so long as He lived. But the very same Christ is not yet fully resurrected in His believers; rather has He only begun in them as a first-fruit, to be resurrected from the dead.'[220] 'So far as Christ is risen in us, we are without law, sin and death. But so far as He is not arisen in us, we are under law, sin and death.'[221] Those were some of the theses Luther set himself to defend and maintain, but in the discussion that followed he expanded them as follows: 'A Christian is a person who is buried with Christ in His death, he has died to sin, the law and death, and every other such tyrant. But we do not see that, for it is hidden from the world; it does not appear, does not strike us in the eye (1 Peter 3:4 and John 3:8 are then cited). For the Christian is not in this world. He does not live, he is dead. He stands in another life, the heavenly, which is far beyond that which we have here. And yet what troubles and work and what plagues we shall have to experience before we reach there ... But the Christian lives here as there through God's imputation, righteous and holy under the wings which like a hen He spreads over us. And yet, so far as the Christian is a fighter and is engaged on military service, he is still under the law here and under sin, for he is still in this life. Daily he feels and experiences the struggle with his flesh

179

and lives only too close to it (Romans 7:23, 25) ... A man who believes in Christ is through divine imputation righteous and holy; he already lives in heaven for he is surrounded with the heaven of mercy. But here while we are embraced in the Father's arms, clothed with the best robe, our feet stick our from below the mantle, and Satan tries to bite them if he can. Then the child whimpers and cries and feels that it still has flesh and blood, and the devil is still there ... Thus we are holy and free in the Spirit, not in the flesh ... For the feet have still to be washed, for they are unclean and so Satan bites and attacks them until they are clean. You must pull your feet under your cloak else you will have no peace.'[222]

Two particular points must be emphasised in this connexion:

(*a*) Luther distinctly thinks of the resurrection of the body as in some real sense begun in the believer. 'This is done by the Holy Spirit who sanctifies and awakens even the body to this new life, until it is completed in the life beyond.'[223] It was in line with this that Luther expounded the meaning of the 'spiritual body' of the resurrection. *Spiritual* does not mean *of spirit* simply, but that the body, the same body which we have now, will be controlled by the Spirit, potentiated by it and clothed with light.[224] Commenting on John 3:3: 'Except a man be born again he cannot see the Kingdom of God', and John 3:6: 'That which is born of the flesh is flesh', Luther says: 'But that flesh and blood that is baptised in Christ is no more flesh and blood (for it is born anew of the Spirit) even although it was flesh and blood. Naturally it is flesh and blood, but spiritually it is not, because through Christ it is become clean in baptism and is taken into the Kingdom of God. Therefore it cannot be called mere flesh and blood any more, externally according to the body. For properly speaking flesh and blood mean *der alte Mensch nach seiner Vernunfft* ... Because flesh and blood cannot enter into the Kingdom of God it must cease, die and pass away and rise in a new spiritual being in order to reach heaven. Therefore He warns them as Christians that they must become new men, so that on that day they may not be found as flesh and blood.'[225]

This renewal of flesh and blood, the renewal of the whole man in the unity of body and soul, has already been begun. 'Let us learn to understand and distinguish these words properly, "natural" and "spiritual" according to the Scriptures – not as though the body is to be separated from the soul, but that the body must become spirit or live spiritually, as we have already begun to do through Baptism: so that we live spiritually in the soul, while God looks upon the body and reckons it to be spiritual, although it must take its departure from this temporal life and be fully renewed and be wholly spiritual living only by and through the Spirit. Jesus Christ our Lord is the second Adam, resurrected to a spiritual life, so that He no longer suffers from bodily wants, as He did when He was on earth, but He has a proper and true body with flesh and blood, as He showed to His disciples. He it is who has in His own person established the heavenly, spiritual life in order that He might first begin it in us and complete it altogether on that day.'[226] '*Non solum habebimus in futurum sed etiam iam habemus, sed in fide.*'[227] That follows from the fact that we are joined to Christ as members of His Body, for 'the whole body hangs together'. 'Because Christ has begun our resurrection more than half has already taken place.'[228] That teaching comes out with particular force in the doctrine of Baptism.[229] The Sacrament was not to be thought of as '*momentaneum negotium*' but as '*perpetuum*', whose reality (*res*) reaches out already to the future life.[230] 'It is nothing else than the killing of the old man in us and the resurrection of the new man, both of which will continue in us all our life long. Hence a Christian life is nothing else but a daily Baptism once begun and daily continued . . . Therefore everyone should regard Baptism as a garment for daily use.'[231] 'We begin then to leave behind this corporal life, so that there is already a *realis et corporalis transitus* from this world to the Father.'[232] As the outward man perishes the inward man is renewed, but the very renewal of the inward man already spells judgment to the outward man in effective anticipation of the final judgment when we shall be made over again completely.[233] 'Spiritual birth takes its rise in Baptism, proceeds and increases, but only in the last day is its significance fulfilled. Only in death are we rightly lifted out of Baptism by the angels into eternal life.'[234]

(*b*) Between Baptismal resurrection and death or the resurrection of the body at the last day Luther thinks of the Christian's life in terms of progress and advance, 'so that he can meet the coming Saviour'.[235] Here we see that for Luther faith is not simply pure encounter *vis-à-vis* the Word of God but in relation to the Incarnate word it has permanence in time, reaching out through time towards future fulfilment in the resurrection. That dynamic view is applied to the whole Kingdom, for '*das Reich Christi stehet im Werden, nicht Geschehen*'.[236] The believer must not imagine that he is perfect, but like St Paul must forget the things that are behind and reach out towards the things that are ahead, counting not that he has apprehended. Thus '*Christianus non est in facto, sed in fieri ... Summa, proficiendum est, non standum et secure stertendum. Homo noster vetus debet de die in diem* (*ut Paulus*) *renovari*' (2 Corinthians 4:16).[237] Thus 'sanctification once begun daily increases, for the Holy Spirit is continually at work in us, by means of the Word of God, and daily bestowing forgiveness on us, till we reach that life where there is no more forgiveness, all persons there being pure and holy, full of piety and righteousness, delivered and free from sin, death, and all misfortune, in a new immortal and transfigured body.'[238] 'Thus we constantly grow in sanctification and ever do become more and more "a new creature" in Christ. The Word is *Crescite* (2 Peter 3:18) and *Abundetis magis* (1 Thessalonians 4:1).'[239]

Both of these two points Luther regards in a corporate way, though this emphasis is not so strong. The resurrection of the new man is to be understood as part of the resurrection of the whole body already begun in Christ, in which the individual's resurrection is already implicated; and so the progress or daily renewal of the believer is thought of as operating through the sacramental ministry of the Church as the Body of Christ, which as a whole daily grows in cleansing and sanctification.[240] 'Our Lord Jesus Christ has begun the resurrection in His own body, but that resurrection is not yet complete for we must also rise again. Just as His suffering and death are not complete, so that we follow on and suffer and die with Him as members of whom He is the Head. As St Paul says, he makes compensation in his flesh for what is yet wanting in the affliction in Christ (Colossians 1:24). Similarly His resurrection is not yet complete, for we follow on and rise from the dead. He is our Head, and we are the members of His Body.'[241]

THE CHURCH

This brings us to the point where we must examine Luther's doctrine of the Church, but we may say now that Luther's doctrines of imputation, regeneration and Baptism point to the new life in Christ as an enduring new creation in and under our existence in the two kingdoms. That helps to underpin his sharp distinction between the spiritual and the corporal, between grace and nature, but those distinctions are still maintained in their sharpness. That is apparent, for example, even in the doctrine of Baptism, which means mainly Baptism into the death of Christ, burial in the grave of Christ, so that the new creation remains wholly concealed until the advent of Christ.[242] There is a distinct failure at crucial points to give the doctrine of the resurrection its full significance and weight. Thus even when speaking of the resurrection, he tends to interpret it dialectically as crucifixion, as a death to death, and therefore as life. 'Against my death which binds me, I have another death, that is to say, life which quickens me in Christ: and this death looses and frees me from the bonds of my death, and with the same bonds binds my death. So death which bound me is now fast bound, which kills me is now killed itself by death – that is to say, by the very life itself.'[243] 'I live for I am quickened by His death and crucifixion through which I die: that is, forasmuch as by grace and faith I am delivered from the law, sin, and death, I now live indeed. Wherefore that crucifying and that death whereby I am crucified and dead to the law, sin and death and all evils, is to be resurrection and life. For Christ crucifies the devil, He kills death, condemns sin and binds the law and I believing this, am delivered from the law, etc. The law therefore is bound, dead, and crucified unto me, and I again am bound, dead, and crucified unto it. Wherefore by this very death and crucifixion, that is to say, by this grace or liberty, I now live.'[244] And yet on the other hand this means that so long as we are in this life waiting for the manifestation of Christ, we can never leave the death of Christ behind, even though we are risen with Him. Even though we are *justus* we are still to be considered *justificandus*, as we saw earlier. So that the very fact that Luther keeps up the dialectic of death and life to the very end is an indication of the dynamic character of Christian faith; its progress is through

183

continuous death and resurrection.[245] In other words, the progress envisaged does not cease to be eschatological, for the progress itself comes under judgment, real though it is. It is progress toward the last day. '*Reformamini in novitate sensus vestri* (Romans 12:2). *Hoc pro profectu dicitur. Nam loquitur iis, quia iam incoeperunt esse Christiani. Quorum vita non est in quiescere, sed in moveri de bono in melius velut egrotus de egritudine in sanitatem, ut et Dominus ostendit in homine semivivo in curam Samaritani suscepto . . . Semper homo est in non esse, in fieri, in esse, semper in privatione, in potentia, in actu, semper in peccato, in justificatione, in justitia,* i.e. *semper peccator, semper penitens, semper iustus*'.[246] Therefore 'progress is not by sight, but always unto clearer faith, from faith to faith, always by believing more and more so that '*qui iustus est, justificetur adhuc*' (Revelations 22:11).[247]

A better word than *progress* to express this kind of eschatological advance is another word that Luther uses, *pilgrimage*. That way of expressing it is more frequently taken by Luther towards the end of his life, for example in the exposition of Genesis, where certainly the material lends itself to this interpretation, but where too more and more he is to be found using the Epistle to the Hebrews, in which the thought of the Church as the pilgrim people of God is powerfully set forth. But here is a description from a sermon of 1531 which is very clear: '*Zu solchem ewigen Leben sind wir getaufft. Dazu hat uns Christus durch sein Tod und Blut erlöset, Und dazu haben wir das Evangelium empfangen. Als bald man ein Kind aus der Taufe hebet und im das Westerhembd anzeucht, So wirds von stund an eingeweihet zum ewigen Leben, das es hinfurt die zeit seines Lebens nur ein Pilgerim und Gast sey in dieser Welt Und sich also drein schicke, das es dis zeitlich Leben gedencke zu lassen und auff jenes unvergengliche Leben imerdar hoffe und warte.*'[248] We are not baptised for this life but are by Baptism so inserted into the Kingdom of God that we live our life in this world as those who really have a new life already in Christ, hidden from this world which can only be according to the natural *Vernunfft*, and who therefore enter upon a pilgrimage towards the manifestation or appearing of our new life in body and soul at the coming of Christ.[249] We can undertake this pilgrimage toward his glorious appearing if we die daily with Him and daily rise with Him in faith and hope, if we realise that in this world we are sown like seed into the ground that we may receive our new body and new life in the harvest of the new world.[250] Because through Baptism we are already inserted into the Kingdom of God, our life in this world is such a pilgrimage that any moment of it may be the *Stündlein* when hope will yield to sight.

This is the perspective within which Luther thinks of the Church. It is essentially the Church of the baptised, but as the operative power in Baptism is the Word of God,[251] the Church as baptised is essentially correlative to that Word, and corresponds to the *Regnum fidei*, where the Word is heard and believed, and the *regnum visibile*, where through preaching and Sacraments 'the visible God', Christ the Incarnate Son, is King and Lord.[252] 'Wherever the Word of God is preached and believed, there is the Church; and where the Church is, there is the Bride of Christ.'[253]

Such a view carries with it a number of important implications:
(*a*) Because the Church is correlative to the Word of God and is 'constructed' in it,[254] the real life and essence of the Church are lodged beyond itself. '*Tota vita et substantia Ecclesiae est in verbo dei.*'[255] As such, however, grounded beyond itself in the Word, the Church is essentially an eschatological community, for 'the Word of God is that by which we receive testimony of future and invisible things.'[256] The definition of faith in the Epistle to the Hebrews: 'Faith is the substance of things hoped for, the evidence of things not seen' (Hebrews 11:1), had very great influence on Luther. It is precisely because the Church is essentially *de fide* correlative to the Word as its creation,[257] that he thought of the Church as hid with Christ in God and waiting for its manifestation in the coming of Christ.[258] Until then the Church continues to exist in history as it proclaims the Word, for it lives by its proclamation. It can even be said that the Church is *praedicatio*. But this means that the Church lives through continuous dynamic movement, through the continuous creation of the Word acting from beyond the Church and impinging on it. '*Ecclesia semper nascitur et semper mutatur in successione fidelium, alia et alia est ecclesia et tamen semper eadem.*'[259] As such the Church lives wherever God dwells, and whenever through the Word the gate of heaven is opened, as Jacob found at Bethel. As such the Church is bound to

185

no time or place and therefore to no 'carnal succession', certainly bound to no *personae*, but it is bound to the Word and the Sacraments of the Word. It is essentially the eschatological community where the Word of God sounds summoning people to a life above and beyond,[260] and where the Sacraments are the signs of the reign and activity of the invisible King.[261] '*Ut sit integra definitio Ecclesiae, quae est habitatio Dei in terra, non ut in terra maneamus: Sed ideo administrantur Sacramenta, ideo docetur verbum, ut introducamur in regnum coelorum, et per Ecclesiam ingrediamur in coelum.*'[262]

(b) The Word of God which is creative of the Church is Jesus Christ Himself, the Word that became incarnate in His historical body. Through the preaching of the Gospel that Word is now embodied in the Church, but embodied in a spiritual way – i.e. through faith – so that the Church is the *corpus vivum*.[263] This doctrine of the Church as the Body of Christ, livingly united to Him the invisible Head of the Body,[264] meant for Luther that the whole conception of the Church built up on a purely historical and physical structure is false.[265] The Church cannot exist except within the realm of physical things and events,[266] any more than it can be understood except in terms of the *regnum visibile* of the Incarnate Son and His mighty deeds of redemption, but the Church is to be understood in terms of His action through the Word upon men within this corporal realm, and therefore even this physical and visible embodiment of the Church in the world has to be understood in terms of the Spirit, i.e. *spiritually*.[267] The Church is at once a '*corpus naturale*' and a '*corpus mysticum*'.[268] At this point the Church in Luther's thought has to be thought of in terms of the *duplicia regiminia*, the *Regnum invisibile* and the *regnum visibile* of Christ discussed above.[269]

(c) As a living body correlative to Christ the Church is the '*corpus fidelium*', the body of believers.[270] In other words, the Church is to be understood in terms of actual people, the people of God, rather than as a great juridical institution.[271] This emphasis upon people believing the Word and united to Christ is most characteristic of Luther and very prominent in all his sermons. 'Where God's Word is there must be the Church; so also where Baptism and the Sacrament are, there must be God's people and vice versa.'[272] 'God's Word cannot be present without God's people, and God's people cannot be without God's Word.'[273] The Church is thus essentially a communion of persons who are of one heart in Jesus Christ,[274] for 'He has set up and founded His Church not on external power and authority or on temporal things but on inner love, and humility and unity'.[275] It is a fellowship or communion of love rather than a historical structure sacramentally impregnated with grace.[276]

FORM AND ORDER

Does this community of believers have any historical form and structure essential to its nature, and therefore in some way a manifestation here and now of what it shall be in the new world?

When Luther expounded the nature and form of the Church in opposition to the worldly and temporal institution of the Papacy he tended to stress the conception of the Church as *Christenheit*, the universal communion of believers scattered throughout the world, spiritually joined to, and correlative to, the ascended and invisible Christ;[277] but when he opposed the 'spiritualising' of the Church by the *Schwärmer* who wanted to resolve away the physical or material aspect of the Church, he insisted that the Church even as *Christenheit* comes under orderly and constitutional forms of human life.[278] Like the family (*oeconomia*) and like the State (*politia*), the Church (*ecclesia*) is one of the three hierarchies that make up our human life.[279] These are not to be regarded on the same level. Before there was any *oeconomia*, or any *politia*, says Luther, the *ecclesia* existed, and has therefore spiritual ascendancy. To that the *oeconomia* was added, so that it was the *oeconomia* that was the form which the *ecclesia* originally took in God's creation.[280] But after sin entered the world *politia* (which might well be called '*regnum peccati*') was added as a 'necessary remedy for corrupt nature'.[281] In the fallen world the Church comes to be actualised as a community of believers by submitting to these three social structures[282] – and here the *oeconomia* is of special importance as the '*seminarium non solum politiae, sed etiam Ecclesiae et regni Christi usque ad finem mundi*'.[283] Of the three hierarchies *ecclesia*, because of its other aspect as *Regnum Christi*, retains a transcendent character. It is the '*porta coeli*',[284] for through it we are called to another end beyond that of this world, and through it we enter into the eternal life of the Kingdom of God.[285] Conformity with the laws and regulations of the social structures of human life does not produce the Church as *communio sanctorum*, but it does enable it under the creative impact of the Word of God to come into being, and to take part in the on-going life of the world.

This participation in the on-going life of the world Luther speaks of in terms of *Beruf* or calling, so far as the individual believer is concerned. Through Baptism every believer is a member of a community where *coram Deo* all are equal, and each has a priestly responsibility for his neighbour or brother,[286] but in this world he has an office or a function to perform, and in it he is commanded by God to do good works. Just because he is by Baptism inserted into the Kingdom of God and given to hope for eternal life he must carry out his calling in this world in accordance with the Word of God, so that his good works issue out of his faith and are well-pleasing to God.[287] If a man does not believe that he is baptised into the victory of Christ and made an heir of eternal life, then he will not be happy or peaceful in this life or in the performance of his duties; rather will he tend to be impatient, will murmur against God, and find his daily life hard and sour; but if he does believe in his Baptism, and looks forward to the new life beyond, then he will fulfil his calling happily and joyfully in the service of God's Word and will actually find his life in this world to be sweet. Thus the hope of eternal life and our daily calling in this life belong together and must not be separated. Eschatology carried with it a joyful ethic within the social structures of this world.[288]

When we come to seek the parallel to that in the life of the corporate community of the faithful, it would appear that this is to be found in *ecclesia* considered as one of the three social structures, along with *oeconomia* and *politia*, and as bound up with them. In this sense the Church does have visible structure in history, but Luther's experience with the Papacy particularly made him feel that the Church as the creature of the Word and as the community of the faithful was constantly threatened and obstructed by historical and visible structure, especially when that laid any claim to institutional independence, for that was to give the Church a *schema mundi* and to drag it down within the world that passes away, thus wrenching it from the Kingdom of God that is neither visible nor temporal.[289] What is at stake here is the self-transcendence of the Church, which knows that its true life under the impact of the Word of God is lodged beyond the external structure of history in the risen Christ Himself. Thus against the whole tendency of the Papal Church Luther insisted that room must be created within the visible and physical world for a Church whose essential nature is determined by union with Christ. It must have freedom to live within the *regnum corporale* in a way appropriate to its inherent spiritual nature, freedom to live within the historical and corporal world and yet to transcend it and to look for its true life and true form in a new world where all that is corporal would be glorified and come under the full control of the Spirit of God.

It is in this light that we are to interpret Luther's stress upon the fact that there is a *duplex communio* in the Church – '*externa et corporalis communio*' and '*interna et spiritualis communio*'[290] – which corresponds to the two regiments we have already discussed, and the two times in which the Christian lives, as '*homo carnalis et exterior*' and '*homo spiritualis et interior*'.[291] How are these two related to each other? There is no doubt that they are thought of as overlapping each other, for the spiritual is not that which is necessarily opposed to, or beyond, the corporal, but the relation of the corporal to the Spirit of God which is mediated and determined by the Word of God. '*So fort an alle das ienige, so unser leib euserlich und leiblich thut: wenn Gotts wort dazu kompt und durch den glauben geschicht, so ists und heisst geistlich geschehen, Das nichts so leiblich, fleischlich odder eusserlich sein kan, es wird geistlich, wo es ym wort und glauben gehet, Das geistlich nicht anders ist, Denn was durch den geist und glauben ynn und durch uns geschicht, Gott gebe, das ding, da mit wir umb gehen, sey leiblich odder geistlich. Scilicet in usu non in obiecto spiritus est. Es sey sehen, hören, reden, greiffen, geberen, tragen, essen, trincken odder was es wölle.*'[292]

THE SACRAMENTAL ANALOGY

Sometimes Luther tends to speak of this in terms of the body and soul,[293] which allowed him to draw a distinction between the corporal and the spiritual in the Church without separating them.[294] A clearer and a more frequent analogy, however, is taken from the Sacraments. According to this he thinks of the communion of saints in Christ as forming an invisible and spiritual body with an external sign.[295] The internal communion is here the communion of faith, hope and love, while the Sacraments are the signs of faith, hope and love.[296] On this analogy, then, the Church is thought of as 'involved in external things' or 'in the flesh', on the one hand, and 'involved in spiritual things', on the other hand.[297] Just because the Church is involved in the flesh it can only exist in a context where there are unjust or unbelievers[298] – which carries with it a *duplex ecclesia* in another sense, the Church of true believers and of hypocrites.[299]

The application of the sacramental analogy to the doctrine of the Church throws light upon the fundamental difficulty in Luther's thought. This helps, in part, to explain why Luther insisted so strongly that the '*Hoc est corpus meum*' involves a direct identity between the elements and the Body of Christ, for that sacramental identity nailed the two communions, the corporal and the spiritual, together – even though that identity appeared to contradict the all-important distinction between the two realms or regiments. But if Luther refused to speak of a spiritual Body and a spiritual eating of the Body in the Sacrament, how could he consistently speak here of the Church as a spiritual Body or a spiritual and inner communion? On the other hand, if 'in, under and with' describe the relation of identity involved in *Hoc est corpus meum*, then we are thrown back upon a conception of the Church as utterly hidden and invisible,[300] and of the outward form of the Church as mere *larva*. This is perhaps mitigated by the notion of consubstantiation, which, as against transubstantiation, would mean that the outer form of the Church could not, in Luther's view, be consistently interpreted in terms of mere *species* or *accidents* as the Roman doctrine analogically would demand. On the one hand, then, the 'in, under and with' might be interpreted eschatologically of the nature and form of the Church which are concealed under the Sacraments, for the Sacraments are '*res sacrae non propter praesentem vitam institutae, sed ideo, ut sint praeparatio quaedam sacra rerum futurarum*'.[301] On the other hand, the element of identity involved in the sacramental relation between the spiritual and the corporal would seem to demand in the polity of the Church a form and order in which there is already manifest something of the future reality. What has Luther to say about that?

Here we have to bear in mind that for him the Sacraments are subordinate to the Word, so that whatever the Sacraments reveal of the form and order of the Church, they are to be interpreted in terms of the action of the Word of God, in terms primarily of *praedicatio* and *ordinatio*.

The whole purpose of the preaching of the Gospel is to collect us and include us 'within the unique revelation of God' given in Word and Sacrament. That is how Luther interpreted the final commands of Christ as recorded at the end of Matthew and Mark. '*Vult nos colligi in verbo et baptismo, tanquam certo et infallibili signo, quod velit nos salvare et adiuvare ... Ideoque collegit et conclusit nos intra limites verbi.*'[302] This compacting of the Church within the limits of the Word is what Luther called '*bona politia*' '*Ubi verbum dei est, ordinatio dei et deus vult bonam politiam.*'[303] It is in this sense that Luther seemed to think of the form of the Church. '*Si quaeris ubi sit Ecclesia? nusquam ea apparet At vero non ad externam formam respiciendum est, sed ad verbum, ad baptismum, et ibi quaerenda est Ecclesia, ubi Sacramenta integre administrantur, ubi sunt auditores, doctores, confessores verbi.*'[304]

Luther thought of the form of the Church, then, in two senses. '*Forma autem haec posita est primum in verbo et donis Spiritus Sancti*' (and he called that '*forma spiritualis*'[305]). '*Deinde in externa administratione seu politia pulcherrimis legibus divinitus instituta.*'[306] Of the latter Luther did not speak very much,[307] and here the contrast between the Lutheran and the Reformed Churches is marked. In the Lutheran view all forms of Church life and order on earth are *adiaphora*, and will come under judgment at the Advent of Christ as part of the *schema mundi*. The Reformed Church laid greater emphasis upon shaping the Church here and now in accordance with the divine commands, and in building up its structure on the Word. For Luther, on the other hand, Reformation meant primarily letting the Word of God act critically upon the existing order and liturgy of the Church.[308] It meant, in fact, such eschatological suspension of order and liturgy as to leave room and freedom in the present for the preaching of the Gospel and the calling out of the community of the faithful.[309] In so far as the Word of God is already the bearer of the final judgment, it interrupts the closed systems of the Church's order and liturgy and keeps them in essentially imperfect condition, in order that they may be open to continual modification, and open towards the new creation that is yet to be revealed.[310] The Church's citizenship is in heaven. It may use the forms of this passing world, but only as garments to be flung aside like Adam's leather jacket when the time for their use is past.[311] Luther's doctrine of the Church is ultimately clear, therefore, only in his negative dialectical idea, in his mighty protest against the tendency of the Roman Church to identify the forms of the Church's historical existence with the pattern of the Kingdom of God.

Luther was mostly concerned with the *forma spiritualis* which is posited in the Word and Sacraments – and here one would expect him to say something of the true and ultimate form of the Church as disclosed by Word and Sacrament, but he hesitates to do so. If the Word reveals Christ to us, does not the form of Christ thus revealed tell us anything about the essential form of the Church? Is there not even in the Word made visible in the holy Sacraments a glimpse of the future structure of the Church? But for Luther the real humanity of Christ is concealed *in* and *under* the sacramental elements, so that even there the real form of the Church lies hidden behind the *larva dei*. That is the point where Luther's tendency towards a docetic view of the risen humanity of Christ proves to be a real weakness in his doctrine of the Church, so that even when he thinks of the *forma ecclesiae* in terms of the Word and Sacraments, it is only to define the Church on earth functionally in terms of its marks or activities, rather than in terms of its essence as the risen Body of Christ within history; the mediaeval notion of *corpus mysticum* still bulks too largely in his thought, though it is combined with the mission of the Church in a new way.

THE CHURCH UNDER THE CROSS

There are, however, other lines of Luther's thought which we must gather up into this discussion, for they contribute to his full doctrine of the Church as eschatological community.

In 1541 Luther published in *Wider Hans Worst*[312] a defence of the Reformation in Germany against the accusation that instead of the ancient Catholic Church Luther had founded a new Church. The argument that Luther developed in his reply was remarkably like that advanced by Calvin earlier in his reply to Cardinal Sadoleto, and may well have been dependent on it, but the interesting thing is that here towards the end of his life Luther propounds a view of the Church not unlike Calvin's view of the Reformed Church as the restoration of the face of the ancient Catholic Church. While admitting that the Church is always *zweyerley* and will be until the end of the world,[313] Luther repudiated the notion of novelty or *neuerey* and claimed *das wir die rechte alte Kirche sind*, demonstrating that along seven lines, with regard to Baptism, the Sacrament of the Altar, the Keys, proclamation of God's Word and the singing of the Psalms, the Apostle's Creed, the *Vater unser*, and finally the ancient Church's respect for the State and its refusal to kiss the feet of the Pope. Before throwing back upon the Papal Church the accusation of novelty and adulteration of the ancient faith, Luther went on to show that through the Reformation '*die vorige alte Kirche*' had begun to shine again, like the sun reappearing from behind the clouds.[314] That is the '*rechte alte Kirche*' which, says Luther, we are who 'with the whole holy Christian Church are one Body and one communion of saints'.[315] What the Reformation has done is to repudiate the devilish adulteration of the Apostolic faith and all the strange novelties that it brought with it, and to restore to the Church its virginity as the pure Bride of Christ.[316] By the purity of the Church Luther means that the Church has returned to the pure Word and Sacraments and is ready to be guided by the Word of God which is the only Way, Truth and Life. The Church of the Reformation acknowledges that before God it is sinful, and that its life lags behind the Reformation in Word and Sacrament,[317] so that though here there are the marks of the true Church, the Church itself remains '*ein hoch tieff verborgen ding*'[318] which faith knows to be holy before God but which before the world appears otherwise.[319] As Luther had said elsewhere, *coram deo* the Church is '*gloria et decor*', but *coram mundo* it is '*opprobrium et abjectio plebis*'.[320]

193

There seem to be three ideas involved here, which though distinguishable do not represent distinctions in actual fact:

(*a*) The Church is at once *justa et peccatrix*, and therefore presents a double front.[321] Externally the Church is still involved in the unredeemed world of the old man, but according to its inner aspect the Church is holy and justified. These two aspects can no more be separated in the Church than they can in the individual believer. 'It is not that a man is two things. So far as we believe we are new, so far as we do not believe, we are old.'[322] It is in that way then that we are to think of the true form of the Church, for the Church is not to be judged by what it is in its wavering life but by Him in whom it believes and by whom it is purified. '*Non sumus sancti formaliter intrinsece, sed extrinsece ab ipso Christo. Sophistae dicunt aliquem sanctum, quod omnia membra et cor sint sancta, a forma inherente dicunt sanctos, sed iusti et sancti a Christo, qui est nostra iustitia, sanctitas, weil wir sein verbum haben, facit nos sanctos, non obstante, quod concupiscentiae manent in carne, illae obscurantur a claritate Christi. Sicut sol obscurat omnem foetorem, quae est in aere, aqua.*'[323] If therefore the Church is said to have a form it is a *forma extrinseca*, and that means that we must believe that the Church, all too visible in its sin and unrighteousness, is yet forgiven and justified and formed in Christ. '*Ecclesia vera est, quae orat ex fide, et serio orat: remitte nobis debita nostra, sicut nos remittimus debitoribus nostris. Ecclesia est, quae de die in diem proficit, quae de die in diem induitur novum hominem et exuit veterem. Ecclesia est, quae primitias Spiritus, non decimas, multo minus plenitudinem in hac accipit. Nondum sumus plane exuti carne, et nudi, sed sumus in exuendo et promovendo seu proficiendo.*'[324] In other words, the *forma*, or the *species*, or the *facies* of the Church has to be interpreted in terms of the eschatological *reputatio*. The Church cannot be thought of as *invisibilis ecclesiola*[325] but in terms of a *Christenheit* with a dual aspect as *justa et peccatrix*.

(*b*) The Church is a '*hoch tieff verborgen ding*' because '*ecclesia non habet externas notas, nisi valde contemptibiles, scilicet verbum, remissionem peccatorum, baptismum in mortem Christi, et coenam domini*'.[326] The Church presents a visible form in this world but not of the kind that the world will accept by its standards, for to it the Church presents a contrary picture as weak and deserted and without sign of power or worth. But that, says Luther, is the *'stulticia dei sub cruce latens'*.[327] Thus whenever we pass judgment upon the Church 'we must not look where there are no offences, but where there is the pure Word, pure administration of the sacraments, where there are men who love the Word and confess the Word before the world. *Haec ubi invenies, ibi statue ecclesiam esse*, whether there are few or many who have and do these things.'[328] It is in the Word and Sacraments that God's *facies* is to be seen, and it is there that the Church receives its true form,[329] but like the face of God it is discernible only by faith, for the Church lies *'pro aenigmate et obscuro verbo per baptismum'*.[330] The point that Luther emphasises again and again here is that the Church is *sacramentally* related to external and corporal things, and that the Sacraments by their very nature tell us that the Church exists on earth only *'sub contraria'*.[331] Where that relation is perverted as in the Papacy the Church only presents a *'falsa species'*.[332] Thus the Papal Church which Luther speaks of as the *'ecclesia diaboli'* also appears in a contrary form. *'Licet foris in speciem Ecclesia diaboli appareat sancta, et velit pro Christo contra diabolum agere videri. Econtra, Ecclesia Christi apparet haeretica, et velut pro diabolo contra Christum agere. Ideo benefacit Christus, qui verbo definit, et fide comprehendi docet, Ecclesiam veram esse contra Ecclesiam diaboli, Nam sensu et specie longe contrarium apparet.'*[333]

(c) The Church is always the Church militant under the Cross (*sub cruce*) and therefore 'according to its external aspect' it appears as afflicted by God (*percussa a domino*).[334] Because the Church in this world always lives *'in medio regni sathanae et in media cruce'*,[335] it always presents a *'scandalosa facies'*.[336] That may be due to its contemptible smallness in the eyes of the world, but is mostly due to the fact that it suffers and is persecuted and is maligned. God hides the Church, therefore, *'sub obscuro et horribili tegumento'*.[337] The Church lives in the flesh and in the world but lives there in no other way than by faith in Christ the Son of God who suffered for the Church. The Church for Christ's sake suffers continuous abuse and vilification, is confounded and rejected by men, is mortified and dies, but it lives in Christ, and therefore all these opprobrious experiences and scandals which the Church has in the World are the precious gems with which God ornaments the Church.[338] This way of regarding the form and order of the Church in this world, as essentially *sub cruce*, is well expounded in Luther's exposition of the Song of Songs, for example, in comments on 1:5: The Church is '*nigra coram mundo, coram deo quia ornata verbo et donis spiritus sancti, habet veritatem, sapientiam divinam, charitatem, patientiam et omnia ornamenta spiritualia, deinde habet externam administrationem divinitus ordinatam, optimis legibus instructam, oportet ein schone ordinatio sey, quam Deus immediate gestelt.*'[339] It is in persecution and suffering for Christ that these spiritual ornaments are bestowed upon the Church and that they shine out revealed and seen in the Word and Sacraments.[340] '*Quanquam sim politia divinitus instituta et ornata verbo Dei, Tamen in speciem miserrima esse videor, Nusquam succedit, paucissimi sunt, qui pacem publicam ament et tueantur. Videor non Politia, sed quaedam seditiosorum hominum colluvies esse. Nolite hac forma offendi. Figite oculos non in nigredinem sed in osculum, quod mihi Deus offert, et suum propter verbum, fidem. Sic Ecclesia Speciem habet meretricis omnium ludibrio expositae, lacerata. Psalms 22 ... opprobrium hominum, sed formosissima intus propter verbum, modo hoc adsit, es gehe denn externe, wie es wolle.*'[341] 'In the School of Christ we learn this hard lesson: *Deducit ad inferos et reducit, mortificat et vivificat.*'[342] That is Luther's constant theme that it is only through *agones* and *tentationes* that the Church exists and fulfils its mission, and therefore he insists on interpreting the whole idea of the essential form of the Church in history in terms of the Cross.[343]

This is precisely the way in which the Church grows and increases until the end of the world, so that 'the world is converted to faith, *scandaloso et miraculoso modo, scilicet per infirmitatem contra omnem potentiam, sapientiam, iusticiam etc, quae manifeste sunt divini miraculi.* For the kingdoms of the world are established not by infirmity but by power against the weak. *Ideo alia ratio est regni Dei propagandi et regni mundi.* This argument convinces us that the Church is the Kingdom of God; all the other kingdoms of the world fight against the one weak and despised Church but do not prevail at all. But the Church itself conquers at last all kingdoms and converts them to itself, by the very power of God. But before it increases like that its weakness and humility is scandalous.'[344] That comes from Luther's exposition of the parable of the mustard seed, but when he goes on to expound the parable of the leaven which a woman took and hid in three measures of meal, it is essentially the same thought that he sets forth. The Gospel preached by the Church is the '*novum fermentum*' which once mixed into humanity does not desist until the end of the world but penetrates the whole mass of those that need to be saved.[345] Here then in the midst of the world Christians and Christ are baked together into '*ein kuche, ein brod*', for Christ as *fermentum* is incorporated into them to become one body with them, and can no more be separated from them than the leaven from the paste. In vain does the devil seek to separate Christ from the Church. '*Der teyg ist geseurt, der teufel wird die seure nicht sondern vom teyge. Er koche oder brate sie, oder röste und börne sie da zu, so ist der sauerteig Christus drinnen, Und sol drinnen bleiben bis an den iungsten tag, das alles durch seuret werde et nihil de pasta infermentatum maneat.*'[346] 'So long as Christ remains Christ and the Church remains the Church, the world will abound in scandals and evils',[347] but all this only serves to further the fermentation of the world through the Church until it is brought under the purpose of God or reduced to faith.

It belongs therefore to the very nature and mission of the Church that it should be hidden in this world and mixed up with hypocrites and unbelievers, and indeed, as we have already noted, it could not exist in the flesh without being so involved in humanity. There were times when Luther rather yearned for a separate Church of the pure and faithful to whom he could preach and minister[348] – though true Christians were too few for that purpose – but he did not wish to withdraw them out of their context in the social structure of the world by setting up a special ecclesiastical structure and so organising a clear-cut, separatist Church, a visible society of the saints, but preferred to allow the Church to work as a leavening *Christenheit* in the social hierarchies of the world, of a family, worship and the state.[349] Certainly the Church was to be visibly marked out by the Word and Sacrament, by confession, from the world[350] but it was to be compacted by the Word within the authority and protection provided by the State. This did not mean that the Church was the tool of the State. How could it be if the Church was ruled by the majestic Word of God[351] and was the instrument of that Word as it exercised its authority over all the kingdoms of the world? The very mixing of the Church as *Christenheit* within the hierarchies, even under persecution, would mean at once the preservation of the world for the sake of the Church and the Gospel,[352] and at the same time the bringing of the world and its institutions under the reign of Christ so that He could use them as His *larvae* for the purpose of the Gospel and the growth of the Church.[353]

As a community of those who confess Christ, who are marked out by the Word and Sacraments, the Church is *'visibilis in mundo'*,[354] but it is *in mundo* and until the day of judgment will always be the Church of hypocrites as well as of true believers, an external *Gemeinschaft*.[355] For that very reason it will always be covered *sub cruce*, discernible only to faith – but that is because of its eschatological and teleological mission until the end of the world. The Church is joined to Christ, who has made it His Body, and as such it is the *Regnum Christi*. *'Idem regnum Christi hic et in futuro: hic per fidem incoatum, in futuro consummandum per gloriam.'*[356] The Church is involved in the world and as such it is involved in its social structures and forms and is given shape within them by Word and Sacrament so that as *ferment* it may pervade and rule over the world and bring it under the *Regnum Christi*. It is only within this double involvement that the Church in Christ wearing the new humanity is to be interpreted – that is, it can be interpreted only dialectically. It is not that Luther does not think of the Church as a *tertium datur* proleptically participant in the new creation, but this is only known to faith in crucifixion and mortification: it is concealed under the Cross and held forth in hope.

In other language, used by Luther early in his theological career, the Church as the *Regnum Christi* is the *Regnum gratiae* or the *Regnum in fide* and remains such *'usque ad iudicium extremum'* until the *'Regnum in quo Christus inquantum homo regnat'*, passes over into the *Regnum gloriae* when Christ will hand over the Kingdom to the Father. Now He rules *'in fide per humanitatem Christi, tunc in specie per revelationem essentiae dei.'*[357] Everything that Luther has to say about the Church in history, its form and polity, its face and visibility, its work and suffering and victory, is said in the context of that eschatological movement from *Regnum gratiae* to *Regnum gloriae*, from enigmatic concealment in grace to the revelation of glory. On the one hand it is the *theologia crucis*, but on the other hand it is the pressure of the *Regnum gloriae* and its imminent revelation, that demand eschatological suspension of form and order in the Church on earth.[358] That does not mean that the Church can do without form and order. On the contrary, but form and order have to be used eschatologically so that they leave room, as it were, for the breaking in of the *Regnum Dei* from above.[359]

In the Book of Revelation liturgy and apocalyptic belong together. The Eucharistic liturgy is part of the great apocalyptic conflict between the Kingdom of God and the kingdoms of this world, and so liturgical forms are understood as an engagement, if only by way of echo, in the conflict that took place on the Cross and from the Cross has been inserted into history. That is the way in which Luther seems to link up his apocalyptic intensity with the eschatological suspension of form and order in the Church and its life on earth. The believer within the Church is caught up in warfare, into the mighty and blessed battle of the Word of God, and his whole life is lived in tension. There can be no doubt that Luther's dialectical eschatology, the tension between *having* and *not-having*, created in him an insatiable hunger for the objective assurance of forgiveness, and threw him at times into great anxiety, an anxiety which he interpreted as real participation in the apocalyptic strife of the Kingdom of God. The term he employed to describe that was '*Anfechtung*' or '*tentatio*'.[360] The sharpness of that strife and the realisation, inherent in the *justus et peccator* dialectic, that before God the believer is always in the wrong,[361] helped him at times to lose sight of the new creation in Christ as already accomplished fact, as a '*perfectum praesens*'. It was not that Luther had no sense of the new creation either as regards the Church or as regards the individual believer, but that his weak stress on the renewal of the whole creation tended to rob it of temporal relevance and force. In the end Luther's doctrine of *Anfechtung*, which corresponds so well to his view of faith, means that the believer does not really learn to live on the resurrection side of the Cross. So far as Luther entered into the triumphant eschatology of the New Testament, it was employed rather as consolation in *Anfechtung*[362] than as actual anticipation of the final victory of the Son of Man. '*Ein feste Burg*' will ever remain one of the great hymns of the Church, but it expresses only one side of the eschatology of the Reformation.

NOTES

1. *WA*, 30/2:367 ff.; 34/1:536 f.
2. *WA*, 10/3:191 ff. At this period (1522), however, Luther had a milder view of Purgatory than that which he adopted after 1530. See *WA*, 7:149, 453.
3. See also the *Exposition of Genesis* 22:18, *WA*, 43:245 ff.; Genesis 25, *WA*, 43:351 ff.; and *WA*, 42:67 f.
4. *WA*, 10/3:192.
5. *WA*, 10/3:194.
6. *WA*, 12:596. Cf. *WA*, 36:349: '*Asbald die Augen zugehen, wirst du auferweckt werden. Tausend Jahre werden sein, gleich als wenn du ein halbes Stündlein geschlaffen hättest. Gleich wie wir, wenn wir nachts den Stundenschlag nicht hören, nicht wissen, wie lange Zeit wir geschlaffen haben, also noch viel mehr im Tode sind tausend Jahre hinweg. Ehe sich einer umsiehet, ist er ein schöner Engel.*'
7. *WA*, 33:404 f.; *WA*, 36:687 f., etc. Compare the beginning and end of the long *Exposition of Genesis* throughout which he expounded again and again the *Regnum fidei* and the *Ecclesia* in terms of *sinus Abrahae, sinus Christi*. At the beginning: '*Dominus noster Ihesus Christus perficiat opus suum quod incepit in nobis, et acceleret diem illum redemptionis nostrae, quem (Dei gratia) levatis capitibus petimus, suspiramus et expectamus . . . Veni Domine Ihesu. Et qui te amat, dicat: Veni Domine Ihesu, Amen*' (*WA*, 42:2). And at the end: '*Das ist nu der liebe (liber?) Genesis. Unser Herr Gott geb, das andere nach mir besser machen. Ich kann nit mehr, ich bin schwach, orate Deum pro me, das er mir ein gutes, seliges stündlein verleihe*' (*WA*, 44:825). Those are the eschatological brackets within which all Luther's life, work and thought are to be understood.
8. But cf. also the sustained exposition of Titus 2 (*WA*, 34/2:108 ff.).
9. *WA*, 14:70 f. Judging by this, Luther's own calculations in the *Supputatio annorum mundi* (*vide infra*) were exercises of the reason, not of faith!
10. Cf. the last four *Theses* of 1517. 'Away, then, with those prophets who say to Christ's people, "Peace, peace", where there is no peace. Hail, hail to all those prophets who say to Christ's people "The Cross, the Cross", where there is no cross. Christians should be exhorted to be zealous to follow Christ, their Head, through penalties, deaths, and hells; and let them thus be more confident of entering heaven through many tribulations rather than through a false assurance of peace' (*WA*, 1:238). See also the Sermon on *Ablass und Gnade*, *WA*, 1:239 ff.; and the Sermon *de Poenitentia*, *WA*, 1:317 ff.
11. This becomes increasingly clear in the early series of lectures on the Bible, Psalms (1513–14; *WA*, 3 and 4 and 9:116 f.), Romans (1515–16; *WA*, 56 and 57), Galatians (1516–17; *WA*, 2:436 ff.), Hebrews (1517–18; *WA*, 57), and Psalms (1519 f.; *WA*, 5). For the importance of his own experience in this connexion see especially *WA*, 1:525, 558; 19:210, 226; 54, 179 ff. The tension Luther interpreted wholly in terms of the death and resurrection of Christ, His descent into Hell and His ascent into Heaven. '*Sic Deus dum vivificat facit illud occidendo: dum justificat, facit illud reos faciendo; dum in coelum vehit, facit id ad infernum ducendo*' (*WA*, 18:633). That was against Erasmus in the *De Servo Arbitrio*, but earlier he had written: '*vivendo, immo moriendo et damnando fit theologus, non intelligendo, legendo aut speculando*' (*WA*, 5:163).
12. *WA*, 56:334 f.; *WA*, 8:99 f.
13. *WA*, 40/2:1 ff.
14. *WA*, 6:322–9. See also the letter to Spalatin about his horrified conviction that the Pope is Antichrist (*WA*, *Briefe*, 2:48).

15. *WA*, 8:106. Cf. the *Sermons on the Law and Gospel* (*WA*, 36:8 ff., 25 ff.
16. *WA*, 56:442. Cf. also pp. 252, 287, 298, etc., and *WA*, 54:179 ff. For a more mature exposition see *Comm. on Gal.* 3:6; *WA*, 40/1:362 ff.
17. *WA*, 56:204.
18. *WA*, 34/2:465: '*Wenn der Tag nicht ein mal kommen solt, so wolt ich eben. So mehr nie geboren sein.*' Cf. *WA*, 8:719; *WA*, 10/1:142.
19. See the valuable discussion by Dr Gordon Rupp, *The Righteousness of God*, pp. 158 ff.
20. *WA*, 56:268.
21. *WA*, 56:269. See the whole section on Romans 4:7, and also pp. 20, 30, 42, etc.
22. *WA*, 56:287; cf. *WA*, 8:92.
23. Cf. *WA*, 40/1:367: 'Christian righteousness consists in these two things: faith which gives glory to God, and in God's imputation. For faith is weak, and God's imputation must be joined with it. Thus a Christian man is both righteous and a sinner, holy and profane, an enemy of God and yet a child of God.' Luther goes on to point out that such contraries are not acceptable to the philosopher or the natural reason or the wisdom of the flesh. 'Here we see that every Christian is a high priest: for first he offers up and slays his own reason – the wisdom of the flesh; then he gives glory to God, that He is righteous, true, patient, pitiful, and merciful. And this is the daily sacrifice of the New Testament which must be offered evening and morning. The evening sacrifice is to slay reason, the morning sacrifice is to glorify God. This is therefore a strange and wonderful definition of righteousness that it is the imputation of God.'
24. *WA*, 40/1:364. '*Fides ergo incipit, reputatio perficit usque ad illum diem.*'
25. *WA*, 40/1:372; *WA*, 8:77, 88 f., 96 f., 104 f.
26. Therefore the counterpart to the duality of imputation is the duality involved in repentance, which Luther thinks of as a 'medium between unrighteousness and righteousness'. 'Thus he is in sin as a *terminus a quo* and in righteousness as a *terminus ad quem*. If we are always repenting, we are always sinners, and yet at the same time we are just and justified, *partim* sinners, *partim* just, i.e. nothing save penitents' (*WA*, 56:442). Cited from Gordon Rupp, *The Righteousness of God*, p. 180.
27. *WA*, 4:364: '*Semper peccamus, semper immundi sumus. Et quia spiritus et caro unus homo est, sine dubio culpa hominis est, quod caro tam mala est et male agit. Quare ... semper sumus in motu, semper iustificandi, qui justi sumus. Nam hinc venit, ut omnis iustitia pro presenti instanti sit peccatum ad eam, que in sequenti addenda est. Quia vere dicit b. Bernardus: "Ubi incipis nolle fieri melior, desinis esse bonus. Quia non est status in via dei: ipsa mora peccatum est." Quare qui in presenti instanti se iustum confidit et stat, iam iustitiam perdidit, sicut in motu similiter patet: terminus, qui in isto instanti est ad quem ipse in sequenti instanti est terminus a quo. Terminus autem a quo est peccatum, a quo semper eundum est. Et terminus ad quem est iustitia, quo eundum est.*'
28. *WA*, 40/1:229, 280 ff.; p. 545.
29. Cf. *WA*, 40/1:378. 'We look for Christ to come again in glory to judge both the quick and the dead, whom we believe to have come already for our salvation. At this day also Christ is present to some, to others He is to come. To all believers He is present; to the unbelievers He is not yet come, nor does He profit them at all, but if they hear the Gospel and believe that He is present to them, He justifies and saves them.
30. *WA*, 40/2:23 f.; *WA*, 34/2:118.
31. *WA*, 40/2:30.
32. *WA*, 38:567. '*Talis est natura regni Dei, ut alius videatur possidere et non possidet.*

Alius possidet et tamen non videtur possidere.' Cf. also *WA*, 34/2:110 f.

33. Cf. *WA*, 40/2:27. 'Faith is the *dialectic* which conceives the idea of whatsoever is to be believed. Hope is the *rhetoric* which amplifies, urges, persuades, and exhorts to constancy, to the end that faith should not fail in the time of temptation but should keep hold of the Word and firmly cleave to it.'

34. Cf. *WA*, *Tischreden*, vol. I, § 491; *Von den Konziliis und Kirchen*, *WA*, 50:509–653; and *An die Herren deutschen Ordens*, *WA*, 12:232–44; *WA*, 42:276 f.

35. *Tischreden*, 4:51, 13.

36. God alone is in this business. We are carried away by Him. We are led rather than lead.' *WA*, *Briefe*, 2:39, 41; cf. *WA*, 2:399.

37. *Von den Konziliis und Kirchen*, *WA*, 50:509 ff. Cf. *An den christlichen Adel deutscher Nation*, *WA*, 6:411. And also *Colloquia*: 'It is my firm belief that the angels are getting ready, putting on their armour and girding their swords about them, for the last day is already breaking, and the angels are preparing for the battle.' Cited from H. T. Kerr, *Compend of Luther's Theology*, p. 244.

38. See Gustaf Törnvall, *Geistliches und weltliches Regiment bei Luther* (Münich, 1947), and Edmund Schlink, *Theologie der lutherischen Bekenntnisschriften* (Münich, 1947), pp. 306 ff.

39. *Comm. on Gal. Intro. Argument*, *WA*, 40/1:46. Of special importance for Luther were the New Testament passages, John 18:36, *WA*, 6:293; and Luke 17:20 f., *WA*, 6:293. See also *WA*, 7:683 f.

40. The conception of the Church as a *civitas Dei* on earth Luther called '*ein grawsamer yrthum*' (*WA*, 6:293 f.).

41. *Comm. on Gal.* 3:23, *WA*, 40/1:525. Cf. p. 522: 'Therefore we must join two things together which are most contrary, to fear and to fly from the wrath of God, and again to trust in His mercy and goodness. The one is hell, the other heaven, and yet they must be nearly joined together in the heart.'

42. *WA*, 34/2:504. '*Christus venit auffzurichten novum regnum, nicht auffzuheben das alte, auch nichts genomen, sed gegeben, was gebuhrt. Ipse utitur mundo, sed non regit, nimpt ein bissen brods, sed non docet.*'

43. Cf. *WA*, 41:483. '*Et quod hoc factum ideo, ut ostenderet suum regnum non debere esse mundanum, potens, dives in terris. Sed omnia da hin gerichtet, quod aliud regnum, quod nach der weltlichen ehr ... prius dedit mundanum regnum Adae.*'

44. *WA*, 49:137–9.

45. *WA*, 43:3.

46. *WA*, 41:483.

47. '*Deus dedit rationem, ut regamus corporales res, educare liberos, administrare domos etc. ad hoc non opus scriptura, hoc donum Deus proiecit inter omnes gentes. Non opus ergo, ut demittat verbum de celo*' (*WA*, 16:353).

48. *WA*, 36:358; 20:530.

49. See the Prefaces, *WML*, 6:412–23. *WA*, 11/1:392; *WA*, 11/2:1 ff., 48–130. Cf. the work of Melanchthon, *In Danielem Prophetam Commentarius* (1543), *CR*, 13.

50. op. cit., pp. 479–88. In the 1522 Preface Luther had written: 'My spirit cannot fit itself into this book.' *WA*, 7:404.

51. This is apparent also in the commentary of Francis Lambert published in 1528, *Exegeseos in sanctam divi Ioannis Apocalypsin*, which appears to have influenced Luther's second preface of 1545; and in the work of Andreas Osiander, *Coniectura de ultimis temporibus ac de fine mundi* (1544), which was undertaken at the request of Melanchthon.

52. *WA*, 12:596.

53. *WA*, 14:71.

54. See *WA*, 40/2:526; *WA*, 39/2:299; *WA*, 40/3:572.

55. '*Quid futurum putamus ante diem extremum, siquidem nunc revelato Euangelio tanta contemptorum est copia, ut verendum sit, ne brevi praevaleant et repleant Mundum erroribus et Verbum omnino extinguitur?*' (*WA*, 42:246; cf. p. 279).
56. *On Secular Authority – To what extent it should be obeyed*, IV, *WA*, 11:251.
57. Cf. 'These and similar thoughts caused us to publish this Prophet Daniel before the others, which have to be published still, that he may see the light of day before the elements shall melt, and he may do his work and console the distressed Christians for whose sake he was written and spared to these last days' (*Luthers Schriften*, Walch edition, 6:893). Cf. the letter to Hausmann of 25th February 1530: '*Nos iam Danielem formamus edendum pro solatio istius ultimi temporis*' (*WA, Briefe*, 5:242).
58. *Preface to Daniel*, Erlangen edition, 41:323; *WA*, 11/2:129.
59. Letter to Melanchthon, of 2nd June 1530, *WA, Briefe*, 5:346.
60. Luther declares he did not want to 'force others to believe as I do; neither will I permit anyone to deny me the right to believe that the last day is near at hand. These words and signs of Christ (Luke 21:25–36) compel me to believe that such is the case' (cited from H. T. Kerr, *Compend of Luther's Theology*, p. 246). But surely this was to judge according to the carnal reason, the very thing Luther condemned so often! Three years later, in 1533, Luther had to deal severely with Michel Stifel for calculating that the world would end at 8 a.m. on 19th October 1533! (*Tischreden*, 4:51, 2.)
61. Erlangen edition, 41:233; *WA*, 11/2:381.
62. *WA*, 53:1 ff.
63. See also *Tischreden* (F.B.), 4:49 f. and 51:4, 8: '*Diese jtzige Zeit, wenn man sie hält gegen die vorigen, vergangenen Zeit, so ist sie kaum einer Hand breit, oder wie ein ubrig Aepfelchen, das an einen Baume ein wenig hanget*' (ibid., 4:51, 3). Cf. *WAT*, 6:497–509.
64. *Tischreden* (F.B.), 4:51, 9. Cf. *WAT*, 5:321.
65. *De Servo Arbitrio*, 19. *WA*, 18:626: '*Sermo enim Dei venit mutaturus orbem, quoties venit.*' Cf. the letter to Spalatin, February 1520: '*Obsecro te, si de Evangelio recte sentis, noli putare, rem eius posse sine tumultu, scandalo, seditione agi. Tu ex gladio non facies plumam, nec ex bello pacem: verbum Dei gladius est, bellum est, ruina est, scandalum est, perditio est, venenum est, et (ut Amos ait) sicut ursus in via et leaena in silva*' (*WA, Briefe*, 2:43).
66. *WA*, 3:386.
67. *WA*, 28:314.
68. *WA*, 39/1:332.
69. *WA*, 40/2:196; cf. *WA*, 30/2:539 and 554; 27:417.
70. *Sermon on John* 1:5 f., *WA*, 15:542 f.
71. See for example, *WA*, 40/1:427; *WA*, 36:568 f. '*Er redet von dem Reich Christi jtst auff erden, welches ist ein Reich des glaubens, darin er regiret durch das Wort, nicht inn sichtlichem, offentlichen Wesen, sondern ist gleich, wie man die Sonne sihet durch eine Wolcken, da sihet man wohl das liecht, aber die Sonne selbst sihet man nicht.*'
72. *WA*, 51:11.
73. *WA*, 45:280; cf. 28:281.
74. *WA*, 45:252, 282, 290.
75. *WA*, 45:280 ff.
76. *WA*, 45:291 f.
77. Cf. *WA*, 42:625.
78. See, for examples, *WA*, 19:629; 30/2:554; 32:159; 49:30; 50:652.
79. *WA*, 45:253; 40/1:293; 51:21, 239; 11:262; 27:417.

80. *WA*, 40/2:292; *WA*, 40/1:292; 45:252.
81. *WA*, 40/1:427.
82. *WA*, 28:311; 32:183; 45:252; 34/1:178.
83. *WA*, 28:281; *WA*, 16:254; 34/1:178; 40/1:395; 45:252.
84. *WA*, 51:11; 36:385.
85. *WA*, 51:11; 20/2:394 f.
86. *WA*, 49:30, 40, 227.
87. *WA*, 40:293 f.
88. *WA*, 45:280, 292.
89. *WA*, 45:252.
90. When Luther thought of the relation between the Kingdom of God and the concrete life of this world he thought of the Kingdom as assuming *three* visible forms or regiments, which he called '*ecclesia*', '*politia*', and '*oeconomia*'; the latter being the *Hausregiment*, but because this belonged essentially to the worldly kingdom as distinct from the spiritual kingdom, it was not regarded as a third in the wider dialectic. See *WA*, 47:853.
91. *WA*, 45:252.
92. *Sermon for the third of Advent*, on Matthew. 11:2–10, *Predigten*, edition by Kreutzer, p. 26 f. Cf. *WA*, 36:385; 20:530; and 52:26.
93. *Sermon for the second Sunday of Advent*, *WA*, 36:379; *WA*, 34/2:111; *WA*, 33:681.
94. '*Christi regnum ist geordnet, hat, finalis causa, endlich darum eingesetzt ut homines nati in peccatis et morte, ut illis geholffen, ut a peccato et morte ad vitam et iustitiam . . .*' (*WA*, 45:252).
95. *WA*, 27:417: '*Sepe audistis, quod praedicemus spirituale et corporale regimina. Spirituale per verbum, seculare per gladium regit.*'
96. *WA*, 34/2:128 f. See also *WA*, 51:261; *WA*, *Briefe*, 5:413; *WA*, 10/1:142.
97. *WML*, 6:417 f.; *WA*, 11/1:403.
98. *WA*, 39/2:282, on 1 Corinthians 15:24.
99. *Comm. on Gal.* 1:3, 15. Jena edition, 4:394 f. Cf. *WA*, 40/1:72 f., 139; *WA*, 14:28.
100. *WA*, 36:568–71.
101. ibid.
102. ibid.
103. Cited from Baier, *Compendium*, 3a:130 f.; *WA*, 34/2:128 f.
104. Cf. also *WA*, 36:661 f.
105. Cf. the Sermon in the previous year on 1 Corinthians 15:44 f. (*WA*, 36:666 f.): '*Du wirst nicht allein an der Seelen getauft und gepredigt und durch Euangelion gesegnet, sondern am Leibe. Es wird dir Christi Leib und Blut am Altare nicht allein in die Seele gegeben, sondern in den Leib. Er soll nicht dahinten bleiben. Und soll werden ein geistlicher Leib gleichwie Christi Leib am Tage der Auferstehung.*' See also the Sermon on 1 Corinthians 15:20–2, 1532 (*WA*, 36:547 f. and *WA*, 49:395 f.).
106. *WA*, 34/2:126 f. Cf. *Tischreden* (F.B.) 4:49, 51. '*Im künftigen Leben, will ich sagen, da werden Kirchen, Weinbeer, Vögel, Bäume, usw, so solls bald da stehen*' (4, 51:10). '*Wenn wir nur Gottes Gnade haben, so lachen uns alle Creaturen Gottes an!*' (4, 49:5). Cf. *WAT*, 6:307; 2:581.
107. *WA*, 40/1:442; cf. *amabilis permutatio*. *WA*, 38:527; and see *WA*, 5:598–673, the *Exposition of Psalm* 22; *Disputatio Heidelbergae habita*, 1518 (*WA*, 1:362): '*In Christo crucifixo est vera theologia et cognitio Dei.*'
108. Throughout the sermon on Titus 2 Luther emphasises the fact that through Baptism Christians are 'inserted into the Kingdom of God', where the new and eternal life is not to be understood according to the judgment of reason (*WA*, 34/2:108 ff., 118 ff.).

109. *WA*, 40/1:361. 'Faith said, I believe O God when Thou speakest. And what does God say? Impossible things, lies, foolish, weak, absurd, abominable, heretical, and devilish things, if ye believe reason' (ibid). Cf. also *WA*, 31/1:249.
110. *WA*, 40/1:227.
111. *WA*, 18:633.
112. *WA*, 56:392. Cf. also pp. 377 f.
113. *WA*, 40/1:174: '*Iam adhuc agimus cum Deo velato, in hac enim vita non possumus cum Deo agere facie ad faciem. Universa autem creatura est facies et larva Dei. Sed hic requiritur sapientia quae discernat Deum a larva. Hanc sapientiam mundus non habet, ideo non potest discernere Deum a larva.*'
114. Cited from H. T. Kerr, *Compend of Luther's Theology*, pp. 247 f (Lenker edition of Luther's works, vol. VII, p. 36). See also *WA*, 43:393.
115. *WA*, 40/1:51, 175–8.
116. *WA*, 40/1:106. Cf. 49:30.
117. *WA*, 18:389.
118. Cf. *WA*, 10/3:14 f.; and *WA*, 38:144.
119. *WA*, 36:568 ff. Cf *WA*, 43:393, 425 f.; 19:652 f.; 2:27.
120. *WA*, 51:239. '*Denn der leidige teuffel hoeret auch nicht auff diese zwey Reich inn einander zu kochen und zu brewen. Die weltichen herrn wollen ins teufels namen imer Christum leren und meistern, wie er seine kirche und geistlich Regiment sol fueren. So wollen die falschen Pfaffen und Rottengeister nicht inn Gottes namen imer leren und meistern, wie man solle das weltliche Regiment ordenen, Und ist also der Teuffel zu beiden seiten fast seer unmuessig und hat viel zu tun. Gott wolt im weren, Amen, so wirs werd sind.*' Cf. *WA*, 15:220; 18:168 f.; 6:430; 11:271. *WA*, Tischreden, 4635 and 6234.
121. *WA*, 40:8. Cf. *WA*, 5:217: '*Alle könige und fürsten, wenn sie der natur und höchsten Weisheit folgen, müssen Gottes feinde werden und sein Wort verfolgen*'; *WA*, 30/1:189 ff.
122. *WA*, 17/1:193 f.
123. Cf. *WA*, 8:539 f., where Luther makes it clear that the 'law' of the *Regnum Christi* is spiritual: '*das lebendige gesetz Christi, welchs ist der geyst gotts, der nicht gegeben wirt, denn durch das wort des Euangelii.*' Cf. *WA*, 11:235: 'He is a King over Christians and rules by His Spirit alone, without law.'
124. *WA*, 6:293 ff.; *WA*, 2:73.
125. Cf. *WA*, 6:297: '*nit das wir sie voneinander scheydenn wollen.*' The spiritual and corporal realms are to be understood on the analogy of spirit and body in the whole man (p. 295 f.). See also *WA*, 12:275 f., 331. Cf. *WA*, 11:255: '*Also gehets denn beydes Seyn miteinander, das du zu gleich Gottis reych und der wellt reych genug thuest, eusserlich und innerlich, zu gleich unrecht und Ubel leydest und doch ubel und unrecht straffest, zu gleich dem Ubel nicht widderstehist und doch widderstehist. Denn mit dem eynen sihestu auff dich und auff das deyne, mit dem ander auf den Nehisten und auff das seyne.*'
126. For a *tertium comparationis* in the future compare *WA*, 51:261: '*Aber unsers Herr Gotts rat ist der beste, das er gedenckt himel und erden jm einen hauffen zu stossen und eine andere newe welt machen, denn diese welt taug nicht, der buben ist zu viel und der fromen zu wenig drinnen.*'
127. *WA*, 11:251.
128. *WA*, 11:251.
129. *WA*, 10/3:49; *WA*, 11:271.
130. *WA*, 12:275 f., 331; cf. also p. 50.
131. *WA*, 27:417. And see *WA*, 11:53, 251.
132. See especially *WA*, 12:485.

133. Letter to Spalatin, de Wette edition, *Briefe*, 2:492; See *WAB*, 3:260.
134. Cf. Luther's part in the *Promotionsdisputation* of Johannes Macchabäus Scotus, *WA*, 39/2:52, 175, 181. In the Exposition of Genesis Luther speaks frequently of the *tres ordines vitae huius, oeconomia, politia et ecclesia* – see Chs. 19, 21, 43, *WA*, 43 and 44.
135. See the *Disputatio anno* 1539 *habita*, *WA*, 39/2:52 ff.
136. '*Ubi verbum Dei est ordinatio Dei*' (*WA*, 31/2:614).
137. Cf. Calvin, *Instit.* 4.17.13, and his reference to Peter Lombard in this connection. In his early days Luther lectured on the *Sentences* of Peter Lombard, the notes of which are still extant (*WA*, 9:1–94).
138. *WA*, 40/1:463: '*Omnes ordinationes creatae sunt larvae dei.*' Because theology has to use creaturely words and concepts, Luther adds: '... *larvae, allegoriae, quibus rhetorice pingit suam theologiam.*'
139. '*Nuda facie non possumus agere cum Deo*' (*WA*, 40/1:174). '*Iam adhuc agimus cum Deo velato, in hac enim vita non possumus cum Deo agere facie ad faciem*' (ibid.).
140. *WA*, 40:175 f. Luther recalls that both *larva* and *persona* were used of the painted mask of the actor on the Roman stage.
141. op. cit., p. 174.
142. loc. cit., p. 173. The first edition of this passage (*Comm. on Gal.* 2:6) had *universa*, the final edition, *tota*.
143. *WA*, 376: '*Omnes creaturae coram Deo nihil erga Verbum.*'
144. *WA*, 40/1:553 f.
145. We have to remember that in Latin literature *larvae* was used to describe the *noxiae infernorum umbrae* and the *daemones aerii*. See Stephanus, *Thesaurus Linguae Latinae*, and Dufresne et du Cange, *Glossarium* in *art. cit.* Cf. the incredible statements of Luther in *WA*, 31/1:249, and 40/1:361; 40/2:53.
146. Cf. *WA*, 40/1:500 f., 553 f., 1:105 f., pp. 112 ff. etc.
147. *WA*, 57/2:67 f.
148. '*In religione loquimur aliter de rebus quam in politia in qua vult honorari istas personas ut suas larvas et instrumenta per quae excercet et regit mundum*' (*WA*, 40/1:176).
149. Although they have to be used *religiose*, these distinctions do not obtain in the Kingdom of God, for *before God* all are equal. Therefore we are not baptised into these distinctions (*WA*, 34/2:116 f.). See also *WA*, 40/1:179.
150. 'When it is a question of religion, conscience, the fear of God, faith, and the service of God, we must put no fear in these outward *personae*, we must put no trust in them, look for no comfort from them, or hope for deliverance by them, either corporally or spiritually' (loc. cit., p. 175).
151. *WA*, 40/1:174. Cf. p. 176: '*Deus dedit omnes creaturis usum, utilitatem, sed non in cultum et religionem. Sicut utor pane, vino, veste, sic fruor omnibus creaturis dei, sed non debeo ea timere, confidere, in eiis gloriari.*' See especially Luther's letter to Amsdorf, de Wette edition, 5:431. *WAB*, 9:608–11.
152. *WA*, 40/1:173. Cf. the 1535 edition, p. 174: '*Universa creatura est facies et larva Dei. Sed hic requiritur sapientia quae discernat Deum a larva. Hanc sapientiam mundus non habet, ideo non potest discernere Deum a larva.*'
153. '*Larva est nec res seria ... Sed nosti, quod Deus has personas seu larvas nihil curat, ut quae non sint regnum Dei, ita ut Paulus audeat etiam Apostolatum appellare larvam Gal. II: Deus personam non respicit*' (De Wette, *Luthers Briefe*, 5:431; *WAB*, 9:610).
154. *WA*, 40/1:178.
155. *WA*, 40/1:175.
156. *WA*, 40/1:177.

157. *WA*, 32:390: '*die zwo personen odder zweyerley ampt auff einen menschen geraten und zugleich ein Christ und ein Furst . . .*'
158. *WA*, 32:473.
159. *WA*, 32:475.
160. *WA*, 19:648.
161. *WA*, 32:390, 475 f.
162. Cf. *WA*, 32:391, 440; 34/1:122, etc.
163. *WA*, 40/1:442 f.
164. Luther uses *larva* to indicate that he is using the term *person* not univocally of Christ's *eternal Person* and *our person*.
165. *WA*, 40/1:443.
166. At this point Luther presupposes the idea that faith contains at its heart union with Christ, fully expounded earlier in this Commentary on Gal. See, for example, on 2:16, *WA*, 40/1:228: 'Christian faith is not an idle quality or empty husk in the heart, but a firm consent whereby Christ is apprehended: so that Christ is the object of faith or rather, He is not the object, but as it were *in faith itself Christ is present.*' See especially the discussion of Gal. 2:20 of the *unio hominis cum Christo*, *WA*, 40/1:280–90.
167. *WA*, 40/1:444.
168. *WA*, 40/1:445.
169. *WA*, 40/1:285.
170. ibid., p. 285.
171. ibid., p. 284.
172. *WA*, 40/1:289.
173. *WA*, 40/1:229. Cf. *Luthers Vorlesung ueber den Hebräerbrief*, 1515/16, edition by E. Hirsch and H. Rückert, p. 235: In a comment to Psalm 30, '*Abscondes eos in abscondito faciei tuae*', Luther says: '*Hoc incipit quidem in hac vita, sed perficietur in futura. Magna itaque res esse Christianum et vitam suam habere absconditam non in loco aliquo ut eremitae nec in corde suo quod est profundissimum sed in ipso invisibili deo, scilicet inter res mundi vivere et pasci eo quod nusquam apparet nisi modico verbi indicio soloque auditu, ut Christus Matthew 4 dicit: "Non in solo pane vivit homo sed in omni verbo", etc.*' See *WA*, 57/3:214.
174. Luther even speaks of faith as imparting *divinitas* to us, '*non in substantia dei sed in nobis*' (*WA*, 40/1:360).
175. Cf. *Luthers Vorlesung über den Römerbrief*, 2:65: '*Deus nos facit, quale est verbum suum, hoc est justum, verum, sapiens, etc. Et ita nos in verbum suum, non autem verbum suum in nos mutat. Facit autem tales tunc, quando nos verbum suum tale credimus esse scilicet justum, verum. Tunc enim iam similis forma est in verbo et in credente, id est veritas et justitia.*' Cf. also p. 160. (*WA*, 57/1:149).
176. *WA*, 42:8; 10/1:158, etc.
177. Luther speaks of the *outward word* in distinction but not in separation from the *inward Word* which is in Christ (*WA*, 40/1:142, 571).
178. *De Servo Arbitrio. WA*, 18:685.
179. *WA*, 52:26. Cf. *WA*, 40/1:500 f.
180. '*Mortificat et vivicat, deducit ad inferos et reducit*' (1 Samuel 2:6). These words had the profoundest impact on Luther. Cf. *WA*, 56:450.
181. Cf. *WA*, 40/1:544: '*Unser Herr Gott habet varias ordinationes quando venit Christus . . .*'
182. Therefore it still comes under a contrary aspect. Cf. *WA*, 56:446: '*Verbum Dei, quoties venit, venit in spetie contraria menti nostrae, que sibi vera sapere videtur; ideo verbum contrarium sibi mendacium iudicat adeo, ut Christus verbum suum appelaverit adversarium nostrum.*'

183. *WA*, 40/1:173.
184. *WA*, 31/1:191, and pp. 189–218.
185. Cf. *WA*, 6:410, where he speaks of the worldly rule as part of the *Corpus Christianum*: '*Seyntemal weltlich hirschaft ist ein mitglid worden des Christlichen Corpers unnd wie wol sie ein leyplich werck hat doch geystlichs stands ist, darumb yhr werck sol frey unvorhindert gehen in alle glidmass des gantzen corpers.*'
186. *WA*, 31/8:190.
187. *WA*, 31/1:195.
188. ibid., p. 195.
189. ibid., p. 196.
190. ibid., p. 217.
191. ibid., p. 217.
192. ibid., p. 218.
193. '*Non tollitur per Verbum Dei ulla ordinatio Dei, sed tantum praefectur Verbum*' (*Opera Omnia*, Jena edition, 3:545b). '*Ubi Verbum Dei est, ordinatio Dei et Deus vult bonam politiam.*' *WA*, 31/2:614; cf. p. 608, '*Politia a Verbo Dei instituta et donata.*'
194. See also the *Short Reply to Duke George*, cf. 1533, *WA*, 38:135 ff.
195. De Wette, *Luthers Briefe*, 1:543. See *WAB*, 2:249.
196. *WA*, 10/3:15. Cf. de Wette, op. cit., 2:137 f. and 141 ff.
197. *WA*, 10/3:15.
198. *WA*, 31/1:206.
199. *WA*, 57/3:144. Cf. *WA*, 5:69: '*Conjungit enim fides animam cum invisibili, ineffabili, innominabili, aeterno, incogitabili verbo Dei simulque separat ab omnibus visibilibus, et haec est Crux et phase Domini.*' Cf. *WA*, 40/1:283.
200. *WA*, 57:144, 214; *WA*, 3:150.
201. *WA*, 40/1:525 f. On the other hand the timelessness of the Kingdom of God is emphasised in contrast to the temporality of this worldly kingdom (*WA*, 34/2:110 f).
202. See especially *WA*, 1:199; 25:238.
203. *WA*, 40/1:291; *WA*, 40/3:572.
204. *WA*, 39/1:299. He also uses the expression *linea mathematica* here.
205. *WA*, 18:633.
206. *Comm. on Gal.* 4:19, *WA*, 40/1:648 f.
207. *WA*, 40/1:281 f.
208. *WA*, 57:93. In some real sense faith is *substantia*, but not in the same way that a body is *substantia* (*WA*, *Tischreden*, 5, note 5345).
209. *WA*, 20/2:408.
210. *WA*, 23:189.
211. *WA*, 40/1:411 f.
212. That is, *secundum novam et theologicam grammaticam*, in which *substance, nature* become altogether new words and acquire a new signification (ibid., p. 417).
213. *WA*, 40/1:415.
214. Cf. *WA*, 34/2:480 f.: '*mirabilis est Christi grammatica.*'
215. *WA*, 40/1:418.
216. This is on the analogy of the *communicatio idiomatum*, ibid., pp. 414 f.
217. *WA*, 40/1:417.
218. Pp. 418: '*Oportet enim primum rationem illustratam esse fide, antequam operetur; habita autem vera opinione et notitia Dei, tanquam recta ratione, incarnatur et incorporatur ei opus, ut quicquid fidei tribuitur, postea etiam operibus tribuitur, sed propter solam fidem.*'
219. Cf. *WA*, 3:182: The Christian as a new man is '*homo spiritualis et interior coram*

Deo', but as a member of this world he is '*homo peccati, homo carnalis coram mundo*'.

220. *WA*, 39/1:356.
221. *WA*, 39/1:356.
222. *WA*, 39/1:519 ff.
223. *On the Councils and the Church*, III, *WA*, 50:627; cf. *WA*, 32:468 f.; 2:728 ff.
224. See *Sermons on 1 Corinthians 15* of 1532, and especially *WA*, 36:661–75; and *WA*, 23:189.
225. *WA*, 36:673.
226. *WA*, 36:665 f.
227. *WA*, 38:554.
228. *WA*, 36:548; also pp. 666. '*Du wirst nicht allein an der Seele getauft, sondern am Leibe. Er soll nicht dahinten bleiben. Und soll werden ein geistlicher Leib gleichwie Christi Leib am Tage der Auferstehung* (*WA*, 36:666). See also *WA*, 34/2:122 ff.; 49:395 ff.
229. *WA*, 49:403 f.
230. *WA*, 6:534; *WA*, 30/1:218 f.
231. *The Greater Catechism*, *WA*, 30/1:220, 222.
232. *WA*, 6:534.
233. *WA*, 2:724 f., cf. pp. 728, 734.
234. ibid. Cf. *WA*, 6:534 f., and *WA*, 2:724 ff.
235. *WA*, 44:776; cf. pp. 82 f.
236. Cited from *Baieri Compendium Theologiae Postivae* (edited by Walther), vol. II, p. 255. *WA*, 10/1:241.
237. *Annotationes in aliquot capita Matthaei*, 1538 (*WA*, 38:568 f.). Cf. also *WA*, 56:239 f.
238. *WA*, 30/1:191.
239. *On the Councils and the Churches*, *WA*, 50:643. Cf. *WA*, 42:248.
240. See the *Exposition of Genesis* 49:11, 12; *WA*, 44:774–8; *WA*, 36:681 ff.
241. *WA*, 49:395 f.
242. See especially the *Treatise on Baptism* of 1519, *WA*, 2:724–37; *WA*, 36:543–54; 97 f.; *WA*, 34/2:108–37.
243. *WA*, 40/1:278.
244. *WA*, 40/1:281.
245. *WA*, 42:146–47: '*aliquosque procedimus.*'
246. *WA*, 56:441 f.
247. *WA*, 56:173.
248. *WA*, 34/2:116.
249. *WA*, 34/2:117 ff.
250. *WA*, 34/2:121 ff.
251. *WA*, 37:630 ff.
252. *WA*, 45:280 f., 291 f.
253. *WA*, 2:208, 239; 5:547; 9:505; 38:352; 39:176 etc.
254. *WA*, 4:189.
255. *WA*, 7:721.
256. *WA*, 3:386. This is of course prominent in the Sacrament of Baptism, where the Word assumes the form of *promise*.
257. *WA*, 42:334: '*Ecclesia est filia nata ex verbo, non est mater verbi.*' Cf. *WA*, 8:491; 3:259, 454; 4:173, 179.
258. *WA*, 44:109; 9:577.
259. *WA*, 4:169; *WA*, 5:58.
260. '*Cuius vita in fide, spe et charitate, totus scil. pendens ex invisibilibus*' (*Luthers*

Vorlesung über den Galaterbrief, edited by Schubert, p. 48).
261. See especially the exposition of Genesis 28:16 and 17, *WA*, 43:597, 601 f., and *WA*, 42:424.
262. *WA*, 43:601.
263. *WA*, 5:289.
264. *WA*, 43:582: '*Nos ergo per fidem rapimur, et efficimur una caro cum ipso, sicut inquit Christus Ioannis* 17 (21). *Ita in ipsum ascendimus, et rapimur per verbum et spiritum sanctum, et ipsi adhaeremus per fidem unum existentes corpus cum eo, et ipse nobiscum. Ipse caput: nos membra. Rursum ipse descendit ad nos per verbum et Sacramenta docendo et exercendo nos in sui cognitione. Prima igitur coniunctio est patris et filii in divinitate. Altera divinitatis et humanitatis in Christo, tertia Ecclesiae et Christi.*' Cf. *WA*, 2:239; 4:715 f., 597; 12:488; 26:506, etc.
265. Cf. *WA*, 42:424; 43:596 ff., 600 f.
266. *WA*, 7:719.
267. *WA*, 23:189.
268. *WA*, 4:289.
269. Cf. *WA*, 6:408: '*Christus hat nit zwey noch zweyerley art corper, einen weltlich den andern geistlich. Ein heubt ist und einen corper hat er.*'
270. *WA*, 4:191; 11:53, etc.
271. Cf. *WA*, 7:683 f.; 21:333 f.; 50:624 ff.
272. *WA*, 50:631.
273. *WA*, 50:629.
274. *WA*, 3:169.
275. *WA*, 2:73.
276. *WA*, 4:607 f.; 2:273 f., 742 ff.; 7:69.
277. *WA*, 12:275 f.; 21:333; 44:110.
278. *WA*, 15:220; 18:168 ff.
279. *WA*, 47:853; 42:79 f., 159 f., 217, 320, 414, 422, etc.
280. *WA*, 42:79.
281. ibid.
282. Cf. *WA*, 30/2:427. 'Take away out of the world *veram religionem, veram politiam, veram oeconomiam*, i.e. true spiritual life, true temporal government, and true conduct of the home; what is left in the world, but flesh, world and devil?' – i.e. *no church*, except what Luther calls 'the devil's *ecclesia*'.
283. *WA*, 42:178, 179.
284. *WA*, 42:79 f.
285. *WA*, 43:600 f.
286. See, for example, *WA*, 7:28: '*Ubir das seyn wir priester, das ist noch vil mehr, den Kuenig sein, darumb das fas priesterhum uns wirdig macht fur gott zu treten und fur andere zu bitten.*'
287. *WA*, 34/2:133–6.
288. *WA*, 34/2:136: '*Ein Christ, der diese zwey stück weis* (i.e. heavenly hope and worldly calling), *hat hie ein süss Leben auff Erden und dort das ewig Leben durch Christum unsern Heyland. Ob er schon viel mühe und unlust hat in seinem Stande, So hat er doch bey seiner Mühe und Erbeit Frewde im Hertzen und ein gut Gewissen, Denn er weis, das sein werck und erbeit eitel gute werck und Gottesdienste sein. Ist er ein Knecht, so ist er frölich und guter ding, Wenn er ins Holtz feret, Auff den Acker reitet, so singet er, Ist sein Herr wünderlich, schilt in und thut im unrecht, So hat er gedult und wartet auff ein ander Leben.*'
289. *WA*, 30/1:100; 34/1:176.
290. *WA*, 1:639; 3:752 f.; 6:64, etc.
291. *WA*, 3:182.

292. *WA*, 23:189. Cf. *WA*, 7:719. '*Quamquam ecclesia in carne vivat, non secundum carnem vivit, Paulus dicit in Galatians 1 and 2 Corinthians 10. Ita in loco, rebus, operibus mundi versatur, sed non secundum haec aestimatur . . . sicut enim ecclesia sine esca et potu non est in hac vita et tamen regnum dei non est esca et potus secundum Paulum, ita sine loco et corpore non est ecclesia et tamen corpus et locus non sunt ecclesia neque ad eam pertinent.*'

293. *WA*, 6:293–97. Cf. 3:103, 199; 4:24.

294. *WA*, 6:296 f.

295. *WA*, 2:752 f. Cf. *WA*, 31/2:696: '*Christiani signati verbo, Baptismo et Sacramento altaris, quibus discernimur ab omnibus aliis gentibus, non solum coram mundo, sed verius in iudicio Dei.*

296. *WA*, 1:639: '*Est autem fidelium communio duplex: una interna et spiritualis, alia externa et corporalis: spiritualis est una fides, spes, charitas in deum, corporalis est participatio earundem sacramentorum, i.e. signorum fidei, spei, charitatis, quae tamen ulterius extenditur esque ad communionem rerum, usus, colloquii, habitationis aliarumque corporalium conversationum.*'

297. *WA*, 3:150; 39/2:149, 161.

298. *WA*, 2:240; 42:187.

299. '*Duplex ecclesia*' is a common expression, especially in the Exposition of Genesis, e.g. on Chs. 4, 21 and 25 (Cf. *WA*, 43:159). Another expression here is *gemina ecclesia, vera et hypocritica* (*WA*, 42:184 f.). '*Usque ad finem mundi adjuncta erit falsa ecclesia verae ecclesiae*' (*WA*, 44:23; 51:477).

300. On one of the few occasions Luther appears to have used the expression '*ecclesia visibils*' it is applied to the Papacy as the false Church (*WA*, 7:710), much like the term '*larvalis ecclesia*' (*WA*, 4:715 f.). Cf. *WA*, 31/2:550; and Erlangen edition 31:304. Cf. *WA*, 38:141–70.

301. *WA*, 43:424. Luther continues a little later: '*Sed ita utor donis spiritualibus, ut, cum cessant corporalia, ex hac vita ad aeternam er immortalitatem deducar.*' See also pp. 425 and 427.

302. *WA*, 44:95 f.

303. *WA*, 31/2:614. But this must not be a *humana politia* (*WA*, 39/2:147).

304. *WA*, 44:111.

305. *WA*, 31/2:657.

306. *WA*, 31/2:658.

307. 'It is to be remembered that for Luther the word of God means primarily Christ Himself, Christ through the Scriptures, but primarily Christ over against the Scriptures, so that if necessary we have to urge the authority of Christ against the authority of the Bible' (*WA*, 39/1:47). The Bible cannot be used legalistically to provide the laws of the Church.

308. Certain elements clearly had to be abolished, such as Papal supremacy, celibacy of clergy, and the sacrifice of the Mass, which he called the '*cauda draconis*' (Mass prayer for the dead). See *WAB*, 5:237, no. 1528; *WAB*, 6:107, no. 1822 *WA*, 38:584, etc.

309. This carried with it an element of freedom in liturgical and ceremonial usage (*WA*, 6:447; 10/3:5 f.; 12:194).

310. Luther's opposition to the uniformity of any liturgy is seen in regard to the Liturgy of Wittenberg as well as in regard to the Roman Mass (*WA*, 19:44 ff., 72; 26:175, 222 f.; *WAB*, 4:115, no. 1036).

311. Cf. *WA*, 19:113; 26:222 ff.

312. *WA*, 51:469–572.

313. *WA*, 51:477.

314. *WA*, 51:486. This is also interpreted in terms of 'the little horn of' Daniel 7. 1541

was the year of the publication of the *Supputatio annorum mundi*.
315. *WA*, 51:487.
316. *WA*, 51:498.
317. *WA*, 51:529 f., 536 f.
318. *WA*, 51:507.
319. *WA*, 9:566 f.
320. *WA*, 4:242.
321. *WA*, 40/2:196, 558, 560; 8:224; 50:238; 49:40; 30/3:409.
322. *WA*, 24:557.
323. *WA*, 31/2:689.
324. Jena edition 4:525 (*Enarr. in Ps. xc*, 1541); *WA*, 40/3:506.
325. Cf. *WA*, 7:683; 12:485; 19:75. Luther does sometimes use the expression '*ecclesiola*' (*WA*, 42:241).
326. Jena edition 4:586b (*Comm. in Cap. VII Michae Prophetae*, 1542). Cf. *WA*, 13:25, 17:3.
327. *WA*, 31/2:506. Cf. 40/2:558: '*Ideo nullus visus apparet in facie ecclesiae quam ea, quae dicuntur: vocatur sponsa diaboli, deserta a Christo.*'
328. Jena edition 4:525 (*Enarr. in Ps. xc*). *WA*, 40/3:506.
329. *WA*, 42:227; 44:129; 31/2:658. Cf. de Wette, *Luthers Briefe* 5:431: '*Oportet enim Ecclesiam in mundo apparere: sed apparere non potest, nisi in larva, persona, testa, putamine et vestitu aliquo, in quo possit audiri, videri, comprehendi: alioque nusquam possit inveniri.*' *WAB*, 9:610.
330. *WA*, 36:570 f.
331. *WA*, 18:652.
332. *WA*, 43:600 f.: '*Quanquam nostra quoque Ecclesia habet corporalia et externa multa, ut est panis, aqua, terra, etc, sed magna diversitas est inter ea, quae iactant Papistae, et quae nos habemus corporalia. Illa enim sunt contra Deum suscepta et usurpata, non pro Deo aut secundum Dei verbum: ideo tantum inanis fucus, imaginatio et falsa species est Ecclesia ipsorum . . . Ecclesia autem Papistica non est regnum coelorum: quia quaerit aurum, argentum, regna, coronas mundi. Hae sunt claves ipsorum,*' etc.
333. *WA*, 38:545.
334. *WA*, 31/2:506.
335. *WA*, 24:466.
336. *WA*, 38:563.
337. *WA*, 44:109.
338. *WA*, 44:110. Cf. *WA*, 57:107.
339. *WA*, 31/2:657 f.
340. *WA*, 44:110.
341. *WA*, 31/2:610 f.
342. *WA*, 38:563.
343. *WA*, 44:111 f.; 50:642.
344. *WA*, 38:563.
345. Luther also applies this thought of fermentation to the operation of Baptism in the individual believer. Cf. especially *Rationis Latomianae Confutatio*, *WA*, 8:107.
346. *WA*, 38:564.
347. *WA*, 38:566. Cf. *WA*, 8:379.
348. *WA*, 19:73 ff. *WAB*, 4:157, no. 1071; Cf. *WA*, 12:169 f.; 2:408 f.; 12:11 f.
349. *WA*, 26:504 f.; *WA*, 30/2:117.
350. *WA*, 39/2:146–49.

351. Cf. *WA*, 51:519: '*Gottes wort sey so ein herrlich maiestetisch ding.*' See also *WA*, 12:192.
352. *WA*, 42:310: '*Etsi Ecclesia est exigua: tamen est rectrix orbis terrarum, et conservatur propter eam mundus*'.
353. *WA*, 21:432. *Vide supra on larva dei.* Cf. *WA*, 31/2:688 f.: '*Nam verbum publice praedicatum cives domum reportant et ex verbo discunt se et suos gubernare. Ita ut ubique experiamur, in templo, in republica, in oeconomia certos verbi fructus, quod ceu fermentum omnes reipublicae partes, officia et status omnes pervadit.*'
354. *WA*, 39/2:149.
355. *WA*, 22:344.
356. *Luthers Briefe*, de Wette edition 2:492. *WAB*, 3:260, no. 724.
357. *Luthers Vorlesung über den Galaterbrief*, 1516/17, edited by Schubert, p. 32.
358. Cf. *WA*, 19:73; 21:432. Luther opposed therefore the use of the Bible as a document to provide the Church with laws for worship and orders. *WA, Briefe*, 1524; de Wette edition, 6:379 f.
359. See the important letter to Amsdorf, de Wette, *Briefe*, 5:431 f. (*WAB*, 9:611) and cf. his attitude to the Mass in this respect, *WA*, 10/3:1 ff.; 12:205 ff.; 18:62 f. and p. 123; 19:14 f., 72 f.
360. Cf. especially Luther's exposition of the 22nd Psalm (*WA*, 5:620 ff.).
361. Cf. *WA*, 8:59 ff., 73 ff.
362. Cf., for example, the sermon for the Second of Advent, 1544 (*WA*, 52:16 ff., and *WA*, 7:784 ff.).

INDEX

(Most theological themes are indexed under Luther)